A Practical Guide to Corporate Finance

A Practical Guide to Corporate Finance

Breaking the Financial Ice

Christophe Thibierge
Associate Professor of Finance, ESCP Europe

and

Andrew Beresford
Adjunct Professor of Business Communications, ESCP Europe

First published in French 2013 as *Comprendre Toute la Finance*
By Les Éditions Vuibert, Paris
First published in English 2015 by
PALGRAVE MACMILLAN

Palgrave Macmillan in the UK is an imprint of Macmillan Publishers Limited,
registered in England, company number 785998, of Houndmills, Basingstoke,
Hampshire RG21 6XS.

Palgrave Macmillan in the US is a division of St Martin's Press LLC,
175 Fifth Avenue, New York, NY 10010.

Palgrave Macmillan is the global academic imprint of the above companies
and has companies and representatives throughout the world.

Palgrave® and Macmillan® are registered trademarks in the United States,
the United Kingdom, Europe and other countries.

ISBN: 978–1–137–49251–7

This book is printed on paper suitable for recycling and made from fully
managed and sustained forest sources. Logging, pulping and manufacturing
processes are expected to conform to the environmental regulations of the
country of origin.

A catalogue record for this book is available from the British Library.

Library of Congress Cataloging-in-Publication Data

Thibierge, Christophe.
    A practical guide to corporate finance : breaking the financial ice / Christophe
Thibierge, Associate Professor of Finance, ESCP Europe, Andrew Beresford, Adjunct
Professor of Business Communications, ESCP Europe.
        pages cm
    Includes index.
        1. Corporations – Finance. 2. Investments. 3. Corporations – Valuation.
    I. Beresford, Andrew, 1965– II. Title.
HG4026.T48 2015
658.15—dc23   2015003820

Writing, when properly managed (as you may be sure I think mine is) is but a different name for conversation.

Laurence Stern, *The Life and Opinions of Tristram Shandy, Gentleman* (1759—1767)

Contents

List of Figures

List of Tables

Foreword

This is an unusual book in the landscape of corporate finance textbooks. Its originality is that it manages to present all the key concepts in corporate finance in an accessible and engaging way, using a conversational tone and a fair share of humour that balances the seriousness of the subject matter: proof that 'funny' and 'finance' can go together!

The format of the book is also quite novel: concise presentations of serious material are followed by entertaining and enlightening conversations between oddball characters who discuss the concepts in a down-to-earth manner, or illustrative anecdotes from everyday life to drive the points home. For example, one story illustrates incremental expenses from the perspective of a young person who has just bought a shiny boat to impress her family. Another illustrates why we need the stock market from the point of view of Captain Nemo, who needs funds to repair his famous ship. Sometimes you feel as though you were reading a novel and looking forward to the next dialogue or anecdote to find out what happens to these colourful characters. There are plenty of mini case studies relating theories and concepts to real-world applications – case studies that readers can work through step by step to consolidate their knowledge. Financial newbies will find clearly marked warnings of common pitfalls to avoid. And to break through the jargon barrier for the uninitiated or the rusty, timely primers on financial vocabulary are strategically placed throughout the text. We all know that the world of finance often delights in jargon at the expense of clarity, don't we?

As a result, this book is extremely accessible to readers with little or no prior knowledge of finance – students and young professionals just getting their feet wet in the business world – but is also recommended for seasoned pros who have specific gaps in their knowledge or who just want a refresher on certain concepts without having to dust off their old college textbooks. Let's not forget that many of our professional contacts (mostly clients and partners, but also our employees and suppliers) show a genuine interest in understanding the underlying mechanics of finance. This book will definitely help them understand what it's all about.

Don't be fooled by the compact size of this book: all the major concepts are covered here, from financial statements and analysis, investment decisions and cash flows, calculating the cost of capital, through to business valuation, with chapters on the stock market and risk management (one of my personal favourites). All the relevant financial theories and equations are included, backed up by concrete calculations presented in straightforward graphs and tables.

All of the didactic material presented here has been tested in a hands-on and interactive way at one of Europe's top business schools – ESCP Europe – and has been honed and refined through countless iterations in both undergraduate courses and graduate seminars (I was there; I know).

Now, as a senior (non-financial) manager in an international company, I find it very useful and refreshing to have this kind of material at hand, when I am faced with various decisions to make or influence in the United Kingdom, across Europe or, on occasions, beyond. Back to basics is sometimes what you need when facing complex situations.

I am honoured to be associated with the publication of *A Practical Guide to Corporate Finance*: *Breaking the Financial Ice*. I would heartily recommend it to all professionals from any discipline, background or industry who want to build their knowledge about corporate finance while having a laugh at the same time.

Ouahcene Ourahmoune
Director of Operations
Railway Systems & Infrastructure
Alstom Transport UK Ltd.

Unpaid Debts

The authors owe a debt of gratitude to:

Pete Baker and Grace Jackson at Palgrave Macmillan, first for their enthusiasm for this project, and also for all their good advice and guidance throughout the publishing process.

Othman Cole and Terence Tse, esteemed colleagues and professors of finance at ESCP Europe (London campus), for their careful reading of early drafts of this book and for their shrewd comments and helpful suggestions.

The KPMG/ESCP Europe Chair on Governance, Strategy, Risk and Performance and the ESCP Europe research department for generous financial support.

And finally, the students at ESCP Europe, undergraduates in finance and also those in executive education and the executive MBA programme. It is their enthusiasm to learn and their eagerness to get to the bottom of things that we have tried to convey here.

Presentation and User's Guide

Guaranteed to be highly effective, generally safe, and mostly painless if used as directed.

The purpose of this book is to help you understand finance, progressively, using imagery and a straightforward approach. To keep it interesting, the material in each chapter is presented in a variety of ways: introduction of concepts, practical illustrations and Socratic-style dialogues. First, we will take a look at the structure of the book and then offer some words of advice before you read it.

This book is laid out like a ten-course banquet

The appetizer

The 'introduction to finance' chapter is an appetizer in the literal sense of the term: its purpose is to whet your appetite. It outlines what is covered by finance and why it is worthwhile to study financial questions: to create value and to better understand companies and their strategies.

The main courses – nine tasty chapters

Following the introduction, the book is structured in nine tasty chapters for readers to savour. As at a well organized banquet, the dishes follow each other in a sensible order – so the guests don't get indigestion. Each chapter contains 'breathers' – pauses in which to sit back and digest before moving on. Readers can skip a chapter if they wish because the footnotes refer back to key ideas and concepts. The chapters are organized as follows:

- Chapter 1. To borrow an analogy from school, the first thing you have to do is learn to read. Just as medical students begin with anatomy, anyone who wants to understand finance must first learn to read and analyse the past performance of companies. This chapter shows the link between accounting documents and basic concepts in finance.
- Chapter 2. Once we've honed our skill at reading past performance, we can begin to reason about the future. This chapter presents the tools used

to compare amounts of money received or paid out over time – even with very distant payment dates.

- Chapter 3. Concepts learned in the first chapters are put into practice by looking at investment projects and their forecasts. This chapter presents the tools that help us make the best choice between several potential investments, for example, investments varying in size, duration and risk.
- Chapter 4. One of the major issues raised in Chapter 3 is the measurement of risk. We will need two chapters to cover this question. This chapter uses a stock market approach to define different types of risk and their love–hate relationship with returns within stock market portfolios.
- Chapter 5. Following the stock market approach, we return to a corporate finance perspective for another view of risk measurement. This chapter covers the risks and advantages of debt financing, and how financial policy impacts a company's cost of financing. This chapter demonstrates the link between risk and expected return, and how to estimate the required return for a given level of risk.
- Chapter 6. Building on previous concepts (forecasting cash flows, discounting over the long term, the notion of risk premium), Chapter 6 presents different models used to perform a company valuation, in a step-by-step, practical approach.
- Chapter 6¾. This chapter is optional, mainly aimed at ardent finance fans and the insatiably curious. It delves into the many practical and technical questions that underlie business and investment project valuations.
- Chapter 7. Behind all these financial models and calculations, there are financial markets, in other words, human beings. This chapter looks at the stock market and the benefits of having a stock market, before explaining all the fuss around the hotly debated idea of *market efficiency*. In this chapter we will see that the human element can greatly perturb many of the so-called rational models.
- Chapter 8. In this chapter, we come back to groundwork finance: cash management. This includes cash budgets and forecasts, short-term risks and how to hedge against them.
- Finally, Chapter 9 offers a conclusion to all these adventures in the land of corporate finance.

Take a breather: boxed texts throughout the book

Even with the best of intentions, any reader will eventually grow weary and start to nod off. And even with the best teachers and methods in the world, any lecture will eventually become boring. This is why each chapter contains recreational 'breathers' – during which we continue to talk about finance without appearing to do so. There are five different kinds of 'breather', presented in the form of boxed texts:

Dialogues

Similar to 'Socratic dialogues', these boxed texts provide more details, usually to help readers understand concepts. They look like this:

DIALOGUE	
Castor:	So these dialogues are a way for readers to find their own questions?
Pollux:	Their own questions, yes, or others that wouldn't have occurred to them.

Dialogues can also be used to criticize the concepts that have just been presented.

Financialese: a language in its own right

> "Why then", pursued the Sirian, "do you cite this Aristotle fellow in Greek?"
> "Because", replied the scholar, "one should always cite what one does not understand in the language one least understands."
>
> François-Marie Arouet (Voltaire), *Micromégas* (1752)

Definitions in a dictionary tend to go round and round in circles (resulting in dizzy readers) because they always define arcane words using other arcane words. We run into the same problem in every discipline. Of course, the more jargon you use the more competent you appear. But to be admitted to the inner circle of those who are *in the know*, you have to master this jargon. Next to doctors and lawyers, the worst offenders, of course, are finance people. This is why you will see 'Financialese' boxed texts cropping up throughout this book. Here's an example.

FINANCIALESE ————————————————————————————
P&L is short for profit and loss statement, also known as a company's **income statement** (which is the term we will use throughout this book). In other words, the company's sales and other income minus its expenses and other costs for the year. Rather simple, really.
————————————————————————————

Slice of life

A 'slice of life' is a slightly quirky illustration to present a real-life situation and raise a few questions. A little boxed text will make this clear:

SLICE OF LIFE •••
Beryl has just won £1,000 in a sweepstake. She can't decide whether to pay off her overdraft (interest charged at 10%) or deposit her winnings in a savings account at 2%. She has to think in terms of opportunity cost and figure out which of these two options offers the better outcome.
••

Vignettes

Sometimes a textual explanation is not enough. An analogy can flesh out the presentation of a concept. For example, when we say that two companies have merged and that this creates synergies, what do we really mean?

VIGNETTE ⁞⁞
Let's take the case of Olaf Singleton. He's unmarried, lives in a one-room flat and detests doing the shopping every week. Sadie Hawkins is also single and finds herself in more or less the same situation: cramped flat, little free time. But imagine that Olaf and Sadie fall in love and move into a two-bedroom flat. Each of them would pay less rent, the grocery shopping would be done in double quick time, they wouldn't have to pay certain bills twice (gas, water, home insurance, etc.) and love would give them an extra boost to launch their plans together.

That's synergy!
⁞⁞

A fool and his money (are soon parted)

From time to time the authors mention common pitfalls and mistakes that are often made – it's well worth paying attention to these!

A FOOL AND HIS MONEY ...————————————————————————
An overworked executive makes a detour (ten minutes out of his way) to fill up at a petrol station that offers lower prices. There are real savings to be had (5 pence per litre: 0.05×50 litres = £2.50), but given the time spent (1/6 of an hour) it is not worth his while unless the executive is paid less than £15 an hour!
——

Digestif

As well as enjoying the 'breathers', whose purpose is to help with the digestion of certain meaty concepts, readers can go to a website (www. breakingthefinancialice.com) containing examples and case studies that go along with this book. This offers limitless advantages:

- provides tools that are 'pre-chewed' (which aids in digestion, as any baby bird will tell you)
- encourages learning through practice
- reduces the number of pages in the book, which reduces printing costs (answering the publisher's most earnest prayer) and hence the cover price – you lucky devils!

Words of advice before starting

1. The chapters try to explain various financial concepts (organized by topic) as clearly as possible. The material gets more advanced and more detailed as you move through a chapter. If you tune out, take a break, let it sit for a while and then start again at the beginning of the chapter.
2. Naturally, the further we advance through a chapter, the more 'finance' we do – which means there are fewer and fewer laughs. But it also gets more and more interesting and profitable (terrific return on investment (ROI), given the ridiculously low cover price). These two points lead to an unexpected conclusion: if you don't feel up to the task of reading the whole book, it's better to read the first quarter of each chapter than the first quarter of the book.
3. Learning is achieved not only through reading, but also through practice. Use the examples provided, download the spreadsheets and take situations from work or your personal life to apply what you've just learnt.
4. The first chapters are rather independent. But the further you get into the book, the more you realize that in finance everything is connected. So while you can start Chapter 2 without knowing anything about financial analysis (dealt with in Chapter 1), it would be very hard to understand cash flow forecasts (Chapter 3 Capital Budgeting or Chapter 6 Business Valuation) without having first read about and absorbed the basic concepts in financial analysis.

Conclusion

The authors do not live in an ivory tower and until a nice one comes on the market at a reasonable price they welcome comments and questions from readers (errors, problems with comprehension) by email at: thibierge@escpeurope.eu or through the book's website (www.breakingthefinancialice.com).

Introduction

Begin, be bold, and venture to be wise.

Horace, Book I, Epistle II

When the average man in the street hears people talking about finance, a stream of mental images immediately forms in his head. He sees sad, grey senior executives with a calculator where their heart should be, or frenzied stock market investors staring at multiple green screens, desperate to get their information fix, investors who – he believes – are making oodles of money. So what is finance really? A cold, rational, perfectly modelled science, while the world around us is dripping with uncertainty? Or, on the contrary, does the term finance cover an array of tips and tricks, midway between plumbing (accounting) and psychic divination? Is it a set of beliefs as intangible as (speculative) bubbles? Conclusion: we really need to define what finance is.

Finance in three questions

All of finance can be boiled down to three questions that, if not existential, are quintessentially human:

(1) How do I get money?
(2) How do I keep my money?
(3) How do I earn more money?

Notice that we did not add 'at any cost' to these three questions – meaning we are not willing to make money 'whatever the cost'. We have to weigh up the advantages and drawbacks of these choices, because there are limits to our decisions. And all the mechanics of financial decision-making basically come down to measuring advantages and risks. Anyone who has to make a financial decision will in fact be responding to a single, primordial question – a sort of Big Bang question that spawns all other financial questions:

BIG BANG QUESTION: IS IT WORTH IT?

All of this still does not constitute an academic definition of finance, because we have yet to define our terms, but it shows that financial decisions are in fact trade-offs – a choice between several possibilities. A financier's skill therefore essentially consists in:

- drawing up a list of the options available, endeavouring not to overlook any;
- establishing an order of priority to determine which options are 'more worthwhile' than others.

Let's take another look at our three questions and try to derive a definition from them.

Question 1 – how do I get money?

The world has always been divided between those who have money and those who need it. In a developed economy, those who have money are households (their savings) and financial institutions (banks, credit unions, insurance companies, etc.). Those who need it are mainly companies and the government (but households may also need money. Some people and institutions simultaneously have money and also need it). There are two ways to match the supply (those who have money) to the demand (those who need it). To clarify this idea, let's take a look at this vignette.

VIGNETTE

Kate was born in Connecticut and her family is very well off (a three-storey house in New Haven, a cottage in the Hamptons, overflowing bank accounts, etc.). Leonardo is from south Chicago and grew up in The Projects. He really wishes he had some assets and his bank manager regularly reminds him of this. Let's imagine a union between Kate and Leonardo. There are several possible types of marriage: an arranged marriage (by the parents, overseen by their lawyers and accountants, and officiated by the minister of their church) or a love marriage. In the arranged marriage, the intermediaries bring the well heeled party and the needy party together. In exchange, these intermediaries ask for some form of remuneration (the patter of tiny feet, legal fees, a donation to the church). In a love marriage, Kate and Leonardo say, 'To hell with this, there has to be a cheaper way! Let's get hitched without any go-betweens!' In this non-intermediated operation there are fewer expenses (but perhaps the risk is higher).

It's the same for capital markets: in an intermediated market, households cannot bring their money directly to companies; they have to go through an intermediary. For example, households deposit their money in a bank account (interest bearing or not), and the bank lends this money to companies, earning an **intermediation spread**. Insurance companies are also intermediaries, collecting premiums and investing them in financial markets. If, like Kate and Leonardo, a household wants to avoid inter-mediaries, it can provide money directly to companies by buying their **shares**; that is, by becoming an investor in the company. One of the actors in this disintermediation process is the financial market, where capital providers and seekers may come into direct contact with each other.

A company therefore has two ways to acquire funds:

● through intermediaries: it can go to banks or financial institutions (investment funds, for example). These intermediaries have money that they have collected and that they are willing to invest for a return.
● without intermediaries: a company can issue shares to be in direct con-tact with households (it offers its shares to the general public) or with banks and financial institutions. Each individual investor can then choose where to place his/her money and in what proportions. Having said that, a household (or an investment fund) will not invest in a com-pany under just any conditions. It will have certain requirements, as we will see in questions 2 and 3.

Question 2 – how do I keep my money?

This question may be surprising. At a time when everyone is trying to make their assets generate more money, why should we be concerned with just keeping the money we started with? Why not just go directly to question 3? Quite simply in order to introduce our age-old enemy: risk.

SLICE OF LIFE ●
Lonnie Ranger is not married, has no children and earns a good living. As he has more money than he needs, he invests the surplus in the stock market. When Lonnie wins, he's happy – after all that's why he plays the market. When he loses, he drowns his sorrows with a bottle of whisky. He suffers no major side effects; only a hangover.

It's a very different story for Mr Brady, who has a wife and six children (including teenage triplets). He deposits all his money in a bank account and leaves it sitting there because he can't afford to lose his savings. He knows that he's missing an opportunity to make more money but he's

3

not willing to take any risks. If he invested in the stock market and lost,[1] he would have to make a tough choice: have a stand-off with his kids' orthodontist (because he can no longer afford to pay for their braces) or quarrel with his wife (who occasionally likes to escape the ruckus at home by going to a spa) or with Alice, their housekeeper (who has been angling for a new vacuum cleaner and a pay rise). Mr Brady doesn't want to complicate his life and he's happy to forgo making extra money if it means reducing the risk of a household budget catastrophe and a lot of sleepless nights.

Keeping your money without trying to make it grow may be a very rational decision and serve a legitimate financial goal. The question, therefore, is not, 'Must I invest?' but rather 'Beyond what level of risk should I refuse to invest?' Risk and our ability to measure it therefore constitute a major dimension of financial decision-making.

Question 3 – how do I earn more money?

> *Antonio: Or is your gold and silver ewes and rams?*
> *Shylock: I cannot tell; I make it breed as fast.*
> William Shakespeare, *The Merchant of Venice*, Act I, Scene 3

Here is an interesting question that will keep us occupied throughout most of this book. The answer is quite simple and comes down to a few ideas:

● To earn more money you have to take risks. These risks may be small (I deposit my money in a savings account) or large (I buy shares in a Brazilian mining company that is prospecting in Mato Grosso).
● The money earned, expressed in terms of a **return on investment**, must be compared to the risk taken. This is called the **risk–return trade-off**. What is important, then, is not the absolute value of the return on an investment, but the return in relation to the risk taken.

---

1. It happens to good people, even though few of them are willing to admit it.

DIALOGUE	
Ginger:	Hey, Fred, guess what? I've invested my money and now I'm earning 6% a year – my bank was only giving me 3%. Don't you think I'm an excellent financier?
Fred:	I don't know. You haven't told me what you've invested your money in yet.
Ginger:	It's a company that's prospecting for oil under the ice floes near the North Pole. They trade with the Inuit using beaver pelts as money.
Fred:	Let's see now. You face an uncertainty risk on the outcome of the prospecting operation, a risk on the price of oil and a currency risk on the price of beaver pelts, not to mention the geographic distance, environmental risks, the risk of polar bear attacks and the risk of catching the flu. A 6% return for all those risks is chicken feed!
Ginger:	Chicken feed? Really?
Fred:	It depends how risky the investment is. A very solid company operating in a known market without a great deal of risk might satisfy investors with a return of 6% a year.
Ginger:	How much of a return should I have asked for on this investment, then?
Fred:	Finance will answer that question for you. A large part of finance is concerned with assessing risks and calculating a matching return on investment or a corresponding risk premium.
Ginger:	Can't you give me more detail than that?
Fred (smiling):	How many hours are you willing to put in to find out? And what return do you expect from the intellectual investment? In short, is it worth it?

The solution to earning more money is simple: **invest in projects that offer a satisfactory return, given the risk involved.** The difficulty lies in putting this method into practice: how do you quantify the return? What is the risk? How do you measure the amount of risk in an investment? How do you determine the ratio between the amount of risk and an 'acceptable' return? These are all fascinating questions, which we will deal with throughout this book.

Definition of finance; deeper into the rabbit hole

Finance is concerned with monetary resources. It deals with the acquisition of monetary resources, investment and redistribution, over time, taking into account all the risks involved.

That's all.

A little jargon about companies

Finance is practised variously in several fields: corporate finance in businesses, market finance in financial markets, public finance in government and public institutions, and personal finances between the kitchen and the bedroom. There's a vast amount of information about companies in the business and economic press. So we're going to give you a few basic terms and some help in understanding them.

SLICE OF LIFE

*Old MacDonald had a farm. He decides to buy another 100-acre plot of land to grow wheat. He has some money saved, but not enough. He asks his brother-in-law, Ronald, and his father-in-law, Donald, to help out. For a plot worth $100,000, Old MacDonald puts up $70,000 of the capital, Ronald contributes $20,000 and Donald kicks in $10,000. These three characters are now 'co-owners' or **shareholders** of the land, according to their respective contributions: Old MacDonald holds 70% of the land,[2] etc. Now they have to buy machines and seeds. The MT Bank offers to lend the three shareholders another $50,000. They buy the equipment and seeds (or **assets**) and Old MacDonald sets to work. A year later, Old MacDonald has blisters on his hands, pain in his lower back and wheat in his field. He takes some of the wheat from the harvest to pay the interest on the loan and another amount to pay his taxes. The remaining wheat is the net harvest or **net income**. Part of this income can be distributed. For example, they distribute 10% of the harvest: 70 tons of wheat goes to Old MacDonald, 20 to Ronald and 10 to Donald. These are **dividends**. Each of the shareholders can use his dividend to make bread (consumption) or he can sell his wheat on the market and invest the money (**reinvestment**).*

*The remainder of the harvest, which has not been distributed as dividends, is stored in a silo as reserves (**retained earnings**). These reserves will be used to seed the field the following year, or they can be sold by the company to buy new farming implements.*

---

2. Why didn't Old MacDonald just buy 70 acres by himself (using the money he already had) instead of 100 acres? Because, whether we are investing in land or a company, there is a minimum size for the venture to be viable. Thus Old MacDonald needed to join with other investors.

DIALOGUE (AND A LITTLE FINANCIALESE)

Laurel:	But who does the land belong to? Does the bank have any claim to it?
Hardy:	The land belongs solely to the **shareholders** and they are co-owners. Moreover, although the machines and inventory have been financed by the bank, the shareholders still own these **assets**. The bank is not an owner; it has lent an amount of money in exchange for income.
Laurel:	What are the bank's rights?
Hardy:	The bank can demand that the contract be fulfilled. The borrower must pay the bank an annual income (**interest**) and reimburse the loan (the **principal**) within the term stipulated in the contract. If the company does not comply with the contract, it will go into **default on the loan** and the bank can take legal action to get paid.
Laurel:	But what exactly is 'the company'?
Hardy:	The company is a **legal entity** that has been created by the shareholders. Just like a natural person, it can hire staff, conclude contracts and go bankrupt. It pays taxes and has a legal existence, but it never goes to the doctor, the cinema or the pub.
Laurel:	How do the shareholders make joint decisions?
Hardy:	Just like a homeowners' association. They hold a **general meeting**, usually once a year, they have an **agenda** and they vote on the proposals. The weight of their vote is proportional to their investment.
Laurel:	Once a year? That's not very practical if you want to vote on buying a new pencil...
Hardy:	That's why the shareholders recruit (appoint) a **general manager**, often called the **managing director** or **CEO** – who may or may not be a shareholder of the company – to make day-to-day decisions. This manager is answerable to the shareholders.
Laurel:	Can a company ever die?
Hardy:	It can commit suicide: the shareholders can decide to **liquidate** the company. They sell all the assets, pay off the debts and what remains (the **net worth**) goes to the shareholders (Old MacDonald gets 70%, Ronald 20% and Donald 10%). Or it can be **taken over**: be bought by another company and merged into that company. When Johnny eats a steak, Steak Co. disappears in its current form and Johnny grows stronger...

Financial Analysis

The world is full of obvious things which nobody by any chance ever observes.

Sir Arthur Conan Doyle, *The Hound of the Baskervilles* (1901)

Financial analysis involves reading a company's financial statements and trying to squeeze the juicy details out of them: how old the captain is, the age of the machines and the overall performance of the business. This requires a minimum skill set and a great deal of ingenuity. Financial analysis is often one of the first steps in business management: a prerequisite for making good decisions is having first understood what the business is all about.

Accounting

A lot of people will never overcome their aversion to accounting. A discipline that is generally deemed to be a bit sad and dreary, accounting is nevertheless – on the scale of human endeavour – what the lone star tick (*amblyomma americanum*) is to the world of living things: something repulsive to the eye, but in reality a marvel of inventiveness. So you will have to set aside your preconceived notions: to work in finance you can get by just fine without any knowledge of the lone star tick, but if you want to survive, you need to understand the mechanics of business accounting.

Financial statements

Every year companies publish several financial statements in their annual report. These statements show what has happened during the year. The two main statements are the balance sheet and the income statement (P&L account). Here is a brief presentation:

BALANCE SHEET

Fixed assets	Equity
Current assets	
Cash and cash equivalents	Debt
Total assets	Total liabilities

Figure 1.1   Balance sheet

INCOME STATEMENT

Sales for the year
− Costs for the year

Net income

Figure 1.2   Income statement

The **income statement** shows the operations that have occurred during the year, so it is like a post-game summary (both half-times[1]) and the bottom line (positive or negative) is the final score of the game. The **balance sheet** represents the state of affairs at the end of the year when the accounts are closed. This is the final standing – the championship ranking.

VIGNETTE⁣‖‖
Mario Imbroglio sets out across Europe in his red Ferrari Testarossa. The 'balance sheet' at the end of the day refers to the final state of the car. For example, the seats, stereo and steering wheel are still there. The tyres are a little worn. There are 22 litres of petrol in the tank and the small tray under the dashboard contains £5.60 in small change, two £100 speeding tickets, and 53 toll receipts. The income statement corresponds to a tally of Mario's exploits: he went to an ATM 12 times, withdrawing a total of £1,250, which he used to pay for 7 fill-ups (£700), 5 overpriced roadside snacks (£200) and 53 tolls (£344.40).[2]
‖‖

---

1. The third 'half-time' would be the annual general meeting, when shareholders vote on the accounts and decide to pay themselves a fat dividend.
2. If we do the maths we get: £1,250 − 700 − 200 − 344.40 = £5.60, which is the amount that will appear under 'cash and cash equivalents' on the balance sheet (sub-heading: plastic pull-out tray). In reality, it is very rare for the published net earnings to match the actual amount in the bank for reasons that we will explain later in this chapter. Meanwhile, we should remember this: net earnings - certain items + other items = cash flow.

Now we're going to set up a concrete illustration that will guide us through
this chapter.

Droids Co. make machine tools. Their customers are automobile factories
with specific needs. Their suppliers are small subcontractors (electronic and
mechanical components, steel, cables and so on) as well as utilities and service providers (energy, insurance and so on). We will read their financial
statements and learn how to interpret them as we go along. Serious readers
can repeat this process every time they want to read a company's financial
statements.

Income statement

Table 1.1 Income statement

Item	2012	2013	2014
Sales	774.7	809.6	848.4
– Cost of goods sold (COGS)	–445.9	–464.4	–485.0
Gross margin	328.8	345.1	363.4
– Selling, General and Admin. expenses (SG&A)	–227.7	–238.0	–249.4
Gross operating profit	101.0	107.1	114.0
– Depreciation/amortization	–25.9	–24.6	–28.0
– Provisions and write-offs	–1.1	–1.1	–1.3
Operating profit	74.0	81.4	84.6
– Interest expense	–16.1	–18.3	–20.7
+ Net financial revenues	0.4	0.3	0.3
Earnings before tax	58.3	63.5	64.3
– Extraordinary items	–2.5	2.2	–2.0
– Tax	–18.4	–21.7	–20.5
Net earnings	37.4	44.0	41.7

---

3. His **net worth** is therefore £5,366 (including the £2,000 of net income for the year). Do this calculation for your own situation. If your net worth is greater than that of the author, go out and buy several
copies of this book.

FINANCIALESE[4]

Sales represents sales revenue (volume sold × selling price). **COGS** (cost of goods sold) is the expenses invoiced by suppliers: raw materials, energy, rent, outsourced work and various other costs. **Gross margin** therefore represents the margin on sales after paying for supplies.

SG&A (selling, general and administrative) expenses include all staff salaries (shop floor workers, salespeople, executives) as well as other payroll costs such as social security contributions. **Gross operating profit** is therefore the margin on sales after paying production costs and overheads.

A word about depreciation/amortization and provisions

Depreciation and amortization are accounting entries which, unlike other items in the income statement, do not correspond to monetary operations. Specifically, **depreciation/amortization**[5] is the process of spreading the cost of a past investment over time. Companies are not allowed to write off an investment as a one-time expense; that would be the equivalent of charging the entire cost of an asset to the accounts of a single year, even though that asset will be used for several years. The accounting solution is to deduct the expense gradually, in instalments, over the useful life of the asset. Some people say that depreciation reflects the wear and tear on the asset, but mainly it is an accounting device to spread out the cost of the investment over time.

DIALOGUE

Rosencrantz:	On Droids Co.'s income statement we see £24M to £28M of depreciation per year. What does that mean?
Guildenstern:	Those amounts correspond to an investment of £250M spread over ten years. The investment actually did occur, but you are not allowed to record –£250M in one go on the income statement. So the expense is spread over time and the accounting representation of this operation is –£24M to –£28M per year over ten years.

Provisions are accounting entries for potential losses such as inventory write-downs or doubtful debt. For example, if an outstanding customer

---

4. The way the income statement is presented differs depending on whether we are following continental European accounting rules or international standards (IFRS). In this chapter we will use the European standards. In the chapters on publicly traded companies we will use the international standards. An appendix at the end of this chapter describes the two systems and their differences.
5. The term 'depreciation' generally concerns tangible assets (machines, buildings), while 'amortization' is used for intangible assets (patents, software). For example, you get married and 20 years later your spouse is depreciated, but your love has not been amortized!

payment is unlikely to be received, a provision is recorded to reduce the net earnings. Should the payment be made after all, the provision is cancelled, thereby increasing the net earnings (see the analysis of the asset side of the balance sheet below).

FINANCIALESE

The **operating profit**, therefore, is what is left of sales revenue after operating costs have been deducted and investment costs and asset depreciation have been spread over time.

Finance costs include the interest payments on debt and any foreign exchange losses. **Financial revenues** may be earnings from (short-term) investments, foreign exchange earnings or earnings from shares held in other companies. The sum of these two lines is the **net financial expense/income**. Adding this figure to the operating profit above gives us **pre-tax earnings**, which therefore relate to the company's ordinary activities, whether operational or financial.

Extraordinary items come from non-recurring operations. Discontinuing a line of business, restructuring costs, severance packages, legal fees and court costs are some examples.

The company pays **corporate income tax** (corporation tax), and what is left after all these operations is known as **net earnings**.

Profit margins

A direct reading of Droids Co.'s income statement provides us with some interesting information: it is a growing business (increasing sales), which generates a profit (the net earnings are positive), even though earnings do not exactly follow the growth in sales. That is about all we can read directly. Now we have to make comparisons between the different fluctuations. The simplest way is to express each line as a percentage of sales, like this:

Table 1.2   Income statement: items expressed as a percentage of sales

Item	2012	2013	2014
Sales	100%	100%	100%
– COGS	–57.6%	–57.4%	–57.2%
Gross margin	42.4%	42.6%	42.8%
– SG&A expenses	–29.4%	–29.4%	–29.4%
Gross operating profit	13.0%	13.2%	13.4%
– Depreciation/amortization	–3.3%	–3.0%	–3.3%
– Provisions and write-offs	–0.1%	–0.1%	–0.2%
Operating profit	9.6%	10.1%	10.0%
Growth in sales		4.5%	4.8%

DIALOGUE

Rosencrantz:	Why did we stop our calculations at operating profit?
Guildenstern:	Because the following results are not really linked to sales. For example, finance costs depend on the amount of debt, not on sales. So expressing them as a percentage of sales would not tell us much.
Rosencrantz:	And what's the point of expressing everything as a percentage of sales anyway?
Guildenstern:	First of all, it allows us to compare one year to another. Then it gives us the margins: gross margin, gross operating margin and net operating margin.
Rosencrantz:	What's a margin?
Guildenstern:	That's what tells us how much profit the company makes on every £1 of sales. For example, here we can say that Droids Co. have improved their gross margin over the years, probably by negotiating better prices with their suppliers or by improving their productivity.
Rosencrantz:	What can we say about the other margins?
Guildenstern:	The other margins benefit from the improvement in gross margin. What is a little surprising is that SG&A expenses are always 29.4% of sales. This might make sense for factory workers (the more we sell, the more staff we need working in production), but not for executives: doubling the sales does not require doubling the number of executives. There were probably some overtime hours or new staff hired, or even hiring and staff training costs.
Rosencrantz:	As for depreciation/amortization and provisions, they don't interest us because they refer to non-monetary operations...
Guildenstern:	Not so fast! Depreciation and amortization are the counterpart to investments that have been made. A company with zero depreciation would be a company that has not invested. So while they are not monetary expenses, they do nevertheless illustrate the company's capital investment decisions.
Rosencrantz:	And another thing, how do you know whether an operating profit margin of 10% (as in this case) is good or not?
Guildenstern:	There is no absolute figure: you have to compare with the competitors in the same sector, by analysing the financial statements of those companies.
Rosencrantz:	OK. Now what do we do with the last lines in the income statement, the ones we didn't express as a percentage of sales?
Guildenstern:	In general, we compare those lines to the items they correspond to: interest payments correspond to financial debt, financial revenue often comes from cash and cash equivalents.
Rosencrantz:	And net earnings?

> Guildenstern: Some people calculate a net margin (net earnings/sales revenues), but that doesn't make much sense because net earnings don't just depend on the amount of sales – there's also the amount of debt, short-term investments, the figure for extraordinary items and so on. In fact, we will compare net earnings to the capital provided by share-holders (equity).

We will take a look at some other ratios in the remainder of this analysis. We have almost finished with the income statement, but we still need to talk about the difference between net earnings and cash flow.

Cash flow, a basic approach

A lot of people confuse net earnings (the bottom line of the income statement) with the notion of cash flow. Droids Co. generated net earnings of £41.7M in 2014, but this amount does not correspond to the money actually generated by the company.[6] We will calculate an initial estimate of cash flow based on the income statement. Then, a few pages later, we will calculate a more accurate cash flow.

DIALOGUE

Guildenstern:	Look at the income statement: most of the items represent money coming in (sales, financial revenues) or money going out (salaries, taxes). The difference between them should be a monetary result, a stream of money – a cash flow.
Rosencrantz:	What about depreciation and provisions?
Guildenstern:	Those lines do not correspond to monetary expenses; they are just accounting entries. All we have to do is remove those two lines from the income statement and redo the calculation to get a monetary result that we will call 'cash flow'. There's another way to do this calculation that is used more often in practice: we take the net earnings and we add back the amount of depreciation/amortization and provisions. For Droids Co., take a look at the calculation in Table 1.3.

---

6. You just have to look at Droids' balance sheet: cash and cash equivalents went from £14.5M to £11.7M between 2013 and 2014; this decrease does not tally with the reported net earnings of +£41.7M.

Table 1.3 Cash flow (basic)

	2012	2013	2014
Net earnings	37.4	44.0	41.7
add back: depreciation/amortization and provisions	27.0	25.7	29.3
= Cash flow	64.4	69.7	71.1

DIALOGUE

Rosencrantz: *There's one thing I don't understand: to calculate cash flow we wanted to **remove** the depreciation/amortization and provisions from the income statement and yet here we're adding them to the net earnings...*

Guildenstern: *That's precisely why I said 'add **back** the depreciation/amortization and provisions'. When you look at the initial income statement, you see that net earnings (£41.7M) is calculated **after** deducting £29.3M of depreciation/amortization and provisions. So the effect of adding back £29.3M will be to cancel out the depreciation/amortization and provisions. By doing that we arrive at the cash flow, which is therefore a monetary indicator that is independent of depreciation/amortization and provisions.*

Rosencrantz: *So what sort of comment can we make here?*

Guildenstern: *My dear neophyte, notice the sizeable difference between what the company reports (a profit of £41.7M) and the more monetary reality (a cash flow of £71.1M). It is more interesting to compare the latter amount to the investments made, for example, or the amount of debt to be paid back, because all those operations require actual cash, not accounting figures...*

A FOOL AND HIS MONEY...

Some people memorize the formula 'cash flow = net earnings + depreciation/amortization' and subscribe to the following (erroneous) logic: 'Depreciation/amortization is monetary because when it is added to profit we get cash flow. Besides, depreciation is money that is set aside to replace machines later on, which is proof that it is monetary. Voilà!'

Their logic is faulty. Depreciation and amortization are non-cash accounting entries that spread out a past investment – nothing more! They are not 'added' to the profit; they are reincorporated into a result that they have been deducted from. To prove it (if you still need convincing), go back and recalculate Droids Co.'s income statement without taking depreciation/amortization into account. The result you get is the cash flow, isn't it?[7] So depreciation/amortization are not components of cash flow.

---

7. If you don't get this figure for cash flow, change the batteries in your calculator and start again!

Let's set this version of cash flow aside for the moment and move on to the company's balance sheet.

Balance sheet

A balance sheet is made up of assets and liabilities. If the accountant is sober, the total for the asset side will be equal to the total for the liabilities side.

Assets

Table 1.4 shows Droid Co.'s assets for the past three years.

Table 1.4   Assets

Assets	2012	2013	2014
Gross assets	554.2	581.3	612.1
– depreciation	−364.3	−388.9	−416.9
Net assets	**189.9**	**192.5**	**195.2**
Gross inventory	112.5	122.9	135.0
–provisions	−6.8	7.5	−8.3
Net inventory	**105.7**	**115.4**	**126.8**
Gross accounts receivable	328.4	381.7	448.0
–provisions	−3.2	−3.6	−4.2
Net accounts receivable	**325.2**	**378.1**	**443.8**
Cash and cash equivalents	17.7	14.5	11.7
Total net assets	**638.5**	**700.5**	**777.5**
Total gross assets	1,012.8	1,100.5	1,206.9

To comment on these accounts, we could express all the lines as a percentage of net assets. We won't, though, because we don't feel like it.[8] We'll just point out that, roughly speaking:

- Receivables accounted for half of net assets in 2012 and their proportion has increased (57% of net assets in 2014); this means that there is more and more money 'outside' the company.
- Assets have been heavily depreciated: last year depreciation accounted for two-thirds (416.9/612.1) of the historical value of the investments. This could mean that these assets are not being replaced often enough.
- Provisions for doubtful debt are small in proportion to receivables (but we're still talking about millions of pounds), while provisions for inventory are relatively large: 6% of inventory has been depreciated (8.3/135), which may represent a significant loss.
- Finally, cash and cash equivalents are small compared with total assets. Obviously, it is never a good thing to leave money 'uninvested', but cash also enables the company to deal with emergencies, such as unexpected expenses.

DIALOGUE	
Rosencrantz:	Let's talk about depreciation. Why doesn't the depreciation on the balance sheet (416.9 last year) match the depreciation on the income statement (28.0 last year)?
Guildenstern:	On the income statement we have the depreciation for the year. On the balance sheet, however, we have the cumulative depreciation for all the years together (and the same goes for provisions). In 2013, the depreciation recorded on the balance sheet was 388.9. In 2014, it was 416.9, an increase of 28, which is the figure we find for that year on the income statement.
Rosencrantz:	So assets were depreciated last year by 28/612 = 4.6% of their purchase cost and 68.1% of assets have already been depreciated (416.9/612.1).
Guildenstern:	That's right, which means that the machines are aging, have not been replaced or are being depreciated quickly.

Now let's take a look at Droids Co.'s liabilities.

---

8. These calculations – and a ton of others – can be downloaded **free of charge** from the book's dedicated website (www.breakingthefinancialice.com). But we'd be willing to bet a fiver that diligent readers will do the calculations themselves. Learning through doing is really the only way.

17

Liabilities

Table 1.5 Liabilities

Liabilities	2012	2013	2014
Capital stock	57.0	57.0	57.0
Net earnings	37.4	44.0	41.7
Retained earnings	197.6	214.3	249.5
Shareholders' equity	**292.0**	**315.3**	**348.3**
Long-term debt	190.0	204.4	230.9
Current liabilities	106.7	119.1	133.8
Short-term debt	49.8	61.7	64.5
Total liabilities	**638.5**	**700.5**	**777.5**

First, we observe that total assets are equal to total liabilities, which is rather reassuring. Let's begin our guided tour by listening to that tiresome Rosencrantz and the rather clever answers from Guildenstern.

DIALOGUE	
Rosencrantz:	I get what the assets side is all about: stuff that you own and that you've put money into. But what about liabilities?
Guildenstern:	Liabilities represent the claims that various investors and partners have on the company's assets. Imagine that the company were to be liquidated, meaning that all the assets were to be sold off. The machines and inventories would then be turned into cash. If we look at the liabilities side, we see the claims that investors and partners would have on this cash: 133.8 in accounts payable, 64.5 in short-term debt and so on.
Rosencrantz:	But there's no guarantee that the assets will be sold at their book value: 777.5. How can we be sure that all the investors will be paid in full?
Guildenstern:	We're not sure. The ones who are taking a big risk are the shareholders, because shareholders' equity will be paid last. For example, if they sell the assets for 750, they will be short 27.5 to pay everybody – and the shareholders are the ones who will get less.
Rosencrantz:	Does that mean that the banks and suppliers will be fully paid, but the shareholders will only get 320.8 (348.3 minus the missing 27.5) instead of the full 348.3?
Guildenstern:	Bingo!

This discussion is important and is worth a closer look. Liabilities represent the claims on the company's assets and allow us to see the financing breakdown that everyone has agreed to. Shareholders have a claim over 348.3/777.5 = 44.8% of the assets, while banks have a claim equal to (230.9 + 64.5)/777.5 = 38% of the assets, and so on.

FINANCIALESE

Shareholders' equity represents what belongs to shareholders and this has two possible sources: either (a) the shareholders provided it, or (b) the company generated profits for the shareholders.

(a) The money the shareholders provide is called **capital stock**. This represents the amount invested in the company by shareholders either at its founding (initial capital) or during subsequent **capital issuances**.

(b) But the company also makes a profit for its shareholders: net earnings, which is the bottom line on the income statement. This amount is included in shareholders' equity because it represents a claim that shareholders have on the profits earned. Given that shareholders not only have a claim on the year's profits but also to all past earnings since the formation of the company, the balance sheet also shows the sum of past earnings, minus any dividends paid: this is recorded under **retained earnings**.

For Droids Co., then, shareholders have a claim of £348.3M, which is made up of £57M provided by shareholders (capital stock) and 41.7 + 249.5 = £291.2M of profit generated (present and past), minus any dividends that may have been paid out.

Financial debt, whether short term or long term, is money that has been lent by banks or other financial institutions. The company should therefore try to remember to pay back the capital on time!

Finally, **current liabilities** includes accounts payable (money owed to suppliers), taxes (VAT, corporation tax payable) and payroll charges (social security, premiums). The company has been granted a certain amount of time to pay. These are non-interest-bearing debts, but they may have a social or business cost.

Capital structure ratios

To comment on these statements, we will first calculate **capital structure ratios**, essentially based on debt.

Table 1.6 Capital structure ratios

Name	Ratio	2012	2013	2014
Financial leverage (debt-to-equity ratio)	Debt / Equity	82.1%	84.4%	84.8%
Proportion of short-term debt	Short-term debt / Total debt	20.8%	23.2%	21.8%

We observe that the company has almost as much debt as equity. The bank's risk is therefore almost as high as that of the shareholders. Banks often prefer not to go beyond 60% of equity. We consider therefore that this company is heavily in debt, which is not necessarily a bad thing, but requires vigilance concerning the company's ability to make interest payments and pay back the principal.

Furthermore, one-fifth of this debt is short-term, which therefore must be paid back within one year. Caution must be exercised if short-term debt accounts for too large a portion of total financial debt.

Liquidity ratios

> *But then the entire economy is affected by the emergence of a series of disorders, occurring rather quickly and persisting for varying lengths of time.*
>
> Dr Georges Thibierge (1856–1926), *Maladies vénériennes et cutanées*, Masson (1891) (Translation by the authors)

Table 1.7   Liquidity ratios

Name	Ratio		2012	2013	2014
Cash ratio	$\dfrac{\text{cash and cash equivalents}}{\text{short-term debt}}$		0.4	0.2	0.2
Quick ratio (acid test)	$\dfrac{\text{accounts receivable} + \text{cash and cash equivalents}}{\text{current liabilities} + \text{short-term debt}}$		2.2	2.2	2.3
Current ratio	$\dfrac{\text{inventories} + \text{accounts receivable} + \text{cash and cash equivalents}}{\text{current liabilities} + \text{short-term debt}}$		2.9	2.8	2.9

DIALOGUE	
Rosencrantz:	What are liquidity ratios?
Guildenstern:	They're ratios that measure a company's ability to meet its immediate obligations. For example, the cash ratio answers this question: 'if I have to repay my short-term debt immediately, do I have enough cash (or cash equivalents) to do so?'
Rosencrantz:	Well here we only have 0.4 so there isn't enough cash to pay off the short-term debt. Oh dear! The company's going bankrupt!
Guildenstern:	If that were the case, it would have gone bankrupt three years ago. It may look alarming, but we have to take a look at the other ratios. For example, the quick ratio

	broadens the question: we now include not only cash, but also accounts receivable (money that will be received soon). And we compare the money that is readily available with the debts that must be paid soon: short-term debt and current liabilities.
Rosencrantz:	*So in our case the amount of money that will be received in the coming months is twice as much as what has to be paid out. The company is liquid. Hurray!*
Guildenstern:	*...as long as the customers pay on time. Lastly, the current ratio expands the question to include inventories: they are turned into sales that become accounts receivable, which in turn become cash. Once again we compare what we expect to receive (the top part of the ratio) with what we have to pay (the bottom part).*
	These liquidity ratios introduce a crucial notion: payment and production deadlines. This notion brings us to an indicator that will be central to many financial operations: net working capital (NWC). We will take the time to study this in detail.

Net working capital (NWC)

Net working capital (NWC, often used synonymously with 'working capital'[9]) is a crucial indicator for the financial management of companies. Whenever you need to calculate cash flows, talk about liquidity or do a business valuation, you will find NWC. It is therefore very important to understand this indicator.

Without further ado then, here is the equation for NWC and the calculation for the year 2012 at Droids Co.

Net working capital = Inventories + Accounts receivable – Current liabilities[10]

Table 1.8 Net working capital

	2012
Inventories	105.7
+ Accounts receivable	325.2
– Current liabilities	–106.7
= Net working capital	324.2

9. Depending on the context, we will use different denominations. While we prefer the term 'net working capital' (NWC), we will also refer simply to 'working capital' for brevity, and 'working capital requirements' (WCR) when it comes to calculating cash flows. Some professionals also speak of 'operating working capital' (OWC).
10. The detailed equation adds this: + other current receivables – other current liabilities.

Now we're moving full steam ahead! But what do these figures mean and why is this indicator so 'crucial'? The eternally patient Guildenstern responds to that wooden-headed Rosencrantz.

Explanation of net working capital (NWC)

DIALOGUE	
Guildenstern:	Let's look at the indicators in order, starting with inventories. What does the £105.7M of inventories in 2012 mean to you?
Rosencrantz:	That means that we have raw materials, but also work-in-process inventories and finished goods. It includes all the products in various stages of production and they are worth £105.7M in total.
Guildenstern:	Ah, so they're worth that amount, are they? And how did we value these inventories?
Rosencrantz:	The same as for any asset: using their historical value – either the purchase cost (for raw materials) or the production cost (for work-in-process and finished goods).
Guildenstern:	So here we come to the first very important thing: these inventories represent costs, which are past expenses. In other words, saying 'I have 105 million pounds' worth of inventory' really means 'I have spent £105 million on purchases and production expenses to build my inventory.' But it's not at all the same thing. Inventories are often seen as assets, but they are actually accumulated expenses!
Rosencrantz:	Mother-of-pearl, that's right!

So that's the first important thing about NWC: inventories – normally seen as assets that are worth money – are first and foremost an accumulation of past expenses. Hush! Rosencrantz and Guildenstern are still conversing, let's listen in ...

DIALOGUE	
Guildenstern:	Now let's move on to accounts receivable. What does the £325M in 2012 represent?
Rosencrantz:	That's money our customers owe us to pay for goods that we delivered to them. So that's good news!
Guildenstern:	No, not really, because we have to remember that today's accounts receivable were yesterday's inventories. And those receivables are built on past production expenses and cash outlays. Truth be told, a company that delivers a product is a company that plays the role of a bank: it made cash outlays to purchase materials and produce goods.

And there's the second thing to remember about NWC: accounts receivable are never good news because, just like inventories, they required the company to spend money without receiving anything in exchange. We know for a fact that we haven't received anything yet, because the very definition of accounts receivable is: 'the money our customers still owe us'.

DIALOGUE	
Rosencrantz:	Yet when we make a sale (we ship something to the customer and we send them an invoice) we earn a profit that should compensate for all that. So the company wins in the end, right?
Guildenstern:	Yes, but the company still has its money tied up for months. Even when they invoice their customers, they still have to wait for them to pay! In some cases, the company only receives payment seven or eight months after expenses are incurred.
Rosencrantz:	All right, so there's a delay, but it's just a matter of time. When the customer pays, the deficit is covered.
Guildenstern:	Not at all! When a customer pays March's invoices in June, that will cover the expenses for March, but in the meantime, the company has already incurred the production costs for April, May and June. They're constantly pushing things forward; the company spends the money to continue to produce and deliver its goods.
Rosencrantz:	Gadzooks! So, if I look at my previous table, that means the company has laid out 105.7 + 325.2 = £430.9M!
Guildenstern:	Well, you've got the idea, but that number is a little overestimated. In fact, the company hasn't actually incurred all those expenses – for two reasons. First, accounts receivable also contain a profit margin, which is not an expense. To be perfectly rigorous, we would have to subtract the margin from our calculation. In the interests of keeping things simple, though, very few companies bother to do this. Second, the company may have incurred the expense, but luckily for us, it hasn't paid everything yet. To see this, let's look at **current liabilities**. In the table, they amount to £106.7M in 2012. That means that of the £431M in expenses incurred, £106.7M has not yet been paid to the company's suppliers. This is why they have been removed from the calculation.
Rosencrantz:	Hang on, I think I'm starting to get it! Listen to this and tell me if I've got it right: in recent months, the company has incurred £105.7M in expenses to build inventory and it has delivered £325.2M worth of goods to its customers. These accounts receivable are in fact production costs + a profit margin, so we can say that the company has incurred a total of 105.7 + 325.2 = £430.9M in expenses (not counting the margin).

> – of the £431M there is £106.7M that has not yet been paid. This means that (by subtraction) 431 – 106.7 = £324.3M has already been paid. That's the NWC. It's the same as saying that over the past few months the company has paid out £324.3M to keep its business operating.
>
> Guildenstern: That's exactly right! And it refers to **operating cash outlays** that have already been made.

Let's summarize this rather long, though necessary, discussion:

- Net working capital (NWC) is, in every respect, a monetary investment. It corresponds to the amounts of money paid out by the company so that it can produce goods and services for its customers. It is therefore an obligatory investment if the company wants to sell its products and get paid.
- Investing in fixed assets (machines, buildings and so on) is not enough. A company that neglects to plan its investment in NWC is a company that will not be able to produce its goods, much less sell its products. There are therefore two types of investment to consider: fixed assets and NWC. And of these two types, the more important is probably NWC. Indeed, although there may be companies that have no fixed assets (everything is rented), **every company has NWC,** because they all have an operating cycle, with customers and suppliers.

Analysis of Droids Co.'s net working capital

Creditors have better memories than debtors.
Benjamin Franklin, *Poor Richard's Almanac* (1758)

Let's calculate Droids Co.'s NWC for the past three years in order to assess its evolution.

Table 1.9 Net working capital 2012–14

	2012	2013	2014
Inventories	105.7	115.4	126.8
+ Accounts receivable	325.2	378.1	443.8
– Current liabilities	–106.7	–119.1	–133.8
Net working capital (NWC)	324.2	374.4	436.8

We observe an increase over the years. Given what we have just said about NWC, this increase is bad for the company's cash flow. The increase amounts to 436.8 – 324.2 = £112.6M. The company has therefore invested an additional £112.6M in its NWC over the past two years.

What might be the cause of this change?

- Either there has been mismanagement (inventories have increased too much, customers have been paying later)
- Or there has been an increase in business volume. For example, if production increases, inventories will increase.

To separate these two possibilities, we have to look at the change in NWC with respect to the change in business volume (sales):

Table 1.10 Growth in NWC compared with growth in sales

	2012	2013	2014
NWC	324.2	374.4	436.8
Growth in NWC		+15.5%	+16.6%
Sales	774.7	809.6	848.4
Growth in sales		+4.5%	+4.8%

We observe here that NWC has grown faster than sales. This is not a good sign. Normally, **NWC will increase along with sales, but it must be kept under control**:

- The more the company produces, the more it consumes, the more it sells and the more it invoices.
- So inventories (production) keep pace with sales.
- Accounts receivable (invoices) keep pace with sales.
- Accounts payable (purchases) keep pace with production (All of this because if sales are anticipated, the company must purchase materials before producing, selling and invoicing.)

In this example, for a 4–5% increase in sales (and therefore probably the same increase in production) we observe a 15–16% increase in NWC. Of course, it may be a temporary increase (excess inventory), but it causes a significant cash outlay (reminder: there is a variance of + £112M).

We can express NWC directly as a percentage of sales:

Table 1.11 NWC as a percentage of sales

	2012	2013	2014
NWC/sales	42%	46%	51%
(NWC/sales) × 365 days	153 days	169 days	188 days

We observe that the proportion of NWC has gone from 42% of annual sales to 51%, which is not good (disproportionately large NWC in relation to the volume of business). If Droids Co. was managed well, we would have an NWC that was holding steady at 42% of sales, or even diminishing.

Some financial analysts do not like this 'percentage of sales' metric because they consider it to be too abstract. They calculate the same indicator but express it in terms of 'days of sales'. Thus we see in the table that NWC represented 153 days of sales in 2012 and by 2014 had gone up to 188 days, which is more than six months of sales. This metric gives us a better idea of the change in NWC because we can break it down into its three main components:

Table 1.12 Breakdown of NWC

	2012	2013	2014
(Inventories/sales) × 365	50 days	52 days	55 days
+ (Accounts receivable/sales) × 365	153 days	170 days	191 days
− (Current liabilities/sales) × 365	50 days	54 days	58 days
= (NWC/sales) × 365	153 days	169 days	188 days

Now we can explain this worsening situation by breaking NWC down into its individual components. We observe that inventories represent more and more 'days of sales' and this means many days of sales that are not converted into cash because they are tied up in inventory. But the main problem is with customers: in 2012 they were paying within five months (153 days), but now they are taking more than six months to pay (191 days). That is a lot of cash that is not going into the company's bank account. Late customer payments are probably causing Droids Co. to run overdrafts and pay fees to its bank.

At the same time, we see that the company is playing the same game with its suppliers, though to a lesser degree. Unpaid current liabilities amounted to 50 days of sales and now they are up to 58 days. This is an improvement, but these eight days 'saved' do not offset the 38 days lost to customers. Ultimately, the change in NWC can be explained by the changes in the timing of these three components.

The course of action that we might recommend to the company's managers derives directly from these observations: keep an eye on inventory levels, try to speed up customer payments and see if the company can negotiate better payment deadlines with suppliers. The aim is to improve the company's cash flow by not tying up too much money in NWC.

DIALOGUE	
Rosencrantz:	I'm wondering about those 'days' that were mentioned. Is it really fair to compare current liabilities (which stem from materials purchases) to sales? They're not the same thing...
Guildenstern:	Indeed. 'Days of sales' is just a unit of measurement here, nothing more. It allows us to compare different items and explain the change in NWC. But it would be false to say that 'the suppliers are paid in 58 days' or that 'inventories are used in 55 days'. The purpose of these calculations is to show the current trend (improvement or deterioration).

Overview of working capital

Net working capital (NWC) is an investment that is necessary to keep the operating cycle going.

- Under ideal conditions, NWC is correlated to growth in sales. That means that it represents a steady proportion of sales (as a percentage or in days) and any change in sales will lead to the same change in NWC.
- NWC is therefore a recurring investment. The more a company grows, the more it will have to invest in NWC ... in advance (because it has to purchase raw materials before producing and selling goods[11]). In the cemetery of still-born companies, many have the following epitaph on their tombstone: 'Though they had all the capital necessary to finance their machines, they forgot they had to finance their NWC ... and, most importantly, their growth.' It is a cruel paradox: the companies whose sales grow quickly are the ones most at risk of going bankrupt.
- NWC taps into a company's cash (as we will see in a moment) and is therefore part of the cash flow calculation.

---

11. It would be a mistake to think that only manufacturing companies suffer from excessive NWC; service companies are also bound by the same constraints. The main problem is seldom production time, but rather the gap between customer payments and supplier payments (especially payroll). Think about a freelance consultant who carries out a project. When will he/she be paid?

The financial presentation of the balance sheet

A balance sheet complies with rules of classification that differ from the priorities of a financier. An accountant is interested in assets and in the company's rights and obligations. A financier would just like to have investments on one side and the company's financing on the other. Let's take Droids Co.'s balance sheet and rearrange it.

Table 1.13 Balance sheet: initial financial presentation

Assets	2012	2013	2014	Liabilities	2012	2013	2014
Fixed assets	189.9	192.5	195.2	Shareholders' equity	292.0	315.3	348.3
Inventories	105.7	115.4	126.8	Long-term debt	190.0	204.4	230.9
Accounts receivable	325.2	378.1	443.8 ←	Current liabilities	106.7	119.1	133.8
Cash and cash equivalents	17.7	14.5	11.7 →	Short-term debt	49.8	61.7	64.5
Total assets	**638.5**	**700.5**	**777.5**	**Total liabilities**	**638.5**	**700.5**	**777.5**

The arrows indicate the modifications we are going to make to this balance sheet.

- First, we are going to move current liabilities to the assets side, with a negative sign. Thus the liabilities side will contain only resources provided by investors (shareholders' equity and borrowings) and the assets side will be made up of operating elements (inventories, accounts receivable and current liabilities).
- Second, we are going to move cash and cash equivalents to the liabilities side, also with a negative sign, so they will be deducted from the short-term debt. If we look at the table above, there is 49.8 of short-term debt and 17.7 of cash in 2012. That means that 17.7 of the 49.8 in debt can be paid off immediately, leaving 49.8 – 17.7 = 32.1 of short-term debt. (To this we will add long-term debt because that also has to be repaid.)

The revised balance sheet is as follows:

Table 1.14 Revised balance sheet

Assets	2012	2013	2014	Liabilities	2012	2013	2014
Fixed assets	189.9	192.5	195.2	Shareholders' equity	292.0	315.3	348.3
Net working capital	324.2	374.4	436.8	Net debt	222.1	251.6	283.7
Capital employed	**514.1**	**566.9**	**632.0**	**Capital employed**	**514.1**	**566.9**	**632.0**

This has a twofold advantage:

- Assets now contain only investments (fixed assets and NWC).
- Liabilities now contain only financing items (the amount of debt indicated is what remains after any potential repayment).

And it's easier to read!

DIALOGUE	
Rosencrantz:	So we've changed the terms. Before, in the accounting presentation, we had assets and liabilities. Now, with this financial presentation, we're taking about capital employed.
Guildenstern:	That's right. Since we have modified the presentation of the balance sheet, the numbers are no longer the same and so we use a different term.
Rosencrantz:	And capital employed can be expressed either as Fixed Assets + NWC or as Shareholders' Equity + Net Debt?
Guildenstern:	Correct, although we prefer the Fixed Assets + NWC calculation, because what interests us is what has been put into the business: the investments that have been made. That said, it also corresponds to the capital provided by investors.

Returns

A 'return' is a profit made on an investment. If you invest £100K in a small rental flat and it generates £6K per year in rent, that is a return of 6% per year. For a company, we can consider two different kinds of return that correspond to two kinds of investment:

- what has been invested in the business activity. This is called capital employed, and the **return on capital employed** is an indicator of the company's economic performance.
- what the shareholders have invested. This is called shareholders' equity, and the **return on equity** indicates what shareholders get from their investment.

Let's look at these two in detail for Droids Co.

Return on capital employed (ROCE)

We have just seen a balance sheet with **capital employed**. This represents the investments made in the company's business. The capital employed generates sales revenue. When operating expenses (raw materials, supplies, wages) are deducted, we are left with the operating profit. The ratio of operating profit to capital employed is the pre-tax **return on capital employed** (ROCE). For Droids Co. this is shown in Table 1.15:

Table 1.15 Return on capital employed

	2012	2013	2014
Operating profit	68.6	74.0	81.4
/Capital employed	514.1	566.9	632.0
= Return on capital employed (ROCE)	13.3%	13.1%	12.9%

FINANCIALESE

Return on capital employed is abbreviated to ROCE (sometimes pronounced 'rocky' or rō-kee'). You will also hear ROI (return on investment) and the rather melodious ROIC (return on invested capital), and sometimes even RONTA (return on net trading assets).

The calculations for Droids Co. show that the return from its business is decreasing. While it is true that the operating profit is increasing, every pound invested in capital generates less and less profit. This may mean that the business is running out of steam (insufficient operating profit) or that it is getting too bulky (too much money invested in capital employed). To delve further into this question, let's break down the ROCE.

A word of advice: these are not complex equations, so don't be put off by them! Let's take the ROCE ratio and break it down into two other ratios:

$$\frac{\text{Operating profit}}{\text{Capital employed}} = \frac{\text{Operating profit}}{\text{Sales}} \times \frac{\text{Sales}}{\text{Capital employed}}$$

Breaking it down like this allows us to express the return as the outcome of two strategies:

$$\text{ROCE} = \text{operating margin} \times \text{capital turnover ratio}$$

Let's illustrate this with Droids Co.'s accounts.

Table 1.16 Breakdown of ROCE

	2012	2013	2014
ROCE	**13.3%**	**13.1%**	**12.9%**
= Operating margin	9.6%	10.1%	10.0%
× Capital turnover ratio	1.51	1.43	1.34

We see that this breakdown can help to explain the decreasing return:

1. The profit margin has improved slightly (a pound of sales generated 9.6 pence and then 10 pence of profit), perhaps owing to better cost control or an increase in prices.
2. At the same time, however, the capital invested is not being used as effectively: one pound invested generated £1.51 of sales in 2012 and only £1.34 in 2014. So either there has been a slowdown in sales (but that is not what we have observed here) or there has been an intensification of investment. Either way, the volume of sales is not keeping pace with investments and that is hurting performance.

This breakdown helps us refine our reading of the company's financial statements and is even used to categorize companies: those that sell a lot and earn small margins; those that reduce their investments to increase their asset turnover ratio; and those that opt for a high added-value strategy.

VIGNETTE – BARFLIES

> *I drink when I have occasion,*
> *and sometimes when I have no occasion.*
> Miguel de Cervantes, *Don Quixote de la Mancha* (1605)

Wilbur: *Clyde, I don't get this business about asset turnover and margins...*

Clyde: *Take a look at your shot glass there in front of you. See it?*

Wilbur: *Sure thing, Clyde. I got it lined up in my sights!*

Clyde: *So I grab the bottle of Jack and fill your glass up to the brim and mine just half-full. What d'ya say?*

Wilbur: *I'd say you're a pal, Clyde!*

Clyde: *Right, but now here's the trick (he tosses back his drink). While you're raving about what a swell guy I am, I drink quickly and I refill my glass before you've even touched yours.*

Wilbur: *Don't you fret, Clyde, I'm gonna catch up...*

Clyde:	Don't bet on it. What the ROCE equation says is that a half-filled glass that you drink twice as fast is the same as a large glass that you drink slowly. Small margin × fast turnover = large margin × slow turnover.
Wilbur:	Then the best thing would be a large margin × fast turnover...(reaching for a larger glass)
Clyde:	Yep, but that's a rare combination. To earn a big margin you often need to make a lot of investments, so that means a large amount of capital employed. And then the asset turnover would be low. Get it?
Wilbur:	Perfickly. Thanksh.

We have one last point to cover here. ROCE benefits from one of its weaknesses; it does not take the company's financing choices into account.

- This is an advantage because it allows us to compare companies without having to take their capital structure into account.[12] Whether they are in debt or not, they will still have the same ROCE.
- But investors (shareholders) are worried about the company's borrowing strategy: every pound paid out in interest is one less they will receive in dividends. We therefore need another indicator, one that will measure final performance.

Return on equity (ROE)

Remember, a return is a profit made on an investment:

- What have shareholders invested in the company? Whether actively or passively,[13] they have invested the equity.
- What is the return for shareholders? Their return is the net earnings, whether distributed as dividends or retained in the company.

We can compare the earnings generated for shareholders by their investment: this will give us the **return on equity**. Let's do the maths for Droids Co.

Table 1.17   Return on equity

	2012	2013	2014
Net earnings	37.4	44.0	41.7
/Shareholders' equity	292.0	315.3	348.3
= Return on equity (ROE)	12.8%	14.0%	12.0%

---

12. Take another look at the ROCE equation: neither the amount of debt nor the amount of interest paid is included.

13. Actively by providing capital; passively by leaving money that might have been paid out in dividends.

This return could be compared with what shares in another publicly traded company operating in the same sector generate. Here we do not have that information, so we will proceed in a different way:

- We have seen that ROCE measures the company's economic performance, independently of the amount of debt.
- In contrast, ROE measures the final performance for shareholders after the interest expense has been deducted, thus taking the company's borrowing strategy into account.
- **So the difference between ROCE and ROE is the impact of the company's borrowing decisions.**

When we analyse this impact we are measuring the company's **financial leverage**.

Financial leverage

Under certain conditions, a company's borrowings will create an additional return for shareholders. This is based on a simple idea:

SLICE OF LIFE● ●
If Lotta Doe borrows money at 8% to invest in a business that generates 11%, that means that each dollar of debt produces 8% for the bank (which receives what it asked for) + 3% for Lotta, the shareholder. Thus, those dollars of debt (dollars that were not provided by Lotta) earn an additional return for the shareholder.

And the greater the amount of debt, the greater the leverage.
● ●

Let's illustrate this idea with Droids Co. First we have to calculate the interest rate. We can get a rough idea by comparing interest expense to financial debt:

Table 1.18 Average cost of debt

	2012	2013	2014
Long-term debt	190.0	204.4	230.9
Short-term debt	49.8	61.7	64.5
Total financial debt	239.8	266.1	295.4
Interest expense	16.1	18.3	20.7
Interest expense/financial debt	6.7%	6.9%	7.0%

We observe that the average cost of debt has increased slightly, perhaps owing to an increase in interest rates or less effective negotiations with the bank. In spite of this increase, the money borrowed was invested in capital employed and has produced a return: the return on capital employed (ROCE).

We can calculate the difference between the two rates of return (ROCE and the cost of debt):

Table 1.19   Differential

	2012	2013	2014
ROCE	13.3%	13.1%	12.9%
–Average cost of debt	– 6.7%	– 6.9%	– 7.0%
= Differential	6.6%	6.2%	5.9%

This difference represents the first component of leverage, which we call **the differential**. (The other component is **leverage** (or gearing), which we will see in a minute.)

DIALOGUE	
Rosencrantz:	What, in plain English, is this difference between the rates of return?
Guildenstern:	For 2012, it means that Droids Co. borrowed money at 6.7% and those sums were invested in assets that generated 13.3%. Out of the 13.3% they paid the bank 6.7% and there was a 6.6% return left over for the shareholders.
Rosencrantz:	So where's the magic in that?
Guildenstern:	This gain was achieved for the shareholders using borrowed money. In other words, they generated a return for the shareholders using money that the shareholders didn't provide.
Rosencrantz:	What can we say about the change from 2012 to 2014?
Guildenstern:	Make an effort, you old codger! The difference is still positive, which is good, but it is diminishing, either because of a decrease in the operating return (ROCE) or because of an increase in interest rates.

Now let's measure how much debt Droids Co. is carrying, because that is another component of leverage.

Table 1.20 Leverage

	2012	2013	2014
Total financial debt	239.8	266.1	295.4
/Shareholders' equity	292.02	315.32	348.32
= **Leverage**	0.82	0.84	0.85

For every £1 provided by shareholders, the banks provided between £0.82 and £0.85 depending on the year. This is not really a measure of the company's debt burden, but rather a measure of the relative contributions of shareholders and banks to the company's financing. But this measure does enable us to calculate the **leveraged return**:

Table 1.21 Leveraged return

	2012	2013	2014
ROCE	13.3%	13.1%	12.9%
– Average cost of debt	–6.7%	–6.9%	–7.0%
= **Differential**	6.6%	6.2%	5.9%
× Leverage	0.82	0.84	0.85
= **Leveraged return**	**+5.5%**	**+5.2%**	**+5.0%**

Thus, Droids Co.'s debt financing strategy has allowed its shareholders to earn an additional return of +5.5% and then +5.0%. As we see, everything begins with the difference between the rates of return, and leverage is a multiplier of this difference: the more debt the company carries, the greater the impact of leverage (if the company were losing money, the losses would also be magnified).

To sum up, the shareholders will get a return made up of two elements:

- From their own investment as shareholders they will get the ROCE. The capital they put into the company is invested in a business that generates a return on capital employed (ROCE).
- From the money borrowed by the company they will get an additional return, called the leveraged return.

If we look at the figures for Droids Co. we obtain:

Table 1.22 Total shareholder return

	2012	2013	2014
ROCE	13.3%	13.1%	12.9%
+ Leveraged return	+5.5%	+5.2%	+5.0%
Pre-tax return for shareholders	18.8%	18.3%	17.9%
Compared with ROE	12.8%	14.0%	12.0%

Several observations can be made about this calculation:

- Shareholders get a return that mainly comes from the company's business operations – fortunately for them – but they enjoy an additional return stemming from its debt financing strategy.
- If we show the final return (ROE calculated as net earnings/shareholders' equity), we see that it differs from the pre-tax leveraged return calculated (18.8% compared with 12.8% in 2012). This does not mean that the leveraged rate of return equation is wrong, just that it is calculated before tax and does not take into account financial revenues and extraordinary items. We will leave the discussion of financial leverage there because what is important here is to understand where the additional return comes from and how it changes over time.[14]

Cash flows

For a financial manager or an investor the only reality is the money coming in minus the money going out. But accounting entries (and therefore financial statements) do not show this information clearly either on the income statement or on the balance sheet. A third statement is therefore needed: the cash flow statement. We are going to look at the beginning of this statement in detail, but first we will explain the concept of cash flow.

In the section 'Cash flow, a basic approach' (above), we made an initial estimate of the company's cash flow. Before we continue, it would be a good idea to go over that part again carefully, moving your lips as you read so that it sinks in better.

Ready? Ok, let's move on.

The cash flow that we calculated there is not really an instantaneous flow of cash into your bank account, for two reasons:

---

14. More detailed calculations are provided on the website (www.breakingthefinancialice.com).

1. Depreciation/amortization and provisions are not the only non-monetary accounting entries.
2. There is the problem of the gap between payment dates.

Let's start with **point 1**. There are certain non-cash accounting adjustments made to the income statement, called **changes in inventory**, whose purpose is to **record only what has been used during the year**, instead of recording everything that has been purchased (this is mandatory: for a given year a company may record only what has been used for that year). These accounting adjustments correct the inventory figures to show only what has actually been purchased and consumed. However, cash flow is based on net earnings and this is calculated after inventory changes. But since financial analysts want to know the reality of every payment, they will remove these inventory adjustments when calculating cash flow.

Now let's look at **point 2**. For a given year's sales, there's a difference between the amounts invoiced and the amount of money actually received. A company may invoice £100M and only receive £70M. The remaining £30M is added to the accounts receivable line and will be paid later by customers. Thus, there's a difference between the 'potential' cash flow and the cash flow actually obtained. What interests the company's accountants is what they have immediately available in the company bank account. This is the money they will use to pay their suppliers and employees and to cover other expenses at the end of the month. Variations in accounts receivable will also have to be removed from the cash flow calculation because the £30M has been invoiced (hence present in sales), but not received (not present in cash).

The same procedure is followed for purchasing: if the company has recorded £80M in purchases but paid only £60M to suppliers, its current liabilities have increased by £20M (the difference). In calculating net earnings (and hence cash flow), there was –£80M in purchases recorded, whereas in reality there was only –£60M in cash disbursements, so we have to add the difference in current liabilities to the cash flow (+£20M in this case).

We are going to do this calculation for Droids Co.

Calculating the operating cash flow

In the first section on cash flow ('a basic approach'), we performed the following calculation:

Table 1.23 Cash flow (basic)

	2012	2013	2014
Net earnings	37.4	44.0	41.7
Add back:			
+ Depreciation/amortization and provisions	27.0	25.7	29.3
= Cash flow	64.4	69.7	71.1

We now know that this cash flow measurement suffers from certain shortcomings. We are therefore going to apply the calculations from **point 1** (changes in inventory) and **point 2** (accounts receivable and current liabilities).

Table 1.24 Changes in inventory, receivables and liabilities

	2012	2013	2014
Inventories	105.7	115.4	126.8
Changes in inventory		9.7	11.3
Accounts receivable	325.2	378.1	443.8
Changes in accounts receivable		52.9	65.7
Current liabilities	106.7	119.1	133.8
Changes in current liabilities		12.3	14.7

Note that these changes are all increases here. Now let's include **points 1 and 2** in the calculation:

Table 1.25 'Immediate' cash flow

	2012	2013	2014
Cash flow	64.5	69.7	71.1
– *Changes in inventory*		–9.7	–11.3
= **Potential cash flow**		60.0	59.8
– *Changes in accounts receivable*		–52.9	–65.7
+ *Changes in current liabilities*		+12.3	+14.7
= **Immediate cash flow** (operating cash flow)		19.4	8.8

We can now make several observations:

- As we only have data for three years, we can calculate only two changes and therefore two cash flows.
- The term 'potential cash flow' does not actually exist; we used it here to show the real monetary result generated by the company. But since

some of this monetary result has not yet been received/disbursed, it is the 'immediate cash flow' that interests us: this is what we have at the moment in our bank account.

- We realize that most of the cash flow of around £70M is tied up in receivables and is therefore not available: the immediately available cash flow is only £19.4M (2013) and £8.8M (2014).

Most importantly, there is one last point that the sharpest readers will have already spotted: these changes remind us of something... inventories, accounts receivable and current liabilities. By Jove, that's it! The net working capital (NWC)! In fact, **these three changes taken together correspond to the change in net working capital.**

Table 1.26 Operating cash flow

	2012	2013	2014
Inventories	105.7	115.4	126.8
+ Accounts receivable	325.2	378.1	443.8
– Current liabilities	–106.7	–119.1	–133.8
Working capital	324.2	374.4	436.8
Change in NWC		*50.3*	*62.3*
Cash flow	64.5	69.7	71.1
– Change in NWC		*–50.3*	*–62.3*
= Immediate cash flow (operating cash flow)		19.4	8.8

And... drum roll please... we arrive at the same result! Ta-daaa!

FINANCIALESE

The term 'immediate cash flow' does not exist either – a shame because then the nomenclature would be clear. What we have called immediate cash flow is actually known as '**operating cash flow**'. Finally, if we also deduct the year's capital investments, we obtain '**free cash flow**' (see Chapter 6).

Summary of operating cash flow

When you drink the water, remember the spring

(Chinese proverb)

The operating cash flow calculation is done in several stages. We can get a rough idea of it when calculating the first 'gross' cash flow: the result is not the exact cash flow, but it is quick to calculate. If we want to calculate the real cash flow from the company's operations, as it appears in the company's bank account, we have to calculate the 'immediate' (operating) cash flow. Once again we see the importance of the net working capital (NWC) concept. Presented as a necessary cash outflow (see the section on working capital), this indicator is linked to the company's growth. Growth in NWC directly affects cash flow, reducing it by the same amount. In fact, calculating operating cash flow is like asking the following question: 'knowing that my business generates a gross cash flow and that out of this gross cash flow I have to finance my cash disbursements for the year (the increase in my NWC), how much will I have left over at the end?' Answer: the operating cash flow.

A FOOL AND HIS MONEY...

Note that we subtract the **change** in NWC, not the NWC. Cash disbursements from previous years have already been made. Only the cash outflow corresponding to this year's growth will be subtracted.

We will leave the subject of cash flows there. Readers who wish to unravel the mysteries of cash flows from investment activities, cash flows from financing activities or surplus liquidity are advised to pursue their quest for knowledge elsewhere, with our blessing.

Conclusion

> *I could not help laughing at the ease with which he explained his process of deduction. 'When I hear you give your reasons,' I remarked, 'the thing always appears to me to be so ridiculously simple that I could easily do it myself, though at each successive instance of your reasoning I am baffled until you explain your process.'*
>
> Doctor Watson speaking to Sherlock Holmes
> in *A Scandal in Bohemia* (1891)
> Arthur Conan Doyle

Performing a financial analysis is about reading financial statements and trying to interpret them. It is not just the mechanical task of calculating ratios and indicators, but rather a quest for answers. One might even say that good financial analysis is the art of asking the right questions. For this, you need to go beyond the numbers and look at it as an entire system to gain an overall understanding of how the company is evolving. We will see in the coming chapters that the time spent analysing financial statements will be amply rewarded when it comes to making financial decisions.

Summary

In the land of finance, one common tongue
Spoken by all, the rules of accounting
Shape in a thousand ways (and still counting ...)
Financial reports: careful; don't get stung!

First, my good friend, take a look at sales.
Deduct the costs and there's the profit.
Other expenses you must take off it
To find the bottom line and all that entails.

But earnings are not entirely cash flow.
We have to adjust for depreciation.
Self-financing needs cash generation
Lest the icy winds of bankruptcy blow.

Meet the balance sheet: what an abstract maze!
Sturdy assets, pitched against matching debt,
Money to collect (but you won't get it yet),
Receivables you know – like cash with delays.

Working capital is quite the stallion.
Galloping ahead, neck and neck with sales,
Growing, and hungry, it never fails
To chomp through your hay, greedy rapscallion!

Whether NWC or fixed assets,
Capital is employed to run the firm.
Performance is key, we need to confirm:
What is the return the shareholder gets?

Return on capital, ROCE,
Operating margin times the turnover
Assets should be used over and over
Keep shareholders happy, dancing with glee.

Their equity will bring, and here's our last word,
A handsome return, you know this is true
But that is not all; there's borrowing, too.
They leverage the debt ... or so I have heard.

APPENDIX
A tale of two systems

Every portrait that is painted with feeling is a portrait of the artist, not of the sitter.

Oscar Wilde, *The Picture of Dorian Gray* (1891)

For many years, at least two financial information systems have coexisted. On one hand there is the national system of any given country[15] and on the other there are international accounting standards known as IFRS (International Financial Reporting Standards). Every company based in Europe, for instance, must keep its books using the national system (in France, it is the French chart of accounts, *le plan comptable général*; in Germany, the *Grundsätze ordnungsmäßiger Buchführung*; in Spain, the *Plan General de Contabilidad* and so on), but for financial communication, publicly traded companies are obliged to use IFRS for their annual reports. IFRS has become the *lingua franca* of financial communication, an international language that facilitates the comparison of companies from different countries. This is why we use the IFRS framework throughout this book. However, to understand the specificities of the two systems, let's compare them.

We are therefore constantly straddling two accounting systems that do not use the same terminology and, what is worse, do not follow quite the same principles. We show this in detail in Table 1.27.

Table 1.27 Accounting frameworks

Continental European Framework	IFRS Framework
Sales	**Sales**
– External costs	– COGS (cost of goods sold)
Added value	**Gross profit**
– Salaries	– SG&A expenses (selling, general and admin.)
Gross operating profit	**EBITDA (earnings before interest, tax, depreciation and amortization)**
– Depreciation and provisions	– Depreciation and provisions
Operating profit	**EBIT**
– Interest expense	– Interest expense
+ Financial revenues	+ Financial revenues or interest income
Current income before tax	**EBT (earnings before tax)**
Exceptional items	Extraordinary items
– Tax	– Tax
Net earnings	**Net earnings**

---

15. In the United States, for example, it is known as US GAAP (generally accepted accounting principles); in the United Kingdom, UK GAAP. Each country has its own system based on the national accounting framework.

Throughout Chapter 1 we have worked on financial statements following the IFRS framework, which is the column on the right. We will now listen to Winston and Franklin discussing the differences between the two columns.

DIALOGUE	
Winston:	Let's start with the sales revenue, which has the same name on both sides. Is it the same thing?
Franklin:	Yes, for this line we will have the same figure, whichever framework is chosen. However, it changes on the very next line. While COGS covers all direct production costs, the notion of 'external costs' covers all the expenses outside the company – everything that the company buys from suppliers.
Winston:	So what is the difference with the COGS on the IFRS side?
Franklin:	Well, the COGS and SG&A lines on the IFRS side match the external costs and salaries (continental European side), but they are classified differently. Let's take two examples. First, the cost of electricity and supplies. In the European framework all of these will be external costs because they are transactions carried out with external suppliers. But according to IFRS rules, the cost of the electricity that contributes directly to production (powering the machines in the factory) will come under COGS, whereas the indirect part (the electricity used to light the offices, for example) will come under SG&A. The same goes for supplies: the supplies used directly in production will be recorded under COGS, while office supplies will come under administrative expenses. Second, let's take the example of payroll costs. In the European framework, all salaries are recorded under payroll costs. In the IFRS framework, factory workers' salaries are recorded under COGS, whereas sales people's salaries come under selling expenses and accountants' salaries under administrative expenses.
Winston:	What is the reason for this difference in framework and the reclassification?
Franklin:	Historically, for continental Europe a salary is a salary, whatever its purpose – we say that expenses are classified according to their **nature**. But the thinking behind the IFRS standards (as well as in English-speaking countries) is in terms of production costs, so a distinction is made between direct costs and indirect costs. Expenses are therefore classified by their **purpose**. One system isn't better than the other; they are just different approaches.

From this we conclude that the intermediate items (subtotals) do not measure the same thing and do not follow the same logic. The European **added value** measures the profit on sales, after subtracting what has been provided (supplies, services) by the outside world. This **added value** is then used first and foremost to pay the employees (salaries) and the remaining balance is called **gross operating profit**. On the other hand, in the IFRS system 'gross margin' measures earnings from sales: sales revenue minus the costs that can be directly attributed to production.[16] Next, indirect costs and overheads are deducted and we get EBITDA (earnings before interest, tax, depreciation and amortization).

DIALOGUE

Winston: But that is just a different way of organizing the costs. We should end up with the same figure on the gross operating profit/EBITDA line, shouldn't we?

Franklin: Unfortunately, that rarely happens. Beneath these simple reclas- sifications there are a lot of other operations that do not use the same evaluations or the same rules. So a company can report one figure for gross operating profit and a different figure for EBITDA. Nevertheless, the analysis remains the same: on both sides we have an indicator of the profit made on sales, net of operating expenses and before depreciation is taken into account.

The rest of the income statement shows the succession of operations in the same order.[17] Once we have deducted depreciation, we arrive at the oper- ating profit (European system) or **EBIT** (earnings before interest and tax) under IFRS, both also known as **operating income**.

DIALOGUE

Winston: So, as we saw earlier, the value recorded for operating profit will not necessarily be the same as EBIT.

Franklin: That's right, and this will be intensified by certain differences. For instance, many operations considered as 'exceptional' in the European approach will actually be incorporated into EBIT under IFRS.

It follows that even if we begin with the same sales figure in both systems we will not end up with the same value for net earnings on the bottom line of the income statement. As far as possible we must try to compare a

---

16. This concept of gross profit can be roughly equated to what a management accountant would call the 'contribution margin'. But it should be pointed out that not all direct costs are variable costs, just as indirect costs are not all fixed costs.
17. The same order does not necessarily mean the same amounts. There are differences between the two systems in recording and valuing certain operations.

company's accounts with those of other companies that publish under the same framework: a company using Spanish accounting standards compared to other companies using the Spanish system, a company under IFRS compared to its competitors reporting under IFRS.

Practical application to finance

The key advantage of the national systems is this: as they are framed by law, they define the accounting terms used in a very precise manner. In most European countries, the chart of accounts is stipulated by accounting law. For example, in France, 'gross cash flow' (*capacité d'autofinancement*) has an official definition and the formula is set in stone. This ensures that companies can be compared with each other because every company reports a gross cash flow that is calculated in exactly the same way. This is not the case for IFRS, for two reasons – one that affects financial analysis, the other financial management.

The impact of IFRS on financial analysis

Even though IFRS is a coded accounting framework, the rules may be applied differently depending on the company: some companies comply fully with the official framework while others continue to use local terms (is 'operating profit' the same as EBIT, for example?).

Let's see what we can glean from a conversation between Franklin and Charles.

DIALOGUE	
Charles:	Throughout Chapter 1 we have used the IFRS framework to perform our financial analyses. What are the differences when we have to carry out a financial analysis on a company using local standards, for example in Europe?
Franklin:	There is no real difference. The formulas for the ratios change because the income statement indicators change, but the logic behind constructing and understanding the ratios remains the same. We still talk about profit, asset turnover, and return on capital employed. But you have to be aware of the difference between the two income statements as explained at the beginning of this appendix.
Charles:	Are the IFRS accounts more complicated to understand?

Franklin:	Yes, but that's not entirely the fault of the IFRS framework. You have to remember that IFRS is intended for publicly traded companies. It is precisely because they are listed companies that their financial statements may be trickier to read. They have subsidiaries so they produce consolidated financial statements and the whole thing requires more technical analysis than for a single company. So it is not the IFRS standards that are more complicated, but the companies those standards are applied to. We should point out, however, that asset valuation is much more complicated under IFRS standards, because companies regularly have to provide a 'market value' estimate of their assets (something that national standards require much less often).

The impact of IFRS on the ×nancial management of companies

Broadly speaking, as soon as we leave the field of financial communication, things become a little fuzzier. In day-to-day business management, the concept of EBITDA, for instance, varies depending on the company – there is no single formula that is applied by all of them. We therefore have to be very vigilant about what is being referred to by these terms.

DIALOGUE	
Charles:	When we get to Chapter 6 of this book, for example, we will be doing sales and earnings forecasts using the terms EBITDA and EBIT. When do we shift from one accounting framework to the other?
Franklin:	The local national system is used by unlisted companies, usually small businesses, and it is more than sufficient for their financial management. On the other hand, large companies are usually publicly traded and must therefore publish their financial statements under IFRS. They have internalized this language and use IFRS indicators in their daily management. Don't forget, however, that some companies, even though they are 100% local and unlisted, may be the subsidiaries of large corporate groups that think and operate using IFRS indicators.

In summary, and for the sake of comprehension, this appendix is the only place where we will talk about national accounting standards: the remainder of the book is based on the IFRS framework.

2

The Time Value of Money*

> Human: God, you are so powerful! What does time mean to you?
> God: Time is nothing. To me, a thousand years is like a minute.
> Human: (respectful silence) And God, what does money mean to you?
> God: Money is nothing. To me, a billion dollars is like one dollar.
> Human: (dreamy silence) God, could you give me…a dollar?
> God: Sure, hang on a minute.
>
> Anonymous

Interest rates: what's the point?

SLICE OF LIFE●●

One summer day in Ancient Rome two senators are having a conversation outside the Colosseum…

Lorem Ipsum: My dear Sivis, **amicus optissime**, lend me 100 denarii today and I will pay you back 100 denarii in a year's time.

Sivis Pacem: Uh, Lorem, you're my friend and everything, but that's not really fair…Today with 100 denarii I can buy 10 kg of steak. In a year's time, with the rise in the cost of living, 100 denarii will only get me 9.8 kg of steak. It would be more reasonable if you paid me back an amount of money that would allow me to buy 10 kg of steak. You should pay me back taking **anticipated inflation** into account.

Greek chorus: Sivis Pacem is reasoning in **real terms**: the two amounts are comparable because they have the same **purchasing power**.

Lorem Ipsum: All right, lend me 100 denarii and I will pay you back 100 denarii + 2 denarii for the anticipated inflation. With 102 denarii you will be able to buy 10 kg of steak in a year. Shake on it!

Sivis Pacem: Uh, my dear friend, there is also the matter of my…how shall I say…my frustration. If I keep my 100 denarii, I can eat the steak right away. My abstinence has a price…you'll have to compensate me for that too, say, an extra 4 denarii.

Lorem Ipsum: Fine! So I'll pay you back 100 denarii + 2 denarii for inflation + 4 denarii for your 'frustration'. Come on now, let's not spend all day on this.

---

*Consider reading this chapter while listening to 'As Time Goes By' as sung by Dooley Wilson in *Casablanca* (Michael Curtiz, 1941) or 'Avec le temps' by Léo Ferré.

Sivis Pacem: Hmmm, how shall I put this? If I were to put my 100 denarii in the Bank of Helvetica, I would feel safe. I know that the Bank of Helvetica won't go bankrupt or disappear. It has a spotless reputation, a satisfactory **credit history**. Its coffers are full, so there's no **risk of default**. However, if I lend to a high-living, slightly devious character who's as slippery as an eel, then I will require an insurance premium; how shall I say, a **risk premium**. Given your background, my feckless friend, I would think a minimum of 5 denarii would be appropriate.

Lorem Ipsum: Help! Murder! You're bleeding me dry! I think I'll go and ask someone else for the money!

Sivis Pacem: With all due respect, kind Sir, I fear that nobody will agree to less than the amounts that I'm suggesting. Your reputation precedes you, if I may say so.

Greek chorus: And so Lorem Ipsum goes through with it: he borrows 100 denarii and will have to pay back 100 + 2 + 4 + 5 = 111 denarii, broken down into 100 denarii of capital borrowed and 11 denarii of interest, that is: 11/100 = an 11% interest rate. Sivis Pacem is paid for (1) the increase in the cost of living, (2) the frustration of postponing consumption and (3) the risk taken in lending to the dubious Lorem.

What we take away from this scintillating dialogue is that money has a value that evolves over time. And what sums up this evolution is the **interest rate,** which is generally set through a meeting of capital seekers and capital providers.

FINANCIALESE

Sivis lends to the bank at 6% and to Lorem at 11%. The difference between these rates is the **risk premium**, since the Bank of Helvetica here is considered a **risk-free investment**. Examples of investments that are reputed to be risk-free are government bonds and corporate bonds issued by large, solvent companies. **Credit rating agencies** assign a rating to each borrower: AAA is the highest rating, attributed to bonds that are as close as possible to risk-free investments.

The interest rate including inflation is called the **nominal rate** (such as when Sivis lends at 11%). The rate without inflation is called the **real interest rate.** Roughly speaking, the nominal rate = the real rate + anticipated inflation (in this case 11% = 9% + 2%[1]). It is like saying: 'I will lend you 100 denarii at 11%' (nominal rate) or 'I will lend you 10kg of steak at 9%' (real rate), because while the money increases by 11%, the steak increases by 2% (the inflation), which means that in terms of purchasing power (in real terms) you earn only 9%.

---

1. Calculated precisely this is: (1 + nominal rate) = (1 + real rate) × (1 + anticipated inflation). The exact real rate is therefore 8.8% (1.11/1.02).

Let's play with the mathematicians: calculating a future value (FV)

> *Take a board with 64 squares on it. Put a grain of wheat on the first square – two on the second – four on the third. Keep doubling in this manner and you will find there isn't enough wheat in the world to fill the sixty-fourth square. It can be the same with compound interest.*
>
> Harry Stephen Keeler, 'John Jones's Dollar',
> *Amazing Stories* (1927)

Lorem borrows 100 denarii from Sivis at an annual rate of 11%. How much will he owe in one year? Answer: 100 denarii of principal + (100 × 11%) of interest = 100 + 11 = 111 denarii. In finance, we write it like this:

$$\text{Future value} = 100 \times (1 + 11\%) = 111 \text{ denarii}$$

Now, if we suppose that Lorem borrows over two years, how much will he owe Sivis at the end of that time? Let's break it down. At the end of one year, as we know, Lorem owes 111 denarii. This 111 denarii is borrowed for an additional year and generates 11% interest. We can write the future value of the 111 denarii:

$$\text{Future value} = 111 \times (1 + 11\%) = 123.20 \text{ denarii}$$

Now, since the 111 is actually $100 \times (1 + 11\%)$, we can rewrite the equation for two years this way:

$$\text{Future value} = 100 \times (1 + 11\%) \times (1 + 11\%)$$

which can be simplified like this:

$$\text{Future value} = 100 \times (1 + 11\%)^2$$

In the same way, if Lorem borrows for three years, he will have to pay $100 \times (1 + 11\%)^3$. Generally, when we borrow an initial amount for a certain number of periods, we will have to pay:

$$\text{Final value} = \text{initial amount} \times (1 + \text{interest rate per period})^{\text{number of periods}}$$

Or in short,

$$FV = \text{initial amount} \times (1 + i)^n$$

This formula is often used by bankers, financiers and underpaid executives who want to know how much their savings will yield in 15 years.

SLICE OF LIFE: HOW STERLING PRODUCES OFFSPRING••••••••••

One day, Dr Frankenstein deposits £1,000 in an account that pays 6% per year. At the end of a year, the balance in his account is £1,060, which we can break down into 1,000 in capital and 60 in interest. If the good doctor does not withdraw anything, the following year he will have 1,060 × (1 + 6%) = £1,123.60. This amount is made up of 1,060 of capital and 63.60 of interest. We observe that the amount of interest for the second year is no longer 60, but 63.60. Dr Frankenstein's creation has produced its own offspring! But how exactly does this procreation work?

The interest from the first year is added to the capital and in turn generates interest. Thus the interest produced the second year can be broken down into £60 on 1,000 and £3.60 on 60. We say that the interest has been compounded because it has been added to the capital and now contributes to producing more little banknotes.

For this to work, of course, all the money has to be left in the account every year.

••••••••••••••••••••••••••••••••••••

Compounding makes the financial world go round. Like snowballs rolling down a hill, sums of money generate interest, which in turn is reinvested and produces interest on the interest. This is the most common case in finance. The exception is the case where the interest is not reinvested because it is regularly withdrawn from the account. In that case, we would talk about **simple interest** (as opposed to **compound interest**). In the above example, a simple interest investment produces £60 of interest every year, while a compounded interest investment generates 60, then 63.60 then 67.40, and so on.[2]

No future! Calculating present value (PV)

FUTURE, n. That period of time in which our affairs prosper, our friends are true and our happiness is assured.

Ambrose Bierce (1842–1914), *The Devil's Dictionary*

---

2. Curious readers can do this calculation: after 13 years of compounding, the annual interest will amount to 120.70, which is double the amount of the first year's interest. After 20 years, the interest will be 181.54 – three times the initial interest of 60 pounds!

SLICE OF LIFE: HOW TO SPEND MONEY YOU DON'T HAVE......

Rocky Beech lives the life of Reilly, going out and blowing all the money he can get his hands on — to the great displeasure of his poor mother, Sandy. She takes her son aside and tells him: 'You won't get any more money out of me, sonny boy. I won't pay any more of your overdrafts for a year. Find yourself a job, O fruit of my loins! At the end of a year, if you have been good, I will give you £30,000.'

Rocky slinks away with his tail between his legs. What should he do? Suddenly the answer pops into his head, crystal clear: borrow!

But how much? 'Let's go and pay a visit to the banker, Robert Baron,' Rocky soliloquizes.

Some time later...

Beech: Good morning, supercilious banker, I have come to borrow an unknown sum.

Baron: Good morning, atypical client. Since I don't know you (and your credit history is unknown), I will lend you money at 10% per year. How much do you want?

Beech: I have no idea. All I know is that I am going to receive £30,000 in a year.

Baron: Well, that simplifies the task. Let's say you borrow an amount of money that we'll call ☺. In one year you will have to pay back ☺ + the interest on ☺. That means FV = ☺ × (1 + 10%). But the maximum you can pay a year from now is £30,000.

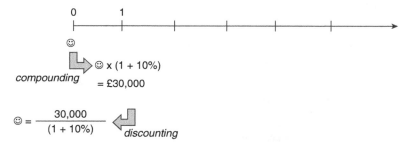

Figure 2.1   Compounding and discounting I

Baron: Take a look at the drawings in Figure 2.1. The future value of your loan must not exceed £30,000 and that sum equals ☺ × (1 + 10%). Rearranging the equation, we see that ☺ = 30,000/(1 + 10%), which equals £27,272. That's how much you can borrow today, because £27,272 + 10% interest will come to exactly £30,000 in one year.

Beech heads home cheerfully with the £27,272 in his pocket. But his mother takes him to task: 'I find you very impulsive, young Rocky. I don't know how you did it, but I suspect you found a way to get around my system. So now I am going to change our contract. Here's the new deal: I won't give you any-thing for five years. If you don't run any overdrafts during that time I will give you £150,000 at the end of it.'

Beech is crestfallen and goes back to see his banker, who reassures him.

Baron: Don't worry, Mr Beech. Have a mint (proffering the tin) while I show you what we're going to do. You want to borrow this amount ⊗ today, know-ing that in five years' time you will have £150,000 to pay back the loan and the interest. First tell me how much you will have to pay back in one year.

Beech: Uh, well in a year I will owe you ⊗ × (1 + 10%), but I still won't have any money to pay you with then.

Baron: That doesn't matter. Let's just imagine that I'm going to 're-lend' you that amount for another year. If I lend you ⊗ × (1 + 10%) in a year's time, how much will you owe me the year after that?

Beech: ⊗ × (1 + 10%) × (1 + 10%), in other words ⊗ × (1 + 10%)^2.

Baron: And if we do the same thing every year, if I agree not to be reimbursed and I lend you the money again, how much will you owe me in five years?

Beech: ⊗ × (1 + 10%)^5. That's actually the future value formula that we saw before!

Baron: In that case, esteemed client, how much am I going to lend you today? An amount ⊗ plus compound interest for five years that can be paid off with £150,000, so that would be ⊗ × (1 + 10%)^5 = 150,000. Therefore ⊗ = 150,000/(1 + 10%)^5 = £93,138.

Baron: Congratulations! As a reward for helping with the calculations, you can keep the mints. On the bottom of the tin is a drawing showing our calculations.

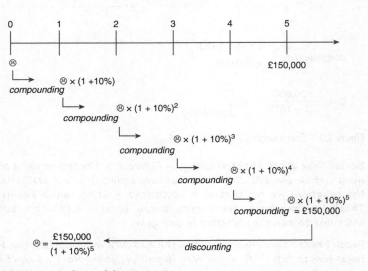

Figure 2.2 Compounding and discounting II

FINANCIALESE

To express a future sum as a **present value**, we perform an operation called **discounting** (the reverse operation of the **compounding** we have already seen), using a **discount rate** (or **opportunity cost**).

The general formula for the present value of a future sum of money to be received after n periods, where i is the interest rate, is the following:

$$\text{Present value} = \text{Future sum}/(1 + i)^n$$

which is,

$$\text{Present value} = \text{Future sum}/(1 + \text{periodic interest rate})^{\text{number of periods}}$$

DIALOGUE

Beech:	What exactly does this £93,138 represent?
Baron:	It represents the present value of £150,000 received in five years. For you, it is an equivalent sum: either you get less today (but you could invest it at 10%) or you get more in five years without having the opportunity to invest. And £93,138 invested at 10% for five years produces exactly £150,000. So the two possibilities are the same for you.
Beech:	It's not exactly the same: in the first case I get the money right away, whereas in the second case it's more frustrating.
Baron:	That's why there is an interest rate. The 10% includes compensation for your frustration. What would really be frustrating is if the choice were between 93 today or 93 in five years' time...
Beech:	Agreed, but all that is based on the discount rate. How can I be sure that the rate will stay at 10% for the next five years?
Baron:	You have absolutely no certainty about that, but it's not a problem. What you are sure of is the interest rate you have been offered. And today I am offering to lend to you at 10% for five years. That's a contract and it won't fluctuate.[3]
Beech:	And what if another banker offers me 8% for five years?
Baron:	Then it would be in your interest to borrow from the other bank. You should always reason in terms of **opportunity cost**; in other words, ask yourself: What is the best opportunity I'm being offered?
Beech:	By the way, you're talking as though I could borrow and invest at the same rate (10%), but that's not realistic...

---

3. 'Unless it's a variable interest rate loan, I suppose?' says Beech. 'Of course,' replies Baron, 'but let's not fry too many neurons at once.'

Baron:	Indeed. When you have to make a decision, you should always consider whether you're a borrower or a lender and take the appropriate opportunity cost into account.
Beech:	I have one last question. We're talking about 'present' value, but when exactly am I supposed to do the calculation?
Baron:	The convention is that we use today's date. Generally speaking, we discount sums to bring them back to the date the decision is made.

Whatever you may think, financiers are active people. They don't spend their time watching the interest accumulate in a bank account; they go out and look for **investment opportunities**. And investment goes hand in hand with renunciation. If I invest a sum today I let go of it (reluctantly), but my consolation will be to reap a larger sum in the future. The problem then is to compare an investment today with a promise of future income. Because a pound (a dollar, a euro) today is worth more than a pound (a dollar, a euro) tomorrow. Discounting allows us to travel along the axis of time and to express any sum of money – whether it is received tomorrow or in 30 years' time – in today's pounds or today's euros or today's dollars (to name a few).

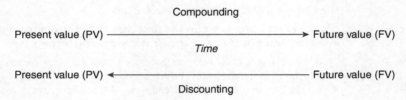

Figure 2.3   Compounding and discounting III

To demonstrate that discounting (and its opposite twin, compounding) is central to finance, we will illustrate our remarks with a few real life subjects (higher education, buying property on a mortgage, investing a sum of money, and valuing an asset).

Do higher education now and put off working until later?

> *If a man empties his purse into his head no one can take it away from him.*
> *An investment in knowledge always pays the best interest.*
>
> Benjamin Franklin (1706–90)

Geppetto is faced with a dilemma: either he gets a job delivering pizzas immediately following secondary school (though at a rather modest salary) or he does a three-year training course to become a professional wood-carver. He would earn a higher salary as a woodcarver, but he would have to pay tuition fees for his training and wouldn't earn a salary during those three years. Cricket gives him the following information:

Annual salary of a pizza delivery guy	£12,000	Number of years of salary as a pizza delivery guy	45
Annual salary of a woodcarver	£15,000	Number of years of salary as a woodcarver	42
Cost of one year of woodcarving training	£ 1,000	Number of years of woodcarving training	3
Interest rate on loan:	6%		

Before jumping into the calculations like frenzied finance fiends (FFF), let's separate the parameters of the **investment decision** by laying out the two possible scenarios: delivering pizzas or training to become a qualified woodcarver.

Table 2.1   Two scenarios

Year	1	2	3	4	5	...	45
Train to become a woodcarver	−1,000	−1,000	−1,000	+15,000	+15,000		+15,000
Deliver pizzas	+12,000	+12,000	+12,000	+12,000	+12,000		+12,000
Difference	−13,000	−13,000	−13,000	+3,000	+3,000		+3,000

There are two advantages to setting out the information in this way. First, it allows us to quantify the different options precisely. The 'difference' line is not merely decorative; it shows that Geppetto will not lose just £1,000 per year of study. In addition to this real expense there is a shortfall of £12,000 per year, so the decision actually concerns a loss of £13,000 per year.

FINANCIALESE

In finance, the bottom line of the chart (*Difference*) is often called **incremental** (or **differential** or **net**) **cash flow**. The notion of incremental cash flow will be of great use to us in making investment decisions (Chapter 3).

The second advantage is that we can now formulate Geppetto's dilemma, which is this: 'is it worthwhile to lose £13,000 per year for three years in order to obtain an additional salary of £3,000 for 42 years?' But something is missing here – you guessed it! – the **opportunity cost** for Geppetto. Cricket helps us out by suggesting that Geppetto take out a loan to pay for his studies. We consider that 6% is the best interest rate that Geppetto will be able to get, and so that is his opportunity cost. By applying what we have learned about the present value of a sum of money, we can cheerfully discount the cash flows.[4]

- the present value of 13,000 lost in year 1 is $-13,000/(1+6\%)$
- the present value of 13,000 lost in year 2 is $-13,000/(1+6\%)^2$
- the present value of 13,000 lost in year 3 is $-13,000/(1+6\%)^3$
- the present value of 3,000 earned in year 4 is $+3,000/(1+6\%)^4$
- and so on.

Now we are going to calculate the **present value** of costs (tuition fees and the salary shortfall) and the present value of revenues (additional salary). A little spreadsheet magic and – hey presto – we get:

$$\text{PV (expenses)} = \frac{-13,000}{(1+6\%)} + \frac{-13,000}{(1+6\%)^2} + \frac{-13,000}{(1+6\%)^3} = -£34,749$$

Thus it makes no difference to Geppetto whether he spends £13,000 each year or £34,749 all at once.[5]

Now let's look at revenues:

$$\text{PV (revenues)} = \frac{3,000}{(1+6\%)^4} + \frac{3,000}{(1+6\%)^5} + \cdots + \frac{3,000}{(1+6\%)^{45}} = +38,348$$

Note that we have discounted the sums starting in year 4, because this is when Geppetto begins to benefit from his additional salary. The dilemma has been simplified thus: 'is it worthwhile to spend £34,749 (in today's pounds) to earn £38,348? Geppetto says 'Si! Si! Si!' and the country soon boasts another expert woodcarver.

---

4. No reason why we can't hum the theme of 'Back to the Future' by Alan Silvestri as we work...
5. And I certainly had better not see this: '13,000 a year makes 3 × 13,000 = 39,000'; otherwise, you will get an F. One pound today is never equal to one pound tomorrow. If you don't believe it, lend me a billion today and I will pay you back a billion in 30 years' time.

We could also have performed the calculation in one go, by computing the **net present value (NPV)** of the investment project, which is the difference between the present value of costs and revenues:

$$\text{NPV} = \frac{-13,000}{(1+6\%)} + \frac{-13,000}{(1+6\%)^2} + \frac{-13,000}{(1+6\%)^3} + \frac{3,000}{(1+6\%)^4}$$
$$+ \frac{3,000}{(1+6\%)^5} + \cdots + \frac{3,000}{(1+6\%)^{45}} = +3,599$$

From this we can infer the **net present value (NPV) rule**: one should undertake projects that have a positive NPV because they procure a net gain – they create value – and inversely we should reject projects that have a negative NPV (for example, spending 100 to earn 90), because they generate a net loss (they destroy value).

DIALOGUE BETWEEN GEPPETTO AND PINOCCHIO

Geppetto:	We haven't taken inflation into account. After all, salaries may increase by, let's say, 2% a year.
Pinocchio:	Nothing is impossible for a woodcarver with a spreadsheet, Geppetto!
	But this technical artifice should not obscure the absolute rule: if you include inflation in future revenues (you use **nominal revenues**), then you also have to use an interest rate that includes inflation: a **nominal interest rate**. In our calculation we used **real revenues**, which are therefore discounted at a **real rate**. Take another look at the dialogue between Lorem and Sivis.
Geppetto:	Thank you, dear boy. But isn't there still an error in using 6% as both the lending and deposit rate?
Pinocchio:	Indeed, it would be more accurate to use 6% as the lending rate and suppose that the student borrows £11,000 a year to live and study. Then we would have to calculate the future value of this loan starting at the beginning of the fourth year. Second, we would have to determine the student's opportunity cost (another interest rate) and calculate the present value (at the beginning of year 4) of the expected revenues. The thoughtful authors of this book have put this calculation on the website to avoid wasting paper and ink.
Geppetto:	But how do we determine the student's opportunity cost?
Pinocchio:	For the moment, all we've got is: 'the opportunity cost depends on the project's risk' and 'you just have to ...'.
Geppetto:	I'm all ears...

Pinocchio:	'You just have to find a listed asset whose expenses and revenues are the same as our project. The return on that asset will correspond to the student's opportunity cost.'
Geppetto:	Indeed...and of course it's so easy to find an asset that costs £13,000 per year for three years and then generates £3,000 a year for 42 years...
Pinocchio:	It's not as hard as you think, papa – can I call you papa? We can put together a portfolio of securities that, when combined, will produce these cash flows. For example, buying 13 £1,000 government bonds the first year is equivalent to spending £13,000. We will see that a project's risk can be summarized with a few indicators that will be largely independent of the revenue flows.
Geppetto:	I can't wait.
Pinocchio:	Let's strike while the iron is hot and move on to the second example.

Buying a house on a mortgage

Debts are like children: the smaller they are, the more noise they make.

Spanish proverb

Kofi and Shugga are looking for a love nest to create some tiny claimable dependants. Swampland Realty finds them a tree house overlooking the Congo for 100 turistas (the local currency).[6] Kofi decides to borrow the money from River Bank. The banker, Mr Ali Gator, a recent business school graduate, rattles off some jargon.

DIALOGUE	
Ali:	I can offer you a nominal rate of 10% per year for a five-year loan. You have three repayment options: a mortgage with repayment *in fine*, a constant repayment mortgage or a constant annuity mortgage.
Kofi:	Ungawa!?
Ali:	Bless you. Here are some tribal arrowheads simulating the three repayment options: interest payments are set against a grey background and payments *against principal* are shown below.

---

6. Social climbers and readers with delusions of grandeur are welcome to replace the amounts with millions or zillions, if they wish; the reasoning will still hold. We've deliberately used small numbers to make them easier to read (and to save our poor publisher ink and paper).

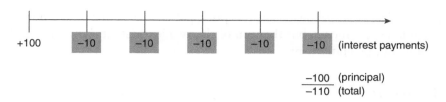

Figure 2.4   First option: mortgage with repayment *in fine*

As you can see, in the first option, a mortgage with repayment *in fine*, you repay the principal in a single payment at the end. The interest, however, is paid in each period (in this case every year).

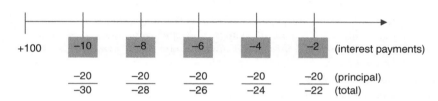

Figure 2.5   Second option: constant repayment mortgage

In the second option, the principal is paid back in equal amounts (**constant repayment** or **constant amortization**). One hundred turistas over five years means a repayment of 100/5 = 20 turistas of principal per year. The interest payments, however, are not constant because the remaining principal diminishes as time passes. The first year, the borrower pays 10% interest on 100 of principal, which is 10. The second year, the remaining principal is only 80 (20 has been repaid), so the borrower pays 10% × 80 = 8 turistas of interest. In constant amortization, the overall payments (principal + interest) are spread over time, but they are not equal.

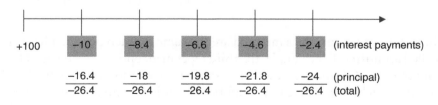

Figure 2.6   Third option: constant annuity mortgage

In the third option the loan is repaid in **constant annuities** and we finally have equal instalments. That's great, but the mystery is how the banker managed it! The payments on the principal are never the same, nor are the interest payments, but the sum of the two is constant. Let's have Kofi express our bewilderment.

DIALOGUE

Kofi: Holy snappin' crocodiles! What kind of a shady racket is this?

Ali: Don't worry, Kofi, I'm not trying to sell you down the river! See for yourself by calculating the present value of the payments. If I type the numbers into my dynamo-powered computer (keep pedalling, please), I get the following result:

$$\text{PV(payment)} = \frac{26.4}{(1+10\%)^1} + \frac{26.4}{(1+10\%)^2} + \cdots + \frac{26.4}{(1+10\%)^5} = +100 \text{ turistas}$$

Not only does that prove that I haven't tried to fleece you, dear Kofi, but it gives us a general proposition: the present value of loan payments (principal + interest) is always equal to the capital remaining to be paid back.[7]

Kofi: Oooiyoiyoiyoiyooiii!

Ali: You can say that again!

Kofi: Where did the 26.4 come from?

Ali: Ah, now that's the real question! How did we calculate this constant payment and how is it divided between principal and interest?

A few simplified (?) formulas; in particular, the constant annuity formula

> But if you observe, people always live for ever when there is an annuity to be paid them; and she is very stout and healthy, and hardly forty. An annuity is a very serious business; it comes over and over every year, and there is no getting rid of it.
>
> Jane Austen, *Sense and Sensibility* (1811)

In certain situations, the sums paid are the same for each period. These are called **annuities**. For example, the third repayment option is made up of five annuities of 26.4 turistas. Another example is Geppetto's additional £3,000 of salary each year. There is a simplified formula for annuities that we can apply. For readers who are not allergic to mathematics, we will explain it in

---

7. The reader will have to check whether this proposition is correct by doing the calculation for the other two repayment options.

a few lines and an equation. Everyone else can skip over the next paragraph, right up to the word 'Caramba'. Here we go ...

Given that these sums are identical from one period to another, we can factorize – an ugly mathematical term for 'simplify' – the calculation as follows:

$$PV(\text{annuities}) = \frac{26.4}{(1+10\%)^1} + \frac{26.4}{(1+10\%)^2} + \cdots + \frac{26.4}{(1+10\%)^5}$$

$$= 26.4 \times \left[\frac{1}{(1+10\%)^1} + \frac{1}{(1+10\%)^2} + \cdots + \frac{1}{(1+10\%)^5} \right]$$

What is intriguing (for those who like maths) is that what is found between the brackets is the sum of a geometric series. Perhaps you don't find that terribly interesting? However, it is worth noting that this sum can be reduced to a single fraction.

Caramba!

$$PV(\text{annuities}) = 26.4 \times \frac{1-(1+10\%)^{-5}}{10\%} = +100 \text{ turistas}$$

There are two advantages to be gained from this formula:

1. When we have a series of identical flows, called **annuities** (rent, monthly mortgage payments, daily wine purchases), we can express the **present value** of this series in an elegant formula. This formula allows us to answer bewildering questions like, 'Is it better to pay for your new car in one lump sum or in 112 monthly payments of £933?'
2. There is a fundamental principle in mathematics (hang on to your hat), which is: *if A = B, then B = A*. Thus the formula becomes:

$$26.4 = 100 \times \frac{10\%}{1-(1+10\%)^{-5}}$$

This formula – which is none other than the previous formula rearranged – is called the **constant annuity formula**. Given the amount of a loan (100 in this case), it tells us how much the annuities are (in this case, five payments of 26.4). Using this formula, the banker was able to calculate the sums owed by Kofi and Shugga. Likewise, when the electronics store salesman tells you: 'Buy this enormous flat-screen TV and pay it off in 36 equal instalments', you can work out whether he's offering you a good deal or trying to rip you off. The general formula is:[8]

$$\text{Constant annuity} = \text{Amount borrowed} \times \frac{i}{1 - (1 + i)^{-\text{number of periods}}}$$

Amortization schedule for a loan

Kofi and Shugga want to understand their financial commitment. So, with the help of Ali the banker, they make an **amortization schedule** for the loan, describing the evolution of their payments. Let's begin with the first line.

Table 2.2 Amortization schedule, year 1

Year	Starting principal	Payment	Interest	Principal	Remaining balance
1	100	26.4	10.0	16.4	83.6
	a	b	c	d	e

We read it like this: at the beginning of the year, Kofi and Shugga still have to pay back 100 turistas (the entire loan), which corresponds to *a*. At the end of the year they pay the annuity of 26.4 (step *b*). But this is not just a payment on the principal borrowed; it also contains interest. How do we separate the two? Very simple: first we remember that the interest rate was 10%, so the interest is 10% of 100 = 10 turistas (step *c*). Thus the 26.4 annuity is made up of 10 in interest and 26.4 – 10 = 16.4 in principal (step *d*). Finally, given that 16.4 of the 100 has been paid back, the amount of principal remaining to be paid is 100 – 16.4 = 83.6 (step *e*).

Let's move right along to the second line.

Table 2.3 Amortization schedule, years 1 and 2

Year	Starting principal	Payment	Interest	Principal	Remaining balance
1	100	26.4	10.0	16.4	83.6
2	83.6	26.4	8.4	18	65.6
	f				

---

8. Be careful: there is a negative sign in front of 'number of periods' in the denominator.

As we have seen, at the end of the first year there was 83.6 left to pay. We use this amount to start year 2 (step *f*). Kofi and Shugga make their second payment: 26.4, which includes 10% of 83.6 = 8.4 turistas of interest and therefore 26.4 − 8.4 = 18 turistas of principal. We finish the second year with a remaining balance of 83.6 − 18 = 65.6 turistas.[9]

We can now fill in the last three lines of the schedule.

Table 2.4 Amortization schedule, years 1–5

Year	Starting principal	Payment	Interest	Principal	Remaining balance
1	100	26.4	10.0	16.4	83.6
2	83.6	26.4	8.4	18.0	65.6
3	65.6	26.4	6.6	19.8	45.8
4	45.8	26.4	4.6	21.8	24.0
5	24.0	26.4	2.4	24.0	0.0

A few remarks on this schedule:

- At the end of the last year the remaining balance is zero. That's reassuring. If you don't get this figure, go back and do the calculation again.
- The annuities are 26.4 every year. That's normal: the principle of a constant annuity is that the payments are constant…
- and yet within these sums that are ostensibly identical from year to year we find a sort of hourglass where the sand shifts from one side to the other.
- During the first years, Kofi and Shugga are paying a lot of interest because they haven't paid off much principal yet. Then, over the years, as the remaining balance diminishes, they pay less interest and an increasingly large share of the 26.4 goes to paying off the principal.
- Logically, this sequence ends with a zero in the final box. Indeed, it is the starting figure of 100 that led us to 26.4. The annuities had to be 26.4 so that the present value of five annuities would be equal to the initial amount of the loan (100).

9. The numbers have been rounded off: 8.36 becomes 8.4.

Toward infinity and beyond, or two other simplified formulas

> *Two things are infinite: the universe and human stupidity; and I'm not sure about the universe.*
>
> *Attributed to* Albert Einstein (1879–1955)

We are starting to get quite sharp at this business of calculating interest. Compounding and discounting no longer hold any secrets for us, but alas we still do not have complete mastery over time. Indeed, for the moment we are bound to a finite horizon (Kofi borrows for five years, Geppetto works for 45 years and so on). But in finance there are assets that have an *infinite* lifespan; for example, land or stock market securities. Even a rental property could be considered as a promise of infinite revenues. Indeed, if we estimate the future rent minus maintenance expenses, our property will last forever.

The previous formulas, bound by the final year, will now be transformed into:

$$PV = \frac{10}{(1+6\%)} + \frac{10}{(1+6\%)^2} + \frac{10}{(1+6\%)^3} + \cdots + \frac{10}{(1+6\%)^\infty} = ?$$

where ∞ is the heady symbol for infinity, akin to saying 'the Day of final Judgment'. The problem is this: a spreadsheet only has a few hundred columns and cannot go quite as far as infinity. Luckily for us, we recognize a sequence here that will simplify things: the sum of a geometric series until infinity. A fat lot of good that does us. But this sum can be simplified thus:

$$PV = \frac{10}{6\%} = 166.67$$

Thus a flat that brings in £10K of rent per year would be equivalent to a present value of £166.67K. To be convinced of this, you just have to deposit £166.67 at 6%; at the end of the year it will generate £10 of interest. If we take away the £10 (if we consume the rent), we find ourselves with £166.67 again. Deposited at 6%, this once again generates £10 of interest the year after and so on. Thus we have a new simple formula for **the present value of a perpetuity**.

$$PV = \frac{CF}{i}$$

Let's be honest: this formula is not used a lot – not because of the infinity part, but because of the assumption of constant cash flows. We need to be more realistic and suppose that the cash flows received will grow each year – to offset the increase in the cost of living, for instance. So let's imagine a flat that, instead of bringing in a constant rent (£10K per year), generates a rent that grows by 2% a year. The landlords will receive £10K the first year, £10.2K the second year, £10.404K the third year and so on. In year n, they will get the rent received in year $n-1$ plus 2%.

$$CF_n = CF_n - 1 \times (1 + 2\%)$$

where CF (cash flow) stands for the rent

If we call the growth rate g, we get:

$$PV = \frac{CF}{i - g}$$

This new formula represents the **present value of a growing perpetuity**, which is the present value of a stream of cash flows that increase by g every year. This formula is often used to value securities and companies because it allows you to project the growth of an activity over the very long term (literally to infinity).

DIALOGUE IN CASABLANCA	
Ingrid:	So, to value a stock you just have to define three figures? Like, 'I think Laszlo stock will pay a dividend of $5 in a year, that this dividend will grow by 2% a year, and I suppose that shareholders want a return of 7%?'
Humphrey:	That's right, kid. In that case, the stock will be worth PV = 5 / (7% – 2%) = $100.
Ingrid:	And what if g is greater than i?
Humphrey:	That's not possible in the long term, baby-doll. And infinity is really, really long term, get it? Whatever business Laszlo is in, it will eventually reach maturity. We might imagine 10% growth for a few years, but as soon as the business develops, the company will see its growth slow down. In a saturated market (for example, when all the consumers have already got the product), the growth rate will necessarily be low.
Ingrid:	Does that mean that this formula should be used only for mature companies?

Humphrey:	That's right, cupcake. If all you had to do was line up three figures to value a stock accurately, then everybody would be doing it. But this formula offers a very simple shortcut that allows us to say things like: 'I can't make any accurate forecasts beyond five years, but I'm going to assume that my business will continue to grow by 1.5% a year until the end of time.'
Ingrid:	Isn't there a sexier name for this formula than 'present value of a growing perpetuity'? A name that would look good on a movie poster, maybe?
Humphrey:	People often call it the Gordon–Shapiro formula, after the two researchers that popularized it.
Ingrid:	And how do we determine *i*, *g* and, most importantly, next year's dividend?
Humphrey:	One thing at a time, sweetheart. First let's get a handle on the basic concepts in finance. We'll come back to valuing companies later on.

Investing a sum of money: period interest rates

> The creditor goes to bed at night and wakes up in the morning better off than when he retired to bed, because his interest has increased during the night, but you grow poorer while you are sleeping, for the interest is accumulating against you.

> Phineas T. Barnum, *The Art of Money Getting* (1880)

We now know how to make calculations on interest rates, even to infinity. But those charming television and furniture salespeople often offer us monthly payment plans: loans that are paid off in monthly instalments. So let's make a foray into period rates: monthly, quarterly, daily and so on.

SLICE OF LIFE •
Pantalone wants to deposit 100 ducats in an interest-bearing account. One banker, Arlecchino, offers him an **annual** rate of 6%, while another, Pulcinella, offers him a **monthly** rate. This means that if Pantalone deposits his money with Arlecchino, he won't see any interest for one year, whereas if he deposits it with Pulcinella, he will get the first interest payment in a month, and then more interest in two months, and so on. Pulcinella says, 'Arlecchino is offering an annual rate of 6%. There are 12 months in a normal year, so the monthly rate that I can offer is 6%/12 = 0.5% per month.' Let's say that Pantalone chooses to invest with Arlecchino: he will get 100 × (1 + 6%) = 106

ducats in one year. But if Pantalone chooses the Pulcinella investment, he will benefit from **compounding**. As long as he doesn't withdraw the interest, he will get 100 × (1 + 0.5%)^{12} = 106.17 ducats, which is 0.17 ducats more than he would get with Arlecchino. For a wealthy Venetian, the 0.17 ducat difference may seem insignificant. But if a zillion Turkish lire were deposited instead, the difference would be enough to buy a few bottles of Arak.

In sum, when Arlecchino proposes an annual rate of 6%, the capital generates 6% annually. So far, so good. But when Pulcinella proposes an annual rate of 6%, with **interest paid monthly**, it generates 6.17% annually.

• •

FINANCIALESE

When Pulcinella calculates a monthly interest rate as 'annual rate/12 months', he gets 0.5% per month, which is called the **(monthly) proportional rate**. When we calculate how much this 0.5% compounded every month generates, we get an **annual percentage rate (APR)** of 6.17%.

Continuing with the example of an annual rate of 6%, we can calculate:

• the weekly proportional rate, which will be 6%/52 weeks = 0.12% per week, and the resulting annual percentage rate, which will be $(1 + 0.12\%)^{52} - 1 = 6.18\%$;

• the daily proportional rate, which will be 6%/365 days = 0.016% per day, and the resulting annual percentage rate, which will be $(1 + 0.016\%)^{365} - 1 = 6.183\%$.

Table 2.5 presents a few equivalents for an annual rate of 6%.

Table 2.5   Interest rate equivalents

Period	Proportional Rate	Converts to	Annual percentage rate
Annual	6% per year	→	6.000%
Quarterly	1.5% per quarter	→	6.136%
Monthly	0.50% per month	→	6.168%
Weekly	0.12% per week	→	6.180%
Daily	0.016% per day	→	6.183%
Hourly	0.001% per hour	→	6.184%

DIALOGUE BETWEEN PANTALONE AND HIS BANKER, PULCINELLA

Pantalone:	I see that when a bank offers me 6% per year, in reality I won't get exactly 6% — it depends on how often the interest is paid.
Pulcinella:	Exactly. It is only when interest is paid annually that the advertised 6% corresponds to the effective (equivalent) rate paid.

Pantalone:	But that's exasperating! If I borrow at 6% annually with monthly interest payments, it's as if I had borrowed at 6.168% annually!
Pulcinella:	Yes. That's why when a bank offers you a loan you shouldn't pay attention to the advertised rate, but rather the annual percentage rate (APR), which gives the 'true' equivalent rate, taking the frequency of interest payments into account.[10]
Pantalone:	So why do banks continue to operate like that?
Pulcinella:	It's a convention. It's easier to calculate a monthly rate by dividing the annual rate by 12 than it is to do a 'twelfth root' that will be perfectly accurate. The bank knows that there is a small approximation error when dividing by 12. You should be aware of that, too...
Pantalone:	But this error comes from the proportional interest calculation, which is a very rough approximation. For an annual rate of 6%, the equivalent monthly rate is not 0.5%, but...uh...uh...
Pulcinella:	Let me help you, kind Sir. We want to know the monthly percentage rate (MPR) such that a 12-month investment will produce an annual percentage rate of 6%. So we want $(1 + MPR)^{12} = 1 + 6\%$. We therefore obtain MPR $= (1 + 6\%)^{1/12} - 1 = 0.487\%$ per month.[11] Look at Table 2.6 and you will see the equivalent rate calculations for each period. As you can see, they have been calculated so that, depending on how often interest is paid, it always produces an annual percentage rate of 6%.

Table 2.6 Equivalent rates

Period	Equivalent Rate	Converts to	Annual percentage rate
Annual	6% per year	→	6.000%
Quarterly	1.467% per quarter	→	6.000%
Monthly	0.487% per month	→	6.000%
Weekly	0.112% per week	→	6.000%
Daily	0.016% per day	→	6.000%
Hourly	0.001% per hour	→	6.000%

10. Please note that we should also include any additional fees (insurance, administrative expenses, net of any possible tax exemption, etc.) to get the effective interest rate that is charged to the customer on a yearly basis.
11. For those that have trouble visualizing or memorizing this formula, remember that it is simply a formula for compounding interest, but instead of compounding over several periods, you compound for less than one period, saying 'one month is 1/12 of a year', which is why the sum in brackets is to the power of 1/12. Take a deep breath and read it again serenely

DIALOGUE	
Pantalone:	So, to summarize: just because banks can't be bothered to explain twelfth roots to their clients, they do a simple calculation that ends up with a higher annual percentage rate (see Table 2.5).
Pulcinella:	I'm afraid so, Signor Pantalone.
Pantalone:	But what really makes my head spin is that **the more frequently interest is paid, the higher the annual percentage rate**: for weekly compounding the annual percentage rate = 6.18%; for hourly compounding the annual percentage rate = 6.184%, and so on.
Pulcinella:	That's right. That's because the interest also accumulates interest (compounding principle). Also, the more quickly the interest is paid, the sooner it starts to accumulate interest and all of that increases the annual percentage rate.
Pantalone:	All right, so it increases with the frequency of interest payments, but is there any limit to this?
Pulcinella:	Yes. It's called the **continuous compounding rate**. It's a rate where the interest is paid every microsecond – what am I saying? – every **nanosecond**, and even better than that – continuously.
Pantalone:	What's the point of this continuous compounding rate?
Pulcinella:	It's often used in financial markets. For example: when they say 'Acme Equipment's profit was £1.4M on 31 December', they are well aware that the profit wasn't all generated on exactly 31 December. It was earned gradually during the entire year. So for every microsecond, Acme Equipment's stock includes a small portion of the profit that is being earned and we need a continuous rate to discount this type of profit that is continuously generated.
Pantalone:	Final question: how do you calculate this continuous compounding rate – just for my personal edification?
Pulcinella:	We use the **exponential growth constant**, which is a mathematical constant called **e** (Euler's number), equal to 2.718 and a bit (it has an infinite number of decimals, like Pi). For an annual rate of 6% with continuous interest payments, the continuous compounding rate = $e^{6\%} - 1 = 6.1837\%$ (rounded off).

Provisional conclusion: the yield curve

*In your experience, which bonds make the best investment?
Municipal bonds, treasury bonds? – As a rule, I prefer to invest
in family bonds.*

Attributed to C. Thibierge

This chapter has been long and the concepts need to be studied, practised and digested. That will take time. We still have two more topics to cover that are often linked: bonds and the yield curve.

Bonds

Let's look at a company that needs a £100M of capital. The executives go to see their banker, who offers them a loan at 7% for five years. The company also has another option: it can issue financial instruments (securities) that pay interest. These securities are called **bonds**. Let's say the company issues 100,000 bonds with a nominal value of £1,000, for five years at a rate of 6%. They sell these bonds on the financial markets for 100,000 × £1,000 = £100M. The company is now £100M in debt to 100,000 bond holders at 6%, but that's better than what the banker had offered them (7%).

FINANCIALESE

The financial instrument described above is a **bond**, with a **nominal** or **face value** of £1,000, **maturity** is in five years and the **yield** is 6%. The bonds have been **issued** (initially sold) **at par** (face value). Generally, the bonds are also redeemed at par, in this case £1,000 repaid after five years. Every year, bond holders will receive an interest payment, called the **coupon**, equal to nominal value × nominal yield. Here, the annual coupon is £1,000 × 6% = £60.

A few calculations on bonds

Let's take a look at the bond described above. At the date of issue, this bond represents a promise that the holder will receive £60 per year for five years and then £1,000 at term. This series of cash flows can be represented on a timeline as follows:

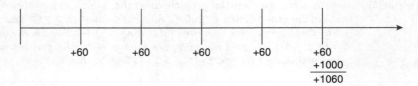

Figure 2.7   Series of payments for a bond

We observe that this diagram represents the repayment series of a loan (just like the *in fine* loan repayment option described earlier), only this time it is from the point of view of the lender.

Now let's imagine two things:

(1) two years have passed (and two coupons have been paid);

(2) bond market rates have fluctuated.

The timeline for the bond holder becomes shorter, as we see in this diagram:

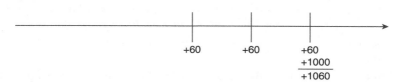

Figure 2.8   Series of payments for a bond, three years before term

Since the market rates have changed, the present value of the bond will also have changed. Let's suppose first that the market yield has remained at 6%. The PV therefore is:

$$PV = \frac{60}{(1+6\%)} + \frac{60}{(1+6\%)^2} + \frac{1,060}{(1+6\%)^3} = £1,000$$

This should not surprise us: a bond with a face value of £1,000 that yields 6% when the market wants 6% will be worth £1,000.[12] Now let's suppose that market yields have dropped to 5%. The PV will now be:

$$PV = \frac{60}{(1+5\%)} + \frac{60}{(1+5\%)^2} + \frac{1,060}{(1+5\%)^3} = £1,027.23$$

When yields decrease, the value of bonds goes up and when yields increase, the value of bonds goes down. To illustrate this, let's listen to a discussion between Mr Bond and Miss Penelope Farthing.

DIALOGUE	
Miss Penelope Farthing:	How do you explain the fact that when yields decrease, the value (price) of the bond goes up?
Mr Bond:	There are two ways to explain this. The first is mathematical: when we calculate a PV, we divide by the interest rate. If the rate decreases we divide by a smaller number so the PV increases.
Miss Penelope Farthing:	And the other explanation...the less mathematical one?

---

12. Note that this calculation will produce the same result regardless of the number of coupons remaining.

Mr Bond:	If bond yields decrease from 6% to 5%, new bonds will be issued at 5%. But we have an old bond that pays 6%, which is more attractive. Thus on a bond market yielding 5%, one that pays 6% will see its price go up.
Miss Penelope Farthing:	How do you explain this new value of £1,027.23?
Mr Bond:	If new investors buy a bond from me, they will get £60 in a year, £60 in two years and £1,060 in three years. If you do the calculation, you will see that at a purchase price of £1,027.23 those investors will earn exactly 5%. This price is therefore an equilibrium price: it makes no difference whether the investors buy the old bond or a new one because they both yield 5%.
Miss Penelope Farthing:	I rather liked the old Bond! Why didn't it stay at the initial price of £1,000?
Mr Bond:	Because at £1,000 it would have been very attractive and everybody would have wanted it, so its price increased to £1,027.23 – the equilibrium price.
Miss Penelope Farthing:	Does that mean that all the investors in the market have their eye on the interest rates and regularly recalculate the present values? And bonds are traded every day like stocks?
Mr Bond:	Indeed.
Miss Penelope Farthing:	So why do people say that bonds are 'safe investments', if their prices fluctuate?
Mr Bond:	First, because their price fluctuates less than that of stocks (so they are less risky) and second, because, regardless of the price, a bond guarantees coupons and a redemption of fixed values. These values do not fluctuate because they are defined by contract at issuance.
Miss Penelope Farthing:	So the uncertainty is about the resale value during the life of the bond. If we keep the bonds until maturity, we are sure of our gains?
Mr Bond:	Precisely. Come on, Penny, let's go and have a gin and tonic. My treat.

The yield curve

In the previous example, we spoke of a bond yield that dropped to 5% and we discounted the cash flows according to the new yield. The assumption that we were making was that the yield is the same for one year, two years and three years. In reality, the yields are not the same for different terms. A bank will not lend you money at the same rate regardless of whether you borrow for one year or for ten years. Likewise for bonds, the one-year cash flow should be discounted using the yield for one year, the two-year cash flow using a two-year yield and so on. The financial press regularly publishes bond yields by maturity date, which allows us to plot a yield curve as shown in Figure 2.9.

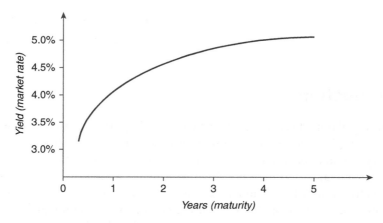

Figure 2.9   Example of a yield curve

Thus, in our example, when we spoke of a market yield of 5%, that was clearly the five-year bond yield. To calculate the real PV of the bond we would have had to take the one-year yield (4% on the chart), the two-year yield (4.5%) and the three-year yield (4.7%). Thus the correct calculation would be:

$$PV = \frac{60}{(1+4\%)} + \frac{60}{(1+4.5\%)^2} + \frac{1,060}{(1+4.7\%)^3} = £1,036.20$$

Compare this value with the £1,027.23 calculated earlier; the difference is not negligible. Imagine enjoying the £9 difference multiplied by hundreds of thousands of bonds... Unfortunately, that only happens in our dreams. Market traders are competent and vigilant. There is a good chance that any variation in the yield curve would be immediately and fully taken into account by investors in their investment strategies. We will return to this idea when we talk about the stock market (Chapter 7).

73

3

Capital Budgeting

You must lose a fly to catch a trout.

George Herbert (1593–1633)

Introduction

Thinking about whether to go to college, deciding whether to buy a company or choosing between two machine tools: these are all investment decisions. You try to make the best decision: the one that is most profitable for the company or for yourself. When choosing investments, we rely on decision-making criteria (not too difficult) and on a forecast of future cash flows (a little more complicated ...). In Chapter 1 we saw how to analyse a company's financial statements and we ended with cash flows – the lifeblood of the company. We will now use this knowledge to make cash flow forecasts. In Chapter 2 we suffered through a few financial calculations, including discounting. We will make use of this knowledge in our decision-making criteria.

One further point, but an important one: for the moment we will assume that the discount rate is given to us by our finance department. This will simplify our work in this chapter; the thorny task of determining the correct discount rate to apply will be saved for later chapters.

What is an investment?

Capital as such is not evil. It is the wrong use that is evil.
Capital in some form or other will always be needed.

'Mahatma' Gandhi (1869–1948)

An investment in the financial sense of the term (sometimes called 'capex', for capital expenditure) means committing a sum of money – usually as a one-time expense – in exchange for the expectation of future revenues (cash flows). The typical variables of an investment project are therefore the initial outlay, the expected lifespan of the project and the cash flow forecast for this lifespan. A few examples of investments are: buying an apartment to rent out, doing an MBA, buying shares on the stock market and purchasing a company. An investment may also consist in incurring an expense to make future savings. For example, buying a house now will save me paying future rent; buying solar panels will save on future electricity expenses; performing an activity in-house will save a company outsourcing costs. Divestment follows the same logic, but in the opposite direction: you receive a sum of money now (the fruit of the divestment) in exchange for a series of future negative cash flows.

In either case, you try to work it so the gains are greater than the costs. And to help you achieve this, there are capital budgeting or investment decision criteria.

Investment decision criteria

> *Good decisions come from experience. Experience comes from making bad decisions.*
>
> Mark Twain (1835–1910)

Normally we determine the cash flows (receipts, disbursements) of an investment first and then we apply decision criteria to see whether the investment is profitable. But since we have just finished the chapter on financial calculations, it is easier to start with the criteria. So let's say we have an investment project to study with all the cash flow forecasts already calculated because our big brother is a corporate financial wizard and he has already crunched the numbers for us. And since he's our big brother, we're sure he hasn't made any mistakes...

Here, then, are the forecasts for the investment project, guaranteed to be 100% correct:

Table 3.1 Cash flow forecast

Year	0	1	2	3	4	5
Projected cash flows (in £)	−50,000	2,640	10,478	15,028	19,578	38,025

Note that this investment involves a significant outlay the first year (purchasing giant flat screens for a bar) and that it generates growing revenues until year five, the last year of the project.[1] How can we tell whether it's worth making this investment?

---

1. By convention, the year of the investment is always year 0. This makes the discounting calculations easier.

Net present value (NPV)

Anyone who hasn't read Chapter 2 will probably just add the cash flows together. But those of us who have read that chapter (several times) are going to discount the figures to get present values (how much those future cash flows are worth today). Our ever-obliging bean counter of a brother tells us that 'the expected return on investment is 9% per year' – so there's our discount rate. We can now perform the discounting calculation:

$$\frac{2,640}{(1+9\%)} = 2,422, \text{ then } \frac{10,478}{(1+9\%)^2} = 8,819, \text{ then } +\frac{15,028}{(1+9\%)^3}, \ \cdots$$

Table 3.2 Present values of future cash flows

Year	0	1	2	3	4	5
Cash flow forecasts (£)	−50,000	2,640	10,478	15,028	19,578	38,025
Present value at 9% (£)		2,422	8,819	11,604	13,870	24,714
Sum of present values (£)	61,429					

The future cash flows[2] are now all expressed in 'year 0 pounds' (present values), so they can be added together. The cash flows generated from year 1 to year 5 have a total present value of 61,429. The question is now very simple: is it worthwhile investing £50,000 (expressed in year 0 pounds) to earn £61,429 (also expressed in year 0 pounds)? The answer is clearly 'yes'. We can also calculate the net gain: −£50,000 + £61,429 = +£11,429. This gain is called the net present value and the formula for NPV is as follows:

$$NPV = -\text{Inv} + \frac{CF1}{(1+i)} + \frac{CF2}{(1+i)^2} + \frac{CF3}{(1+i)^3} + \cdots + \frac{CFn}{(1+i)^n}$$

where Inv is the amount invested in year 0, CFk is the cash flow generated in year k and n is the number of years the project will last.

---

2. We did not have to discount the first amount (−50,000) as it was already expressed as a present value in year 0.

The NPV rule is very simple:

- If NPV is positive, the investment will generate more than it costs, so you should invest in this project. When there are several potential projects, you should invest in the one with the greatest NPV.
- If NPV is negative, the cost of the investment is greater than the present value of the gains; you should not invest.

Here the NPV is positive, so we decide to invest.

DIALOGUE	
Winsom Cash:	What exactly does this figure mean: NPV = +£11,429?
Kristal Ball:	It means that the moment the CEO says, 'Ok, let's invest!' the company will trade £50,000 against the expectation of earning £61,429 and will thus make a net gain of £11,429. The company will therefore be made richer by +£11,429.
Winsom Cash:	But the gain is not guaranteed. It depends on the state of the economy, on our forecasts...
Kristal Ball:	That's perfectly true, but it's the best we can do on day 0. The discount rate is there to 'flatten' the future cash flows, bringing to bear the weight of time and risk.
Winsom Cash:	That's what I mean. We have arbitrarily set the discount rate at 9%. But if I do the NPV calculation at 16%, I get an NPV of −£1,392, so according to the NPV rule we shouldn't invest.
Kristal Ball:	Not so fast, Winsom. The discount rate is not a variable! It is a known value that has been given to us by the finance department and doesn't vary (or at least we shouldn't change it just because we feel like it). But it is true that it's an important value: if the finance department had told us that the discount rate was 16%, this project (with identical cash flows) would have been rejected.
Winsom Cash:	So when are we going to learn how to determine these rates?
Kristal Ball:	In Chapters 5 and 6¾.

FINANCIALESE

When a project has a positive NPV, we say there is **value creation**. Indeed, in the previous example, giving the green light to the project means exchanging an outlay of £50,000 (expressed in today's pounds) for gains amounting to £61,429 (also expressed in today's pounds). The project thus creates a net gain of £11,429.

The internal rate of return (IRR)

Here is a second investment decision criterion. It's not as useful as NPV, because it suffers from several shortcomings. Nevertheless, in spite of its flaws, it is still used a great deal in companies. Let's introduce it properly before we criticize it.

The internal rate of return (IRR) is the discount rate for which the project's NPV is equal to zero. In other words, it's the discount rate at which the sum of the discounted cash flows is exactly equal to the initial investment. For our investment project we obtain an IRR of 15.12%.[3]

Table 3.3 NPV using IRR

Year	0	1	2	3	4	5
Projected cash flows	−50,000	2,640	10,478	15,028	19,578	38,025
Net present value (at 15.12%)		2,294	7,906	9,850	11,146	18,805
Sum of present values	50,000					

Indeed, at this discount rate the sum of future cash flows, when discounted, is equal to £50,000. This means that at this rate NPV = –50,000 + 50,000 = £0.

The IRR rule is as follows:

- If the IRR is greater than the company's discount rate, the project will be profitable and they should invest.
- If the IRR is lower than the company's discount rate, the project will not be profitable and it should be rejected.

In our example, IRR = 15.12% > discount rate of 9%, so the project is profitable.

Criticisms of IRR

Let's be clear: IRR works well most of the time and it usually leads to the same decisions as NPV. But it is this 'most of the time' that makes the red flag pop up. Here is a list of the criticisms that have been levelled against IRR:

---

3. We can find the IRR by successive approximations, by solving a polynomial equation or by using the IRR function on a spreadsheet.

1. There are some projects for which there is no IRR (there is no rate that cancels out NPV).
2. There are some projects for which there are several IRRs (several rates cancel out NPV).[4]
3. When we compare several projects, using the IRR criterion may lead to the opposite conclusion from what we get using NPV.
4. IRR is not a financial indicator, nor is it a rate of return; it is just the result of solving an equation.
5. It is not possible to solve the equation and find IRR unless we assume that intermediate cash flows have been invested at IRR. In our example, that means that we have to be able to invest the intermediate sums at an annual rate of 15.12%...

We won't go into detail on all these points. Suffice it to say that the first three points are the ones that will cause us problems when we have to choose the most promising investment project.

DIALOGUE	
Walter Melon:	How do you explain the fact that this criterion is still regularly used by companies?
Clarence P. Brain:	There may be several explanations. First, the IRR criterion often leads to the same conclusions as NPV. However, NPV does not face the same criticisms. For example, there is only one NPV, not several, and NPV has a fairly clear meaning.
Walter Melon:	So why do some companies use IRR instead of NPV?
Clarence P. Brain:	To tell you the truth, finance professors, researchers and Nobel Prize winners don't really understand why – and it's certainly not for lack of talking about it for the past 80 years. It's probably because IRR is reassuring: it is given as a percentage, which makes you think of a rate of return. For some people, it's probably more meaningful to say 'this project earns us 17%' than 'this earns us £27,000'. But that sometimes leads to the wrong decisions.

---

4. 'Oi, look at this then: our project has a rate of return of +11%, and also +53%, and even –27%! Cool, innit?'

Payback period

The payback period is the length of time it takes to recoup the initial investment. In principle, the shorter the payback period, the more reassuring the project is for the company. In fact, there are two types of payback period: the **simple payback period** and the **discounted payback period**.

Let's do the calculation for our project, first with the simple payback period:

Table 3.4 Simple payback period

Year	0	1	2	3	4	5
Projected cash flows	−50,000	2,640	10,478	15,028	19,578	38,025
Cumulative cash flows	−50,000	−47,360	−36,882	−21,853	−2,275	35,750

The cash flows have just been added together without bothering to discount them. Thus we start the project with an outlay of −£50,000, then we add the first cash flow and we get a cumulative cash flow of −50,000 + 2,640 = −£47,360, and so on. We observe that by the end of the fourth year the cumulative cash flow is still in the red (−£2,275), but at the end of the fifth year the project is in the black (+£35,750).

Thus the initial investment is recovered in less than five years. We can even calculate a more accurate figure:

- At the end of year 4, they only needed £2,275 more for the investment to be paid back.
- Year five generated a cash flow of £38,025.
- If we assume that this cash flow was generated throughout the year, only a portion of year five (2,275/38,025) is needed to arrive at a cumulative cash flow of 0.
- 2,275/38,025 = 0.06 of a year = 0.06 × 365 days = 22 days.

We can therefore say that the simple payback period for this project is 4 years and 22 days. This is the length of time that the cash flows will take to pay back the initial investment.

In this calculation we have made a novice's mistake: we have neglected to discount the cash flows. To correct our error, we will now calculate the discounted payback period:

Table 3.5 Discounted payback period

Year	0	1	2	3	4	5
Projected cash flows	−50,000	2,640	10,478	15,028	19,578	38,025
Discounted cash flows (at 9%)	−50,000	2,422	8,819	11,604	13,870	24,714
Cumulative discounted cash flows	−50,000	−47,578	−38,758	−27,154	−13,284	11,429

All the cash flows are now discounted, that is to say expressed in year 0 pounds. The cumulative totals have changed. At the end of year 4, £13,284 is still needed to pay back the investment. Year 5 generates a discounted cash flow of £24,714. It will therefore take a portion of year 5 to complete the repayment, calculated thus: 13,284/24,714 = 0.54 of a year = 0.54 × 365 = 196 days. The discounted payback period is therefore 4 years and 196 days.

DIALOGUE	
Iona Ferrari:	What conclusion can we draw about this project?
Donna Tellami:	The payback periods are more than four years out of the total of five years, hence this project takes quite some time to become profitable.
Iona Ferrari:	Does that mean that we should always choose projects with the shortest payback periods?
Donna Tellami:	Be careful! The payback calculation ends when the investment has been recovered. The payback period does not take into account the cash flows that will be received afterward and those cash flows may be very large.
Iona Ferrari:	But how can we include those 'post payback' cash flows in our analysis?
Donna Tellami:	By going back to NPV and its decision rule.

Profitability index

The profitability index (PI) measures the payoff of an investment for each pound invested. There are, for example, small projects that generate comparatively more than larger projects. The profitability index is a ratio that tells us the profit for 'each pound invested'. The formula for this index is quite simple:

$$\text{Profitability index} = \frac{\text{NPV}}{\text{initial investment}}$$

For our project we have a PI of 11,429/50,000 = 0.23, meaning that one pound of investment generates a net gain of £0.23.[5] This criterion is particularly useful in two cases:

1. When two projects have essentially the same NPV, they can be differentiated by choosing the one that generates more per pound invested.
2. When our division of the company is undergoing **capital rationing** and is not allowed to launch large-scale projects, it will give preference to projects that have a higher return per unit invested.

Summary in the form of a numerical example

Let's imagine the following three projects: Mizaru, Kikazaru and Iwazaru. The figures and calculations are correct, the projects are mutually exclusive and all three of them last for five years. All we have to do is choose the best one. The company's discount rate is 10%.

Table 3.6 Three potential projects

Project	Investment	NPV	IRR	Payback	PI
Mizaru	−10,000	3,000	15%	1 year 51 days	0.30
Kikazaru	−20,000	6,000	14%	3 years 232 days	0.30
Iwazaru	−10,000	5,000	30%	4 years 7 days	0.50

DIALOGUE	
Yunomi:	So, without any hesitation I would say the Kikazaru project, because that's the one that generates the highest NPV!
Sosumi:	Bingo! The NPV criterion is more important than all the others. What would you say about the other criteria?
Yunomi:	We see that all the projects have an IRR that is greater than the discount rate (10%), so in theory they are all profitable, but they would not be ranked in the same order as they are for NPV. If we relied only on IRR, we would choose the project that is apparently the most profitable (Iwazaru, 30%), though that's not the one that generates the greatest net gain (5,000 compared with 6,000). So here's a good example of a contradictory analysis between NPV and IRR.

5. Another formula is used occasionally: PI = Present value of future cash flows / Investment. Here that would give us PI = 61,429/50,000 = 1.23, which means that one pound of investment generates £1.23 of cash flow (and £1.23 − £1 = an NPV of £0.23).

Sosumi:	Well spotted! And given this contradiction, what would you do?
Yunomi:	NPV is the criterion to follow!
Sosumi:	Great! What would you say about the payback period?
Yunomi:	Not much. Some companies will reject any project that has a payback greater than two years. In this case, that would have ruled out the two most profitable projects in terms of value creation. That's not so smart...
Sosumi:	All that's left is the profitability index (PI). Do we throw that out with the bath water too?
Yunomi:	It depends. We see that even though the Kikazaru project generates the highest NPV, the Iwazaru project has a higher profitability index. Clearly Iwazaru makes better use of the capital invested.
Sosumi:	So what do we decide?
Yunomi:	There are two possibilities: (1) if the company is not rationing capital, it can afford a 20,000 investment without any problem, so it's a no-brainer: the Kikazaru project must be chosen (highest NPV); (2) if the company (or division) has a limited budget, it may consider the Iwazaru project. For half the investment it generates almost the same NPV – we see this in the PI.
Sosumi:	Conclusion?
Yunomi:	Always favour the NPV criterion. In the event of budget restrictions, try to convince your bosses or investors that they're about to miss out on a good project with an NPV of +6,000 and that you'll need more capital. Failing that, fall back on the project with the best profitability index.

That's it, we've finished with investment decision criteria. Now let's see how to make cash flow forecasts.

Making cash flow forecasts

> He went over it in his head, plate by plate, span by span, brick by brick, pier by pier, remembering, comparing, estimating, and recalculating, lest there should be any mistake; and through the long hours and through the flights of formulae that danced and wheeled before him a cold fear would come to pinch his heart. His side of the sum was beyond question; but what man knew Mother Gunga's arithmetic? Even as he was making all sure by the multiplication table, the river might be scooping a pot-hole to the very bottom of any one of those eighty-foot piers that carried his reputation.
>
> Rudyard Kipling, *The Bridge Builders* (1893)

We went through a fairly detailed exploration of a company's cash flow calculations in Chapter 1. If you feel that your knowledge of cash flows, net working capital or operating cash flows is still a bit wobbly, go back and reread those sections in Chapter 1, because those concepts will come in very handy in this section.

A few rules on cash flow forecasts for an investment project

- The calculations are about cash flows, that is to say, everything that is monetary and only what is monetary. So don't worry about accounting entries; only cash receipts and disbursements should be taken into account – on the date they effectively occur.
- Never forget the tax (because the taxman will never forget you).
- Take all the stages of the project into account: investment phase, operational phase, end-of-life phase.
- Look only at **incremental cash flows** – those that are specific to the investment project (we will also talk about **differential cash flows**).

This last point is worth explaining so that it really sinks in.

SLICE OF LIFE...
Soon-Li Qing wants to buy a sailing boat, a twenty-footer, that will make her sister-in-law green with envy. She pinches every penny and invests her savings, which collect compound interest, and finally the golden day arrives when she can buy her boat. Soon-Li's bank account now looks like a dried up creek bed in the Gobi desert, but she doesn't care; she has her twenty-footer!

Then, down at the marina where she wants to keep it, she realizes that there are other expenses involved in owning a boat: mooring fees, fresh water charges, insurance premiums, annual varnishing and maintenance. But Soon-Li is flat broke and the dream is turning into a nightmare.
....

This instructive fable tells us that Soon-Li has neglected to plan for expenses that were a direct consequence of her decision to invest. We say that these expenses are **incremental** (specific to the investment in the boat) because if Soon-Li hadn't bought the boat she would not have incurred said expenses. Two important ideas can be drawn from this.

1. Companies must always think of the expenses that will be caused by an investment. If a company buys a machine to automate production and reduce the number of workers, it has to take into account the costs of redeploying workers (or severance packages for laying them off)

and the cost of training workers to use the new machine. All these expenses are specific to the investment project because they would not have been incurred if the company had not decided to invest.

2. On the other hand, certain expenses will be incurred whatever happens. Whether the company invests or not, it still has to pay its rent, for example. These expenses are non-specific and should not be included in the cash flows of the investment project.

Here's an illustration:

SLICE OF LIFE••

Pasquale Sharkie owns a small pawnshop. He's thinking about opening another branch, which will be run by his sister, Lucretzia Sharkie. Pasquale has had a market study done (cost = £100K), which concludes that there is indeed market potential for a second shop. He now has to determine the projected cash flows for this new business and calculate the project's NPV.

Pasquale estimates the future revenues of the new pawnshop, then he deducts his sister's salary and that of her henchmen, and the cost of their equipment (baseball bats, knuckle-dusters). He also counts the £100K market study and he charges half of his accountant's salary to the project since the accountant who cooks the books for the first shop might as well bake them for the second shop, too. Pasquale calculates the NPV; it is negative. He decides to abandon the project and redeploys his sister as a toilet attendant.

••

Pasquale Sharkie has ruined his sister's life owing to a few misjudgements that we will now elucidate:

• The revenue forecast for the new branch is indeed specific to the project. If Pasquale invests in the second shop, he will get this revenue; if he doesn't invest, he won't. It was therefore correct to include this figure in the calculation.

• The salaries of Pasquale's sister and her henchmen are also specific to the project, as is the henchmen's equipment. They will only be incurred if the second shop is opened. They must therefore be included.

• On the other hand, the market study has already been paid for. Whether he opens the shop or not, this expense has been incurred and so it is not specific to the project. In other words, the decision to launch the project does not trigger this expense. It should not therefore have been included in the project's cash flow forecast.[6]

---

6. There are many misunderstandings in this regard. This expense will be present in the company's accounts and a management accountant would decide whether to record it under one heading or another. But as the expense is not the consequence of a decision to invest, it should not be included in the specific cash flow forecast for the project.

- Similarly, the accountant's salary is not an expense that is specific to the investment project. If Pasquale does not open the second shop, the accountant will still receive his entire salary every month.

We can draw three lessons from this sorry tale. The first is that crime doesn't pay. The second is that you have to reason incrementally, always asking yourself this question: 'if I launch this project, will I have this cash receipt (or expense) that I didn't have before?' If the answer is 'yes', then it is a specific cash flow and should be included. If the answer is 'no', then it would be a mistake to include that cash flow in the project's forecasts.[7] The third idea is that this type of error can cause you to seriously under- or overestimate the project's NPV and therefore make the wrong decision.

The various stages of an investment project

Let's set up an example of an investment project to illustrate the various concepts.[8] You are the general manager of an upmarket bar called Le Select Bistrot, aimed at a well heeled, refined and demanding clientele. Your bar is doing very well, business is thriving, but – greed will be your downfall – you want to make *even more* money. Your cousin, Buddy Light, pitches an idea to you: install giant flat screen TVs throughout the bar so that patrons can watch rugby matches, blind-man's-bluff tournaments and capoeira competitions. Intoxicated with excitement, the bar's customers will drink even more cocktails and these streams of drinks will bring you streams of money.

We still have to calculate the cash flow forecasts, however.

Investment cash flows

Investment cash flows refer not only to the initial outlay (purchase of equipment and tools), but also to the expenses stemming from setting up the new concept (installation, training, etc.). Obviously we must count only the expenses that are specific to the project. The variables of Le Select Bistrot

---

7. We can also reason 'differentially'; in other words, calculate the cash flows with the investment and without the investment, and then subtract to get the difference between the two. We will see that the cost of the market study disappears. These **differential cash flows** are therefore the ones that can be assigned to the project. This is what we did with Geppetto's salaries in Chapter 2.

8. This is a project whose cash flows correspond to the data provided by your big brother at the beginning of this chapter. So the calculations that we performed for NPV, IRR, etc. actually apply to this project. However, to make it easier to read, we will now express the figures in thousands of pounds (£K).

project are as follows. You have to invest in the new equipment (flat screens, sound system, wiring) to the tune of £50K. The screens will be used for five years and the cost will be depreciated using the straight-line method over this period. In addition, you need to make some alterations in the bar to make room for the flat screens. An interior design and remodelling company has already done the work, creating the space necessary to install the new flat screens (cost = £15K).

Now we are ready to calculate the initial outlay. Those of you who calculated £65K, go and stand in the corner. The £15K is an expense that has already taken place, so whether you invest or not, you will still be 15K out of pocket. This is not a specific expense.[9] Those who answered that the initial investment was £50,000 get a Brownie point. Don't get a big head, though; it wasn't that hard. By convention, we consider that the investment took place at the end of year 2015 (or year 0) and that the business activity grows during years 2016–20 (years 1–5).

Operating cash flows

Here we are at the heart of the matter. Operating activities are the cash flows generated by the project during its lifetime. They have to obey the rules for cash flows (monetary, specific, after tax). We are going to learn how to calculate these flows using the Select Bistrot example.

Your marketing manager, Ginger Ayle, has made the following sales forecasts.

Table 3.7 Projected sales revenue

Year	2016	2017	2018	2019	2020
Projected sales revenue without installation of flat screens (in £K)	100	110	120	130	140
Projected sales revenue with flat screens (in £K)	150	170	190	210	230

Direct costs (cocktail ingredients, electricity, etc.) represent 30% of the selling price. If the giant screens are installed, you will have to hire two waiters/waitresses to handle the extra orders (annual cost to the company including benefits: £15K per person). Furthermore, as the bar's annual sales

---

9. It would be rather silly to have these alterations done without knowing whether or not you were going to launch the project. But the point is: they *have been done*. On a differential basis, this expense will make no difference to whether we launch the project or not, so it should not be counted in the project's cash flows.

have exceeded £80K in 2015, you now have to hire a chartered accountant (annual cost to the company, including benefits: £20K).

We can now perform these calculations and make a few remarks:

Table 3.8 Earnings attributed to the project

(in £K)	Remarks	2016	2017	2018	2019	2020
Incremental sales revenue from project	a	50	60	70	80	90
– direct costs	b	–15	–18	–21	–24	–27
– incremental salaries	c	–30	–30	–30	–30	–30
EBITDA		5	12	19	26	33

(a) We count only sales that can be attributed to the investment. For the first year, without flat screens, Ginger Ayle forecast sales of £100K, but with the flat screens they would reach £150K. So the decision to invest in flat screens will generate incremental sales (in other words, sales that are specific to the 'flat screen' project) of 150 – 100 = £50K.

(b) The direct costs are 30% of incremental sales.

(c) The 'incremental salaries' are only those of the waiters/waitresses (2 × 15 = £30K). The accountant's salary was a sneaky trick (teachers always set traps in exercises to compensate for their existential void), because even without the investment in flat screens the total sales would continue to exceed £80K.[10]

Let's carry on with our calculations. Now we have to compute the income tax. The corporate tax rate should be stable at 35% for the coming years. But tax is not calculated directly on EBITDA; depreciation of equipment is a tax-deductible expense and it would be a mistake not to take advantage of that. Here is the dilemma we are faced with: our pristine cash flow table – which is supposed to contain only monetary items – is going to be fouled by the introduction of depreciation – fetid accounting abomination! Come on then, let's include the depreciation in our calculation, but only temporarily; once it has served its purpose, we'll cancel it out. And just so that we don't forget that it is non-monetary, we'll put it in italics.

---

10. It would have been different had we said, 'When sales reach £150K you will have to hire a CPA.' In that case, investing in the flat screens would have increased the sales to that limit and the CPA's salary would have been a consequence of the decision to invest. His salary would then have had to be included in the project's projected costs.

Table 3.9 Cash flow after tax

(in £K)	2016	2017	2018	2019	2020
EBITDA	5.0	12.0	19.0	26.0	33.0
– Depreciation	–10.0	–10.0	–10.0	–10.0	–10.0
Operating profit (EBIT)	–5.0	2.0	9.0	16.0	23.0
– Tax (or Tax credit if +)	+1.8	–0.7	–3.2	–5.6	–8.1
Earnings after tax	–3.2	1.3	5.8	10.4	14.9
(+ add back depreciation)	+10.0	+10.0	+10.0	+10.0	+10.0
Potential cash flow	6.7	11.3	15.8	20.4	24.9

There are several important points to note here:

- Depreciation is calculated using the straight-line method over five years (£50K/5 years = £10K/year). First, it is deducted to calculate the tax on the project's earnings; then, the depreciation is added back. This is therefore a neutral operation (–10.0 + 10.0 = 0, remember?). Please do not infer from this that depreciation is part of cash flow, or you'll be sent to your room without any dinner.[11]
- The tax is calculated on the operating profit (after depreciation) and if there is an operating loss, there will be a **tax credit** (in 2016, for example). This tax credit is justified here because the investment project takes place within a bar that is otherwise profitable. The project's losses are imputed to the bar's profits and the result is a tax saving for that year.[12] It would have been completely different if the investment project had been set up as a separate entity. There would not have been a profit from which to deduct the project's losses, but the company could **carry forward the loss**. It would not have produced the same cash flows, nor the same NPV. Thus **the fiscal structure in which an investment project operates may have an influence on its cash flows and its NPV**.
- Finally, we see the term 'potential cash flow', which we have already seen in Chapter 1; our dear old friend 'net working capital' is probably just around the corner...

---

11. See the basic cash flow calculation in Chapter 1.
12. This tax credit is clearly a gain that is specific to the project.

VIGNETTE

Megan Bucks has just turned 18. She decides to buy a small factory with her trust fund money and start a business. Her parents authorize the bank to give her $100M. She makes a budget, buys a factory ($50M) and machines ($40M) and incurs various other expenses amounting to $10M. Megan considers herself to be a good business manager; she's thought of everything. She's all fired up and ready to conquer the world.

Justin Time, her childhood friend, points out that if Megan doesn't buy some raw materials she won't conquer anything at all. So Megan spends $20M on a load of raw materials, running up her overdraft by this amount. Justin reminds her that she needs to hire workers and pay them to transform the raw materials into goods for sale. Megan does so, but at the end of the month the factory still has not produced any goods. Nevertheless she still needs to pay her workers (adding $30M to her overdraft). Finally, the glorious day arrives when the goods are ready. Megan transports them to her first customer and asks for payment. The customer smiles and says that she'll pay in 60 days — that's standard in this business. Megan wipes a tear from her eye and does her accounts: in addition to spending $100M on her factory she has shelled out $50M more to finance her business. If she had known, she would have asked her folks for at least $150M before starting out!

Let's meditate on this silver-spoon tragedy. The overdraft of $50M represents the Factory Project's **net working capital (NWC), or working capital requirements (WCR),** as we will refer to it here.[13] Every investment project needs cash outlays to 'prime the pump'. These outlays regularly tap into the company's cash flows because (as seen in Chapter 1) working capital increases (or should) at the same pace as sales. The more you sell, the more money you need to inject into your production. The funniest part is that not only is Megan up the creek without a paddle for 60 days, but the situation is going to get worse during those two months. Megan is not going to loaf around sipping herbal tea and having manicures; she's going to prospect for more customers, have them sign contracts, make production commitments... and as a result she will end up buying more raw materials (and paying her workers to transform them). Her working capital will increase along with her sales and her overdraft will reach unprecedented depths.

---

13. Please note that these terms are synonymous. Net working capital (or simply, working capital) is more frequently used in the context of financial statement analysis, whereas working capital requirements (WCR) is often used when we talk about future cash flows and what we need to keep the business running. We like the term 'requirements' because it represents the cash that the company needs to pay out in advance (this is explained in detail in the following paragraphs).

Now back to our Select Bistrot project to apply this freshly acquired knowledge. The barman, Desmond 'Des' Perado, tells us that the inventory of cocktail ingredients (alcohol, fruit, juice, soda, plastic cocktail umbrellas, ice, etc.) is equal to 60 days of sales, that all the suppliers are paid in 30 days (expressed in days of sales) and that customers pay cash (that's the only bit of good news in the whole cockamamie project). We can therefore apply the net working capital formula learned in Chapter 1 and calculate working capital in days of sales.

Working capital requirements (WCR) = Inventory + Accounts receivable – current liabilities

so WCR = 60 + 0 – 30 = 30 days of sales.

Now let's calculate the project's working capital requirements in £K and, more importantly, the *change* in WCR over the duration of the project.[14]

Table 3.10 Change in working capital

(in £K)	2015	2016	2017	2018	2019	2020
Incremental sales revenue for project	0.00	50.00	60.00	70.00	80.00	90.00
Working capital requirements (WCR)	0.00	4.11	4.93	5.75	6.58	7.40
Change in WCR		4.11	0.82	0.82	0.82	0.82

Working capital requirements are equal to 30 days of sales in our example, so we calculate the amount in pounds like this:

$$WCR_{2016} = \frac{30}{365} \times 50 = £4.11K$$

and the change in WCR is the difference between two years, for example:

$$WCR_{2017} - WCR_{2016} = 4.93 - 4.11 = £0.82K$$

DIALOGUE	
Sleepy:	Why do we worry about the change in WCR, and not only the WCR, as a cash outflow?
Happy:	Because once the initial WCR has been paid out it's no longer a problem. What matters are the new cash outlays that have to be made every year – the changes in WCR. Get it?

---

14. As with all the other tables, there may be a few rounding errors. The tables that are available online – free of charge! – are of course accurate to the 10,000th decimal place.

Sleepy:	It's about as clear as the Mississippi...
Happy:	Wake up, sleepyhead. Just look at the table. In 2015, the WCR for the project was 0, which is normal because there's no project yet and so there are no cash outlays to make. Now, in 2016 they had to pay out 4.11 in WCR. In your opinion how much was the cash outflow?
Sleepy:	4.11. You just said it...
Happy:	Exactly. This 4.11 appears in the second line as the change in WCR (cash outflow) for 2016. Now this is where it gets interesting. How much is the WCR for the project in 2017?
Sleepy:	4.93.
Happy:	So why did the WCR increase from 4.11 to 4.93?
Sleepy:	Because the project's sales increased and since WCR correlates to sales, it increased at the same time. In other words, the more you sell, the more you have to produce and so of course you have cash outflows. You expand your WCR.
Happy:	Now you're awake! Now tell me why we are only interested in the 0.82 change in 2017.
Sleepy:	The 4.11 was paid out in 2016 so it's done. It impacted our cash flow in 2016 but we don't talk about it any more. Now, in 2017, sales have increased, so the WCR has necessarily increased as well – to 4.93. Given that 4.11 was already paid out in 2016, an additional WCR of 4.93 – 4.11 = 0.82 was needed in 2017. It is therefore just this amount that is drawn from 2017's cash flow.
Happy:	You've made me even more happy! Now let's go and explain it to Grouchy...

Now we can go back to our cash flow calculations. We are going to remove the change in WCR from 'potential cash flow' and we will get what we are looking for: operating cash flow.

Table 3.11 Operating cash flow

(in £K)	2016	2017	2018	2019	2020
Potential cash flow	6.75	11.30	15.85	20.40	24.95
– growth in WCR	-4.11	-0.82	-0.82	-0.82	-0.82
Operating cash flow	2.64	10.48	15.03	19.58	24.13

Table 3.11 is worth commenting on:

- First, we did not use the term 'change' in WCR this time, but 'growth' in WCR. This is more precise since, after all, a change can be an increase or a decrease. It is therefore better to say: 'we must subtract the growth in WCR from the cash flow'. Thus in the event of a drop in WCR, we will know to *'add the drop* in WCR to the cash flow.'

- We observe that, apart from the first year, the changes in WCR are quite small, which may explain why some people think they can just forget about this item. But be careful, not all projects are the same. Remember: Megan had working capital that amounted to half her material investment. And back in Chapter 1, more than ¾ of Droids Co.'s cash flow was eaten up by the growth in its working capital. The longer the production cycle (inventories), the later customers pay (accounts receivable) or the earlier suppliers are paid (current liabilities), the more WCR will draw on the company's cash flows.
- Even at this point some readers and students still won't understand why we subtract that darn change in WCR from the cash flows. And the authors can't blame them: with WCR, either you've got the hang of it or you haven't.

For those of you who haven't, we'll try one last time to explain.

VIGNETTE

Cyrano de Bergerac: Why do we subtract the growth in WCR? Varying the tone, we might say:

- *Colloquial:* 'We have to shell out the cash to build up inventories and ramp up production to sell more stuff. And since those slow-as-molasses customers of ours don't pay up until they're good and ready, we have no choice but to finance our little operation ourselves.'

- *Logical:* 'In the cash flow forecasts, sales and costs are for a 12-month period. But the sales made in November and December of 2017 won't be paid for until 2018 because of our customer payment terms. The change in WCR serves to set the record straight: of the 12 months of sales recorded in 2017, we won't receive payments for the last two months (they will remain stuck in the working capital).'[15]

- *Pragmatic:* 'I take a look at my bank account. In January I spend £10 on raw materials and I pay £10 in wages. I'm down £20. At the end of January I deliver the goods to my customer and I invoice £30. They laugh and tell me to come back in a month. Meanwhile, in February, I spend £15 on raw materials and pay £10 in wages. Now I'm at −£45. At the end of

---

15. An even more logical reader might say: 'Yes, but at the start of 2017 we will have received payment for the sales made in November and December of 2016. So that makes 12 months!' True, good reader, but if the business is growing, then the sales from the end of 2016 will be less than 2017 sales. So we are always playing catch-up with our WCR!

> February I deliver to customer n° 2 and I invoice £35. They also laugh. Meanwhile the first joker pays me £30. Where am I? Sales on my books: £65; costs on my books: £45; profit on my books: +£20. Reality in my bank account: −45 + 30 = −£15. Difference between the two: the receivable from customer n° 2, recorded but not received. This receivable increases my WCR (because the payment hasn't been received). All in all, I have +20 profit −35 change in WCR = −£15 cash.'

Now we just have to look at the final stage of the project: the end.

End-of-life cash flows

When an investment project reaches its end, you have to 'dismantle' the assets and this causes final cash receipts and expenses. For example: cash received from selling off equipment (if it still has a resale value), the cost of dismantling the facility and possibly restoring the premises to their prior condition. At this time, we will recover the working capital paid out before, which generates a cash inflow (this will be explained in detail below).

As usual, we will use the Select Bistrot case to illustrate these ideas.

Divestment

At the end of the five years of operation, the flat screens will be out of date and you will get rid of them. Your technician, Jacques Danielle, believes you can sell this used equipment for £15K. This gain is taxable because it is a capital gain of 15 on the resale. You are selling equipment that has been completely depreciated (book value = 0). In addition, you have to count the severance pay for the two waiters and renovation work to restore the bar to its previous condition (filling the holes in the walls, and so on) at an estimated cost of £5K.

This gives us a net gain of 15 − 5 = £10K.[16]

The corporate income tax will therefore be 35% × 10 = £3.5K and the after-tax gain will be 10 − 3.5 = £6.5K.

---

16. You may be surprised by these expenses; why not simply buy new flat screens, install them (without filling in the holes) and continue to employ the two waiters/waitresses? In practice, that is probably what the bar would do. But our project ends here. For the sake of coherence, we have to pursue the incremental cash flow reasoning and ask this question: 'At the end of the project, what cash flows will we have that we wouldn't have had if we hadn't invested in the project?' Answer: the severance packages and dismantling expenses. With this type of reasoning we ensure that each project is analysed independently.

Recovering working capital

Now let's look at the question of recovering working capital. Why do we recover working capital at the end of a project?

There are several ways to explain it:

- This cash outflow was only an advance. Once the project is finished, we pay the last suppliers and sell the remaining inventory (which becomes accounts receivable), and the last customers pay us. In fact, recovering working capital means collecting the last accounts receivable in cash, minus payments to suppliers.
- Working capital correlates to sales. When sales increase, working capital increases, as we have seen. Conversely, when a project's sales fall to zero (which is the case at the end of the project), working capital also falls to zero. During the project, the company pays out money as working capital is growing, and at the end of the project it recovers money from the diminishing working capital. Table 3.12 illustrates this mechanism in the last column (2021), which we have added to the previous calculations.

Table 3.12 Change in working capital

(in £K)	2015	2016	2017	2018	2019	2020	2021
Incremental sales revenue for project	0.00	50.00	60.00	70.00	80.00	90.00	0.00
Working capital	0.00	4.11	4.93	5.75	6.58	7.40	0.00
Change in working capital		4.11	0.82	0.82	0.82	0.82	–7.40

DIALOGUE

Zippy: What do we do with this –7.40 in the last year of the project?

Grouchy: Try to focus, you nincompoop! We said that we either subtracted growth in working capital from the cash flow, or we added a decrease in working capital to the cash flow. So which is it?

Zippy: Uuuh, we add the 7.40 to the final cash flow?

Grouchy: Right! Because it's a cash inflow. We've finally got back all the cash outlays we made before.

Zippy: But why did they put this amount under 2021 in the table? That's rather a long way off, isn't it?

Grouchy: True. We put it in 2021 for the purpose of illustration, but it doesn't take a whole year to recover the working capital because customers usually pay within two months. In fact, most of the time, working capital recovery is placed in the final year (2020 in our example). That's more realistic. And that's what we will do in the summary table.

Summary of all cash flows

We've come to the end of our road and we now know how to make cash flow forecasts. Thanks for playing! Now let's step back and take a look at our work as a whole:

Table 3.13 Summary of all cash flows

Investment cash flows	2015	2016	2017	2018	2019	2020
Purchase of flat screens	−50					
Total investment cash flows	−50	0	0	0	0	0
Operating cash flows	**2015**	**2016**	**2017**	**2018**	**2019**	**2020**
Projected sales without flat screens		100.00	110.00	120.00	130.00	140.00
Projected sales with flat screens		150.00	170.00	190.00	210.00	230.00
Incremental sales revenue from project		**50.00**	**60.00**	**70.00**	**80.00**	**90.00**
− direct costs		−15.00	−18.00	−21.00	−24.00	−27.00
− incremental salaries		−30.00	−30.00	−30.00	−30.00	−30.00
EBITDA		**5.00**	**12.00**	**19.00**	**26.00**	**33.00**
− Depreciation		−10.00	−10.00	−10.00	−10.00	−10.00
Operating profit (EBIT)		**−5.00**	**2.00**	**9.00**	**16.00**	**23.00**
− Tax (or + tax credit)		1.75	−0.70	−3.15	−5.60	−8.05
Earnings after tax		**−3.25**	**1.30**	**5.85**	**10.40**	**14.95**
(+ add back depreciation)		10.00	10.00	10.00	10.00	10.00
Potential cash flow		**6.75**	**11.30**	**15.85**	**20.40**	**24.95**
− increase in WCR		−4.11	−0.82	−0.82	−0.82	−0.82
Total operating cash flows		**2.64**	**10.48**	**15.03**	**19.58**	**24.13**
End-of-life cash flows	**2015**	**2016**	**2017**	**2018**	**2019**	**2020**
Working capital recovery						7.40
+ Sale of assets − capital gains tax						6.50
Total end-of-life cash flows	0.00	0.00	0.00	0.00	0.00	13.90

Table 3.14 Cash flows by project phase

Summary	2015	2016	2017	2018	2019	2020
Investment cash flows	−50	0	0	0	0	0
Operating cash flows	0	2.64	10.48	15.03	19.58	24.13
End-of-life cash flows	0.00	0.00	0.00	0.00	0.00	13.90
Total cash flows	−50	2.64	10.48	15.03	19.58	38.03

Note: Total cash flows can also be called free cash flows, which are basically all operating cash-flows (including end-of-life cash flows) minus investment cash flows.

DIALOGUE	
Smarty:	Beautiful, isn't it?
Sloppy:	Yes, but there's one thing that still bothers me…
Smarty (sighing):	Go on, what is it?
Sloppy:	What if we had financed the purchase of the flat screens with debt? Then we would have had to include the interest payments in the cash flow calculations, wouldn't we?
Smarty:	Nope. We're dealing with investment decisions here, not the company's capital structure policy. We just want to find out whether the project is profitable. A project's profitability depends on its economic characteristics (market potential, profit margins, useful life of equipment, etc.), not the way it is financed.
Sloppy:	Any chance you could be a little less verbose?
Smarty:	The value of a factory doesn't change, whether it is financed through debt or equity. Its value depends only on its economic characteristics, and that's what we measure in an investment decision: the economic value of the project.
Sloppy:	But if I decide to finance my flat screens with debt anyway, can't I deduct the interest payments? (Smarty shakes his head disconsolately) Where will they appear, then?
Smarty:	We never show the interest payments in a project's cash flow statement. The discount rate that has been set for the project is where we will find the company's capital structure policy.
Sloppy:	So the discount rate actually represents a finance cost?
Smarty:	Yes, mainly. Now go and have a lie-down. We'll look at this in more detail later (Chapter 5).

You may think we've finished with this investment project, but there is actually one more important thing to do: the sensitivity analysis of our assumptions. Let's get on with it!

Sensitivity analysis

> *To torment and tantalize oneself with hopes of possible fortune is so sweet, so thrilling!*
>
> Anton Chekhov, *The Lottery Ticket* (1887)

In finance, there is often a paradox: we think that what takes time is running financial models, whereas in reality, as the first chapters in this book illustrate, we spend much more time determining the values to input than we do running the models. Anyone with a spreadsheet and the IQ of a tomato can calculate an NPV, as long as you give them the cash flows (which is what we did in the beginning). On the other hand, it takes a subtle and refined mind to determine cash flows precisely and to judge their relevance.[17]

Performing a sensitivity analysis takes things to the next level: we vary the values of our cash flows to see the impact this would have on the result (on NPV). Every sensitivity analysis is based on the question: 'what if ...'. What if we didn't set the margin at x, but half of that – what would be the impact on our NPV? What if sales growth were less than our forecasts; would our NPV become negative? And what if Godzilla attacked the Tower of London; would our NPV be affected? What is the goal of this mental exercise? To measure the **sensitivity** of our project to the economic context. In short, to judge whether our NPV is as solid as a rock – it won't budge come hell or high water – or if, on the contrary, the slightest breeze would blow our project away like a wisp of straw. It is an assessment of the risk involved in the project.

Let's go back to our Select Bistrot investment project. Here is the table of the main variables:

Table 3.15 Select Bistrot investment project

	2016	2017	2018	2019	2020
Incremental sales revenue from project	50	60	70	80	90
Sales growth		20.0%	16.7%	14.3%	12.5%
Direct cost of supplies	30%	30%	30%	30%	30%
WCR (in days of sales)	30	30	30	30	30
Depreciation	-10	-10	-10	-10	-10
Resale value					15

---

17. Otherwise we get caught in the GIGO syndrome (garbage in, garbage out), because when the data is mouldy, the results are no better. As my grandmother would have said, 'If you try to make jam with cheese rinds, don't be surprised if it stinks.'

Now let's play the 'What if ...' game (we just change one variable at a time).

- What if the jump in sales wasn't 50 the first year, but only 40 (maintaining the same sales growth rate for subsequent years)?
- What if incremental sales started at 50, but then grew more slowly? For example, 2 percentage points less each year (18% instead of 20%, 14.7% instead of 16.7%, etc.)?
- What if the direct cost of supplies was 31% every year?
- What if WCR was 35 days of sales for each year?
- What if the flat screens were depreciated using an **accelerated method** (instead of the straight-line method), like this: –20, then –15, then –5 for the last three years?
- What if you were unable to sell the flat screens at the end of the project (resale value = 0 in 2020)?

The hardworking authors of this book have already done the number crunching for you and offer you the results on a silver platter, with outcomes compared with the NPV calculated initially (£11,430 or £11.43K):

Table 3.16   Sensitivity analysis

Variable	New NPV	Initial NPV	Difference
Initial sales of 40	–12.46	11.43	–209%
Sales growth rate –2 percentage points	7.17	11.43	–37%
Direct cost of sales 31%	9.7	11.43	–15%
WCR: 35 days of sales	11.2	11.43	–2%
Accelerated depreciation	12.38	11.43	8%
Resale value = 0	5.09	11.43	–55%

DIALOGUE	
Jimena:	How appalling! If anything goes wrong we stand to lose loads of money!
El Cid:	Yes, dear.
Jimena:	Mind you, it makes you think, doesn't it? The time when NPV really takes a nose dive is when the initial sales are lower than our forecast. We have to make sure that the 50 in sales the first year is achievable, because our NPV is very sensitive to this variable.
El Cid:	Yes, dear.

Jimena:	The second variable that sinks us is the resale value of the flat screens. After all, how can we know what the resale value will be in five years? Out of prudence, we should really set that at zero, but then our NPV, while not negative, is not nearly so stellar. The value of the project – and its benefit to the company – drops off sharply!
El Cid:	Yes, dear.
Jimena:	We also have to pay close attention to our sales growth and our direct costs; it only takes a slight drop in either of these indicators for our NPV to be affected.
El Cid:	Yes, dear.
Jimena:	On the other hand, WCR doesn't seem to be such a crucial variable. Let's see now: if WCR were to increase to 60 days, we would have an NPV of...hmm...10K! That's 12% off our initial NPV. Not worth crying over, really. I have an idea: we could offer to pay our suppliers earlier (which would worsen our WCR), if in exchange they would give us a rebate (which would improve our direct costs). Imagine if we paid our suppliers in cash and that reduced our direct costs to 28% of sales. The NPV would go up £13.5K, which is +18%! Phenomenal!
El Cid:	What you've just done, darling dearest, is a scenario analysis: you're changing several variables at the same time. That's taking the thing to a higher level: a multi-criteria sensitivity analysis. Some people even go as far as performing 'Monte Carlo simulations' – scenarios with probabilities.
Jimena:	Pipe down, Cid, I'm thinking...Heavens! The depreciation method (straight-line or accelerated) has an impact on NPV! And yet, depreciation is a non-cash item, that's queer...Oh, I see: depreciation is part of the tax calculation. If we depreciate a lot the first years, we pay less tax, and since the first cash flows are discounted less than later ones, that improves the NPV. I've figured it out, I'm as sharp as a tack!
El Cid:	Yes, dear.

A FOOL AND HIS MONEY ...

Sancho Panza: What if we varied the discount rate? Wouldn't that be something to do in a sensitivity analysis?

Don Quixote: ¡Qué no, amigo! We're not going to vary the discount rate, just as we're not going to vary the income tax rate, because those are givens, not variables.

Sancho Panza: But at the beginning of Chapter 2, we saw that the discount rate was linked to risk. Isn't the sensitivity analysis supposed to measure the project's risk?

Don Quixote: Indeed it is, but the risk measured is the risk to future cash flows – things that we have control over: sales, costs, dates and so on.

Sancho Panza: And we don't have any control over the discount rate?

Don Quixote: Go and see your shareholders and your investors and try to convince them to change their return expectations...Basically, the sensitivity analysis serves to highlight the key success factors: variables that have a significant impact on NPV and which therefore need to be estimated correctly and controlled. There's no point in selling a project to your superiors if you know that you can never achieve the projected sales.

And this, without further ado, brings us to our conclusion.

Conclusion

> *In any moment of decision the best thing you can do is the right thing, the next best thing is the wrong thing, and the worst thing you can do is nothing.*
>
> Theodore Roosevelt (1854–1919)

Forecasting is not the same as achieving. Just because your spreadsheet displays lovely round figures does not mean that your investment will live to see the end of the year. Nothing ever happens as planned. Making a forecast does not provide any guarantees. Any intellectually honest person knows that merely building an investment forecast cannot make the universe spin in your favour. So why make a forecast?

- We make forecasts so that we have a model to help in decision-making. The operative word here being 'help'. It is not the spreadsheet that decides, but the person in charge. That person can decide to go against the model, but if things go badly, he can only blame himself. And if he does follow the model and everything goes well – human nature being what it is – he will often attribute this success to his own cleverness: 'all these theoretical models don't do anything that I can't already do with my natural flair for business'. Until the next time.
- We make forecasts to understand the project and its risks better. Building a cash flow forecast involves a lot of suffering and effort, but above all it

101

is about asking the right questions. Is this expense specific to the project? Are my forecasts reasonable? Below what level of sales would my NPV become negative?

We never calculate cash flow forecasts 'just to have an NPV'. We do it to understand the business and to make enlightened decisions.

4

Risk and Profitability – Stock Portfolios

When the shares had fallen to fifteen francs, and anyone who bought it was looked on as a madman, he had put his whole fortune, two hundred thousand francs, into the affair, at a venture, without calculation or instinct, through obstinate confidence in his bull luck. Now that the discovery of real and important veins had sent the price of the shares up above a thousand francs, he had make fifteen millions; and his imbecile operation, which ought to have caused him to be shut up somewhere else, now lifted him to the rank of great financial intellects. He was saluted and consulted more than anyone. Moreover, he placed no more orders, seeming to be satisfied, enthroning himself henceforth upon his unique and legendary stroke of genius.

Émile Zola, *Money* (1892)

Introduction

Risk in finance

Risk usually characterizes our **uncertainty,** faced with the unknown. We cannot accurately predict the future, and some decisions may have consequences that are more costly than others. It follows that the notion of risk encompasses two different things:

- the probability that the worst – or the best – will happen;
- an assessment of the cost of the worst outcome vs. the benefit of the best.

SLICE OF LIFE ●
Ryan Coke is in an existential quandary. If he gets home late, there is a 14% probability that his wife will pack her bags (in this case, Ryan would lose her salary and the family allowance benefits), a 36% probability that his better half will crack his head open (then he would run up hospital bills

that are not covered by his complementary insurance) and a 50% chance that she will have her nose buried in a book and won't even notice he's late (no damage there, except to his pride). On the basis of this information, Ryan Coke rationally decides that there is enough time for another glass of Wild Pheasant.

Clearly, being in a situation of risk means not being able to predict exactly what will happen. But, as this slice of life shows, within the range of possibilities, there are some that are less risky than others:

- either because there is only a small probability that the 'worst case scenario' will happen (14% risk of his wife leaving);
- or because the 'cost of the most probable' is not very high (50% risk of being ignored – just a small blow to his pride).

It is the same when we decide to invest money; we may lose everything (the 'worst case'), but it's not sure we will lose (probability). Understanding this logic is the key to understanding the nature of risk in finance and the notion of risk premium. To illustrate this, we will look at two types of financial asset: government bonds and stock market shares.

Risk-free assets

> *You're looking for a risk-free investment that pays 18% per annum?*
> *Pay off your credit cards.*

Let's take a look at a bond issue carried out by the German central bank a few months ago: maturity was 15 years, the annual yield 4% and the nominal value €1,000.[1] Adam Zappel decides to invest €1,000 and for the moment he intends to keep this bond until maturity. Here is the timeline of expected cash flows.

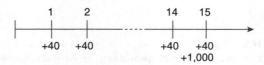

Figure 4.1 Cash flow timeline

---

1. Go back to the section on bonds at the end of Chapter 2 to refresh your memory.

If Adam keeps his bond until maturity, he will get €40 each year (1,000 × 4%) and in the final year the nominal value of bond will be redeemed: €1,000. For this government bond there is no uncertainty. Therefore, as long as Adam keeps the bond until maturity:

- he will receive the amounts shown on the timeline, as stipulated in the contract;
- there will be no problem with payments given that the German government is considered solvent (and hopefully this will be the case for at least the next five years).

In sum, the payment dates and amounts are guaranteed. We call such a bond a **risk-free asset,** because there is no uncertainty about the schedule of payments to receive. But Adam Zappel is still doubtful and so he has a tête-à-tête with his German financial advisor, Herr Dreyer.

DIALOGUE	
Adam Zappel:	It's supposed to be a risk-free asset, but there's no guarantee I will get €40 a year; it depends on the interest rates...
Herr Dreyer:	Ach, nein. The bond yield is set by contract at 4%. Even if market rates fluctuate, the German government – which is more reliable than a Swiss clock – will pay 4% of €1,000 each year and €1,000 at the end. So there's no risk.
Adam Zappel:	But this asset is a bond, and in Chapter 2 we saw that the value of bonds fluctuates on the market. So how can my yield be guaranteed?
Herr Dreyer:	Because you are keeping the bond until maturity. Whatever its market value, it will be redeemed for €1,000. On the other hand, there is a risk if you decide to sell the bond before maturity. Then you would be facing uncertainty about its resale value. But if you keep it until maturity, you are sure to receive €1,000.
Adam Zappel:	What about the solvency of the German government? Very recently, we've seen several countries that are unable to honour their debts.
Herr Dreyer:	That's true. There is a spectrum of risk and national governments are not all equal. Intuitively, a bond issued by Afghanistan is riskier than a bond from Switzerland. But within this spectrum, Germany is currently quite well ranked.

That said, Adam is right: a **risk-free asset in the absolute sense does not exist**. A revolution, a war or an economic crash could cause turmoil in a government's finances. Nevertheless, many government bonds come very close to the notion of risk-free asset because those countries have always honoured their debts in the past.

FINANCIALESE _____

Examples of risk-free assets are government bonds, known in the United States as **Treasury bonds** (long term) and **Treasury bills** (short term) and in the United Kingdom as **gilts** (gilt-edged securities). In Europe, many stock markets keep an eye on the **Bund**, the German long-term government bond.

Risky assets

Emo Beauty Salons Co. is listed on the stock market and its share price fluctuates according to the economic news and the mood of investors. The following table shows the company's share price over six years.

Table 4.1   Change in share price

Date	Share price	Growth
31 December 2009	£12.30	
31 December 2010	£13.15	+6.9%
31 December 2011	£18.90	+43.7%
31 December 2012	£16.40	−13.2%
31 December 2013	£20.90	+27.4%
31 December 2014	£21.50	+2.9%

As we can see, the share price fluctuates. For example, in the first year the share price went from £12.30 to £13.15, which is a growth of (13.15 − 12.3)/12.3 = 0.069 or +6.9%.

DIALOGUE

Benvolio:	*Does the growth here correspond to a measure of profitability?*
Malvolio:	*Yes, the growth in the share price represents a rate of return for investors. If they had bought shares for £12.30 and sold them at £13.15 a year later, their wealth would have increased by 6.9%.*
Benvolio:	*But shouldn't we include the dividend that the investors received that year?*
Malvolio:	*Yes, absolutely! Calculating the rate of return for investors must include the **capital gain** (the growth in the share price) and the dividend. Let's look at a more detailed table.*

Table 4.2 Total return

Date	Share price	Growth	Dividend	Dividend yield	Return
31 December 2009	£12.30				
31 December 2010	£13.15	+6.9%	£1.00	+8.1%	+15.0%
31 December 2011	£18.90	+43.7%	£1.30	+9.9%	+53.6%
31 December 2012	£16.40	−13.2%	£1.50	+7.9%	−5.3%
31 December 2013	£20.90	+27.4%	£1.70	+10.4%	+37.8%
31 December 2014	£21.50	+2.9%	£2.00	+9.6%	+12.4%

DIALOGUE	
Malvolio:	In the first year, for example, an investor will have made a capital gain of (13.15 – 12.3) = £0.85 (growth of 6.9%) plus the £1 dividend that was paid out (a **dividend yield** of 1/12.3 = 8.1%). Altogether, this investor will have received 0.85 + 1 = earnings of £1.85 for an initial investment of £12.30, which is a 15% return (1.85/12.30).
Benvolio:	So the kinds of stocks that make money are either those whose share price increases (growth stocks) or those that pay dividends (value stocks)?
Malvolio:	Exactly. And the investor's total return is the sum of the two: capital gains plus dividends.
Benvolio:	But we observe that the return really fluctuates! From one year to the next, it went from +53% to –5%!
Malvolio:	Don't forget that by their very nature stocks are risky assets. Contrary to government bonds, their earnings fluctuate – both the capital gains part and the dividends.

So this is the major difference between a risky asset and a risk-free asset: the risky asset has a variable and uncertain return. This uncertainty is a risk for investors. Now let's take a look at measuring this risk.

Measuring risk in finance: volatility

What makes an asset risky is its volatility, that is, the amplitude of the fluctuations in its return. Here are three stocks. Let's take a look at their fluctuations over one year:

Table 4.3 Stock prices

Stock	Cool Jazz	Hard Rock	Heavy Metal
On 1 January	£4.00	£4.00	£4.00
On 31 December	£5.00	£5.00	£5.00
52-week high	£5.25	£7.60	£15.90
52-week low	£3.90	£2.10	£0.35

All three stocks ended the year higher than they began it, with an increase of £1 (25%) in their share price. But during the year the three stocks did not have the same volatility; take a look at the 52-week highs and lows. Heavy Metal wins the volatility award: it ended the year with a share price of £5, but during the year it alternated between peaks (£15.90 or +298% over 1 January) and troughs (£0.35 or –91% compared with the start of the year). Thus, depending on when they bought the stock, investors will have paid up to £15.90 for a stock that is worth only £5 at year's end, while others will have sold a stock that they had paid £4 for at the beginning of the year for as little as £0.35.[2]

In this example, the Cool Jazz stock is the least risky, since it generated the same return as the other two (+25%), but with lower volatility (its share price stayed between £3.90 and £5.25).

Let's return to our Emo Beauty Salons stock.

Table 4.4 Returns for Emo Beauty Salons

Emo Beauty Salons	Return
31 December 2010	+15.0%
31 December 2011	+53.6%
31 December 2012	−5.3%
31 December 2013	+37.8%
31 December 2014	+12.4%
Mean	+22.7%

To make Table 4.4 above we have just taken the 'Return' column that we computed earlier and calculated the mean of the annual returns. On average, then, this stock generated a return of +22.7% over the last five years. But just imagine the faces of investors who were promised '+22.7% on average' and found themselves at the end of 2012 with –5.3%! Clearly, we need to add a variable: we cannot just say 'the return on this stock is +22.7%', but rather 'the return on this stock is +22.7% plus or minus Y'.

It is this 'plus or minus' that we will now try to determine, measured using the notion of volatility. We may as well warn you: this calculation is a little laborious. For those who tire easily, you may want to jump ahead to the paragraph starting with 'And voilà!' – you won't have missed too much. Everybody else hang on tight; we're gonna rock!

---

2. Granted, there would also have been some winners; for example, those that bought at 0.35 and sold at 15.90. But don't dream too much; competition is fierce on the stock market.

We want to calculate an amplitude, that is to say the annual deviation from the average return. Let's add a third column that shows this deviation:

Table 4.5 Deviation from average return

Date	Return	Deviation from mean	Deviation^2
31 December 2010	+15.0%	−7.7%	0.0059
31 December 2011	+53.6%	+30.9%	0.0954
31 December 2012	−5.3%	−28.0%	0.0785
31 December 2013	+37.8%	+15.1%	0.0228
31 December 2014	+12.4%	−10.3%	0.0106
Mean	+22.7%	Mean of squares	0.053
		Square root of mean deviation	23.1%

The *Deviation from the mean* column can be read like this: in 2010, the stock generated a return of +15.0% or 7.7% less than the historic mean (22.7%). The following year, the return was +53.6% or 30.9% more than the average annual return. Thus the *Deviation from the mean* column tells us how much the annual performance differs from the long-term average.

We are now going to calculate the average of these deviations to get an idea of the amplitude of the annual returns with respect to the mean. But we are going to add a complication (see last column): first we will calculate the square of each deviation, then the mean of these squares,[3] and finally the square root of this mean. Squaring allows us to cancel out the negative signs and also gives the result some juicy statistical properties.

And voilà! (Welcome back, arts majors.) We now have an indicator that we'll call the volatility of the Emo Beauty Salons stock: 23.1%.

FINANCIALESE

The volatility of a stock is also called the **standard deviation of the return**. By convention, the symbol for standard deviation is σ (lowercase Greek letter sigma). Volatility squared (σ^2) is known as **variance**. Finally, the historical average return is often used to predict returns and here we speak of the **expected return** E(R).

---

3. Owing to a sorry tale of 'degrees of freedom', the average calculated in our example is the sum of the values divided by 4 (even though there are five values). It is not a mistake, though – that's the charm of statistics!

We can therefore summarize the Emo Beauty Salons stock profile by saying that it has a historical average return, or an expected return $E(R)$ of 22.7% and a volatility σ of 23.1%.

DIALOGUE	
Shylock:	Based on these figures, can I say that the return on Emo Beauty Salons stock is 22.7% plus or minus 23.1%? By that I mean that the worst return is 22.7% – 23.1% = –0.4% and the best return is 22.7% + 23.1% = 45.8%?
Portfolio:	Umm, no. You only have to look at the table with the returns: the stock has already gone below (and above) those figures. In fact, the worst that a stock can do is –100%, when its price plummets to £0. And the best, who knows, might be +200% or +1,000% – there's really no upper limit (or as they like to say on Wall Street, the sky is the limit).
Shylock:	So what is the point of calculating the volatility of this stock?
Portfolio:	To give reasonable boundaries to its fluctuations and to compare it with other stocks. The stock's volatility helps us to define its level of risk.
Shylock:	Go on...
Portfolio:	According to the law of statistics, 66% of returns fall between the mean and plus or minus one standard deviation, and 95% of returns fall between plus two and minus two standard deviations. Let's illustrate this with two stocks.

Table 4.6 Comparison of two stocks

	Emo Beauty Salons	Gothic Apothecary
$E(R)$	22.7%	12.4%
σ	23.1%	18.3%

Portfolio:	Here, for example, an investor might say: there is a 95% chance that Gothic Apothecary's return will fall between –24% and +49%. That gives us an amplitude. In comparison, there is a 95% chance that Emo Beauty Salons' return will be between –23% and +69%.[4]
Shylock:	That range seems enormous!
Portfolio:	You're right. Stocks are risky assets, remember. And that's without counting the remaining 5% of probability that the annual return will fall outside two standard deviations; that is, outside the lower and upper figures we calculated. Now there's a **real** measure of amplitude...

4. The calculations for Gothic are: 12.4% – (2 × 18.3%) and 12.4% + (2 × 18.3%) and for Emo: 22.7% – (2 × 23.1%) and 22.7% + (2 × 23.1%).

Shylock: Just to get an idea, what is the average volatility (σ) of a 'normal'
           American or European stock?
Portfolio: In the range of 30–40%, depending on the period.

How to reduce the risk: combining assets

Stocks are risky assets. So be it. That does not mean, however, that we have
to bear the full brunt of their volatility risk. The entire range of risk levels
and (almost) any return can be achieved by combining assets. A shrewd
investor is therefore one who knows how to combine assets to achieve certain performance goals. We will begin by combining a risk-free asset with a
risky asset and then we will move on to combinations of risky assets.

Combining a risk-free asset with a risky asset

Let's take a risk-free asset as presented in the first part of this chapter (a government bond such as a German *Bund*) and a risky asset (Athos stock) whose
characteristics we outline below. We will then see how to combine them.

Table 4.7   Portfolio: risky asset + risk-free asset

	Expected return E(R)	Volatility (σ)
Athos stock	8.0%	20.0%
Bund	3.5%	0.0%

We observe that, by design, the Bund has zero volatility. As a risk-free
asset, its return is fixed and guaranteed, so there is no deviation in the return,
nor any uncertainty – contrary to Athos stock. We are going to combine these
two assets in a **portfolio**. In fact, we are going to build several portfolios with
different proportions of each asset and then comment on the results.[5]

Table 4.8   Portfolios combining different proportions of risky and risk-free assets

Portfolio n°	Percentage of Athos	Percentage of Bund	Expected return E(R)	Volatility (σ)
1	0%	100%	3.50%	0.0%
2	25%	75%	4.63%	5.0%
3	50%	50%	5.75%	10.0%
4	75%	25%	6.88%	15.0%
5	100%	0%	8.00%	20.0%

5. Rather than go into the mathematical formula in detail, we'll just state the principle:
the return for each portfolio is equal to the weighted average of the assets' returns and the
volatility of each portfolio is equal to the weighted average of the assets' volatility.

Portfolio 1 is made up exclusively of Bund and so it has the same return and the same volatility as the government bond. Similarly, portfolio 5 is only made up of Athos stock: it therefore has the same characteristics as the stock. Moving from portfolio 1 to 5, we observe that the return increases as the percentage of Athos stock increases and that the risk increases at the same time. Let's plot these points on a graph (Figure 4.2).

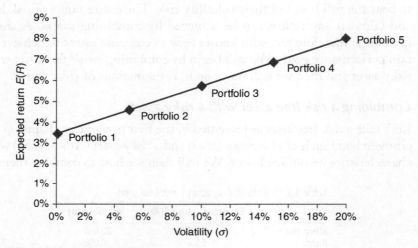

Figure 4.2 Volatility and expected return

Here, we observe two things:

- First, there is a perfectly linear progression: when we increase the portfolio's risk (by adding stock and removing bonds), the return increases proportionally. Each increase in risk always results in an equivalent increase in the return.
- Second, these five portfolios actually cover an infinite number of possible portfolios. That means that whatever the level of risk we choose ('I want a volatility of 17%') or set an expected return ('This portfolio must generate an average return of 7%') we will be able to put together a portfolio that corresponds to our requirements.[6]

---

6. For example, a portfolio that is 85% stock will have a volatility of 17%. With 77.7% stock, the E(R) will be 7%.

Let's illustrate this idea.

What if we added a line to the table, with a sixth portfolio? Here it is:

Table 4.9 Extrapolating the risk–return pair

Portfolio n°	Percentage of Athos	Percentage of Bund	Expected return E(R)	Volatility (σ)
1	0%	100%	3.50%	0.0%
2	25%	75%	4.63%	5.0%
3	50%	50%	5.75%	10.0%
4	75%	25%	6.88%	15.0%
5	100%	0%	8.00%	20.0%
6	125%	−25%	9.13%	25.0%

What's going on here? We've borrowed money (at bond rates, let's say) and bet it all on Athos stock. We end up with a sixth portfolio that is riskier than the risky asset (but potentially more profitable!).[7]

---

7. This type of strategy is possible on certain markets; it is known as 'short selling'. The risk is the exponential function of the investor's greed.

DIALOGUE	
Bonnie:	That's terrific! With this system we can get an even higher return than with Athos stock! In fact, there's no limit, we could aim for a return of...uh...30%?
Clyde:	Of course. But that would make a portfolio with a volatility of...118%. In fact, we can extrapolate the line graph to the right and keep on going.
Bonnie:	Forever, honey?
Clyde:	No, unfortunately it's got to end somewhere: there are two limits. First, we need to be able to borrow the money and it will probably not be at the risk-free rate, but much more expensive. Second, the return on this stock is volatile and that on the portfolio even more so: E(R) = 30% but σ = 118%! However, the loan repayments will not be volatile, they will be set in stone right from the start. All it takes is for the Athos stock to have one bad year and we'll go into default. In other words, if you want to make fast cash, you have to take big risks. Remember that, darling.
Bonnie:	Wouldn't it be less risky just to rob a bank?

In conclusion, combinations with a risk-free asset may turn out to be very risky. Paradoxically, we will now see that combining two risky assets may be a way of reducing risk – under certain conditions.

The strategy with risky assets is important because for the moment we have only played with one stock: Athos. But nobody said it was the most attractive stock. We will now try to find the optimal risky asset, one that will produce the best possible graph. In the end, we will see that this optimal risky asset is not a single stock, but a properly diversified portfolio of stocks.

Combining two risky assets: how to diversify your risk

Let's imagine two very different companies, Porthos and Aramis, Porthos sells bars of soap, Aramis manufactures robots. Both businesses are risky, as we can see from their stock prices shown in Figure 4.3.

Now let's see what happens if we build a 50–50 portfolio: half Porthos and half Aramis. Figure 4.4 shows the trend in the portfolio's value.

We observe that the fluctuations in the portfolio's value are smaller than the fluctuations in the stocks taken separately. By investing in two stocks instead of one we have reduced the volatility, the risk in our investment. That's the magic of diversification!

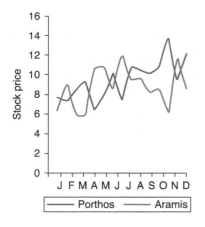

Figure 4.3 Stock prices: Porthos and Aramis

Figure 4.4 Porthos–Aramis 50–50 portfolio

DIALOGUE	
Capone:	Looking at the first picture (Figure 4.3), I see that, often, when one stock price rises, the other falls. So it makes sense to combine them in a single portfolio. The increases in one offset the decreases in the other and the total value of the portfolio is less volatile.
Luciano:	That's right, fella. There is a weak correlation between these two values, perhaps even a negative correlation. This is the key to successful diversification: we need to find securities that are not correlated, that is to say businesses that have nothing to do with each other. Imagine that we combine the stocks of two companies that sell bars of soap. What would we gain with a 50–50 portfolio?
Capone:	Not much. The two values depend on the demand for soap, so it's very likely that their stock prices would always move in the same direction. There's no point in combining them. You may as well just hold one of those two stocks and look for other uncorrelated businesses.
Luciano:	For example, we could combine securities in electronics, petroleum, agriculture and services. As all of these businesses are reasonably uncorrelated, the diversified portfolio that we obtain would be less volatile. To sum up, we reduce risk through diversification when we combine assets that have little correlation between them.
Capone:	Do you think we could find two stocks that have a perfectly negative correlation – where a drop in one would be totally offset by a rise in the other? Let's say, a chemical company that uses a lot of petroleum (for whom petroleum is a cost) and an oil company (for whom petroleum is a revenue).

Luciano: If we were to find two securities with a perfectly negative correlation, the resulting portfolio would be a straight line: there would be no more volatility and we would have totally cancelled out the risk through diversification. That means that the portfolio would be risk free and the return would be...the risk-free rate. Besides, a perfectly negative correlation is a theorist's will-o'-the-wisp. These two stocks may cancel out the 'fluctuation in the price of oil' risk, but they will always be linked by other economic variables: inflation, interest rates, exchange rates and so on. On these items, they will often be influenced in the same direction and will therefore have a positive correlation. Nevertheless, even though it may seem like a pipe dream to find negatively correlated securities, we will see that it is always advantageous to look for stocks that are weakly correlated.

Let's return now to our two stocks. Here are their financial characteristics:

Table 4.10   Market data for two stocks

	Expected return E(R)	Volatility (σ)
Porthos	6.5%	24.5%
Aramis	8.5%	39.7%
Correlation coefficient	0.1	

Porthos is risky (no surprise there – it's a stock), but its business is more stable than Aramis's (people buy more bars of soap than robots). This explains why the volatility of Porthos stock is lower than that of Aramis. Conversely, Aramis is riskier, but its return is also higher.[8] Finally, analysts have calculated the **correlation coefficient** for these two stocks over the long term: it is positive, but weak. This means that the stocks of the two companies move in the same direction 10% of the time and follow independent paths 90% of the time.

We will now combine these stocks in several portfolios, varying their respective weight in the portfolio. Table 4.11 shows the returns and volatilities for these portfolios.

---

8. The stock price tables that this calculation is based on can be downloaded free of charge – it's our treat!

Table 4.11 Expected return and volatility for portfolios

Portfolio n°	Proportion		Expected return E(R)	Volatility (σ)
	Porthos	**Aramis**		
1	0%	100%	8.5%	39.7%
2	10%	90%	8.3%	36.0%
3	20%	80%	8.1%	32.6%
4	30%	70%	7.9%	29.4%
5	40%	60%	7.7%	26.6%
6	50%	50%	7.5%	24.3%
7	60%	40%	7.3%	22.7%
8	70%	30%	7.1%	21.8%
9	80%	20%	6.9%	21.8%
10	90%	10%	6.7%	22.8%
11	100%	0%	6.5%	24.5%

Portfolios 1 and 11 are easy to understand: the former contains only Aramis stock, so it has the return and volatility that correspond to that stock; the latter contains only Porthos stock and therefore has the corresponding characteristics. For the other portfolios, it is better to plot a risk–return graph as we did for the Bund–Athos portfolio.

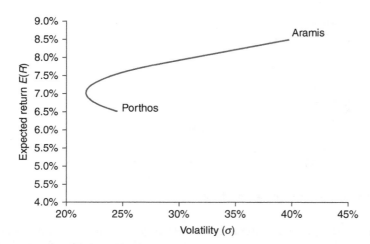

Figure 4.5 Expected return vs volatility

The line graph in Figure 4.5 represents all the possible portfolios that can be made by combining Porthos and Aramis stock. What strikes the trained eye is the curved area to the left of Porthos; we see that there are portfolios made up of the two assets that are less risky than either of the assets individually. Their volatility is even lower than that of Porthos (24.5%).

DIALOGUE	
Capone:	I jus' don't get it. How is it that we can combine two risky assets and get a result that is **even less** risky?
Luciano:	Because the two assets are not perfectly correlated. By combining them, under certain conditions, we cancel out part of their risk through diversification.
Capone:	Does that mean the only attractive portfolios are the ones to the left of Porthos 'cause they're less risky?
Luciano:	No, Al, that ain't it. You're forgettin' about the return. The portfolios that are mostly made up of Aramis have higher returns, though it's true they also have a higher risk.
Capone:	So all the portfolios are attractive?
Luciano:	No. Look at Figure 4.6. Do you think portfolio no. 10 is a good deal?

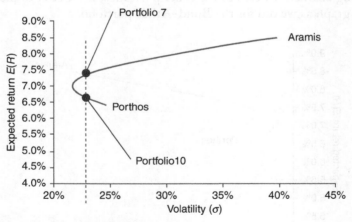

Figure 4.6 Efficient and inefficient portfolios

Capone:	Nah, portfolio 10 doesn't look so good to me. If I draw a vertical line (I'll make it a dotted line, like a stream of bullets), I realize that **for the same level of risk** (22.7% volatility in both cases) there is another portfolio that offers a higher return: no. 7 promises 7.3% whereas no. 10 only offers 6.7%.

118

Luciano:	You got it! That means that some of the portfolios in this chart are **inefficient** because they can be replaced by better portfolios. I'll plot the **efficient frontier** for you below (the solid line). It represents all the attractive portfolios – those that offer the best risk–return ratio. In comparison, the dotted part represents portfolios that are inefficient.

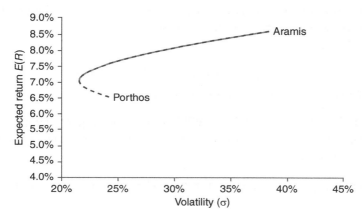

Figure 4.7   Efficient frontier

Capone:	You got a minute, Lucky? I still got a coupla questions.
Luciano:	Sure, Cap, shoot…Just kidding!
Capone:	Wise guy! First, what do we call the portfolio on the far left, the one with the lowest risk?
Luciano:	The **minimum variance portfolio**. A quick calculation will show us that it is made up of 75% Porthos and 25% Aramis.
Capone:	Ok. And since Porthos stock is not on the efficient frontier, does that mean it's no good?
Luciano:	It's not efficient if it is held alone. But, as part of a portfolio it helps reduce the risk. In other words, it would be a bad idea to hold only Porthos stock, but it would be an even worse idea to hold none at all.

A few formulas

When we were discussing the combination of a risk-free asset (government bonds) with a risky asset (Athos) we chose not to show the formula so as not to frighten away the non-maths people. This part is not for the faint-hearted, either. Sensitive souls are advised to skip it and to join us at the section appropriately titled: 'Limited utility of the preceding formulas: a discussion'.

All others, fasten your seat belts! We are going to present the formulas that we used to calculate the tables and draw the graphs.

We are still dealing with a portfolio made up of two risky assets. Let's dispense with the colourful names, though; here we'll just talk about asset 1 and asset 2. These two assets are combined in a portfolio in which w is the weighting of asset 1 and $(1 - w)$ is the weighting of asset 2. First let's formalize the return calculation. The expected return for the portfolio is equal to the average return on the two assets.

So we have:

$$E(R_{\text{portfolio}}) = w \times E(R_1) + (1 - w) \times E(R_2)$$

where $E(Ri)$ represents the expected return of each asset.

Now let's look at volatility. We will have to make a quick detour through **variance** so that it will be simpler to express (reminder: variance is equal to volatility squared).

$$\text{Variance}_{\text{portfolio}} = \sigma^2_{\text{portfolio}} = w^2 \times \sigma_1{}^2 + (1 - w)^2 \times \sigma_2{}^2 + 2 \times w\,(1 - w) \times \sigma_1 \times \sigma_2 \times \rho_{1,2}$$

Here, σi represents the volatility of the different assets and ρ is the correlation between the two risky assets. Furthermore, if we take a close look at the equation, we will see that the portfolio's risk is a function of the risk of each of the assets and a third element (the part starting with the number 2). In this third element, the weaker the correlation ρ, the lower the portfolio's overall risk.[9]

Limited utility of the preceding formulas: a discussion

Welcome back, maths-haters! These formulas are pretty to look at, but the reality is much more complicated. Perhaps you thought we were going to keep working on combinations of two assets? But the world we live in is vast and complex! So we will be combining 20 securities together – what am I saying? – 100 securities or 1,000! That means we need to move on to formulae that can handle multitudes of stock correlations. Let's illustrate this with a few graphs.

Imagine that we take our Aramis–Porthos portfolios and we seek out a third musketeer to join them: D'Artagnan stock. Now we have to vary the proportions of the three stocks. Figures 4.8 and 4.9 below show what

---

9. These formulae are also valid for our first portfolio (Bund–Athos). Just note that the Bund is risk-free (so σ = 0%) and there is no correlation between Bund and Athos (so ρ = 0). The formulae therefore become weighted averages.

may happen if we include D'Artagnan stock. The dotted line represents the initial portfolio (two stocks) and the solid line, the portfolio including D'Artagnan stock.

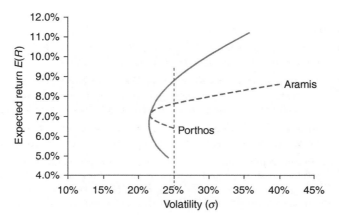

Figure 4.8 Three stocks: increased returns

Adding D'Artagnan stock creates portfolios whose risk has not been reduced but whose return has increased (Figure 4.8). A vertical straight line shows that for the same level of risk, we obtain better returns on the solid line. Owing to its higher return, the D'Artagnan stock has thus improved the overall performance of the portfolio.

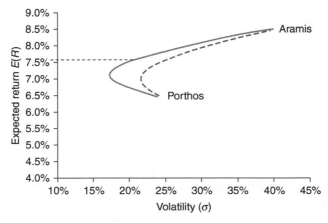

Figure 4.9 Three stocks: decreased volatility

Adding a different third stock (Milady stock) instead of D'Artagnan could improve diversification and cause a decrease in the volatility of the portfolios (Figure 4.9). Following the straight horizontal dotted line toward the left, we observe that adding this stock to the portfolios allows investors to get the same return while lowering their risk.

DIALOGUE

Capone:	Which stocks should we prefer? The ones that help to lower the portfolio's risk or those that increase its return?
Luciano:	In fact, most stocks do both at the same time. And there is really no preference. The ultimate goal is to create a combination of assets whereby the portfolio achieves the best risk–return ratio.
Capone:	And by combining numerous stocks that have little correlation between them, can we obtain a portfolio with 0% volatility?
Luciano:	Ha ha, **ragazzo**, you want to shift the graph as far as possible to the left! I don't want to burst your bubble (nor that of the daydreaming reader, there on the bus), but I think that would be very difficult. Diversification has its limits, as shown in Figure 4.10.

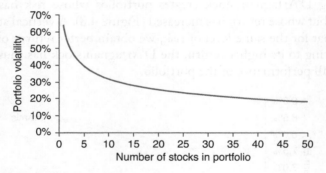

Figure 4.10   Systematic risk

This graph shows how the risk is lowered as we add stocks to the portfolio. Once we have done our shopping and built a portfolio of stocks, we will certainly have reduced the overall risk through diversification, but there remains a residual risk. This risk will never disappear entirely, even if we have several hundred stocks in the portfolio. In other words, in spite of our efforts, the curve will never go below a volatility of 17% in our example. This residual risk is call the **systematic risk**. In contrast, the risk that can be eliminated through diversification is called **specific risk** or **diversifiable risk** or **idiosyncratic risk**.

VIGNETTE |||||||||||||||||||||||||||||||||||||||||||||||||||||||||||||||||||||||||||||||||||||||||||||||||||||||||||||||||||||||
*Chicago 1932. The founder and president of Murmur Incorporated has been assassinated and his young son is the only heir. This is a **specific risk** because a Chicago investor who has diversified his portfolio among several stocks is unlikely to see the presidents of all these companies assassinated the same day (though Capone might well try to pull it off). Similarly, there are risks that are specific to one company: an employee strike, the failure (or success) of an R&D programme, a sales catastrophe or suddenly seizing market share from the company's competitors. Investors can reduce these risks by diversifying the stocks in their portfolio. On the other hand, an economic recession will affect almost all of the companies. The same goes for a corporate tax hike, a rise in interest rates or a general amnesty on corporate fraud. In these cases, even with the most diversified portfolio possible, the majority of the portfolio will be affected. Here we speak of **systematic risk**, because it systematically affects everybody. Zero risk therefore does not exist – especially not in Chicago during Prohibition.*
|||||||||||||||||||||||||||||||||||||||||||||||||||||||||||||||||||||||||||||||||||||||||||||||||||||||||||||||||||||||

Market portfolio

> *I bought a dozen volumes on banking and credit and investment securities and they stood on my shelf in red and gold like new money from the mint, promising to unfold the shining secrets that only Midas and Morgan and Maecenas knew.*
>
> F. Scott Fitzgerald, *The Great Gatsby* (1925)

We will proceed as though we had tinkered with the correlations of a thousand stocks and had obtained the best possible curve. In fact, this is what traders do every day: they tweak their calculations, increase the proportion of one stock, decrease that of another, aiming to make their portfolio as efficient as possible. In the end, **all the investors will have more or less the same curve**.

DIALOGUE	
Capone:	How can we be sure that it is the same curve for everyone?
Luciano:	We're not sure and there are small differences. But if a pension fund manager finds a miracle stock that nobody had considered and includes it in his portfolio, giving him a better portfolio than his competitors, what do you think will happen?
Capone:	People will rush to that pension fund because it provides the best expected return for a given level of risk, and the other fund managers will quickly rework their models to include the miracle stock.
Luciano:	Exactly!

Capone:	Why don't all the funds end up with exactly the same curve, then?
Luciano:	They all have their own optimization model, which is much more complex than the expected return/volatility model that we have been using, and they keep their secret recipe under lock and key. Besides, there is a cost to adding new stocks to one's portfolio, because the transaction cost of investing in a 41st stock will be greater than the marginal gain that it will bring to the portfolio. (This explains why the differences between funds are so small.) There are also certain fund managers who have more in common with used car salesmen than mathematicians, but that's another matter, which we will deal with in Chapter 7, on the stock market.

We are now going to look at a curve that is supposedly shared by all: every investor on the market agrees that it is the best possible curve – with very few variations. This curve is shown in Figure 4.11.

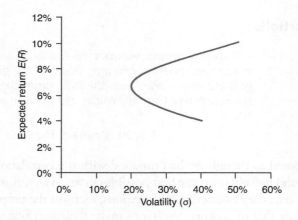

Figure 4.11   Market portfolio

In Figure 4.12, we have traced the previous straight line combining a risk-free asset (government bond) and a risky asset (Athos stock). We will now merge the two figures to ask this question:

- knowing (Figure 4.12) that we can combine a risk-free asset with an risky asset to obtain a straight line (capital allocation line),
- knowing that the best curve for risky assets is the one shown in Figure 4.11,
- **how can we combine the risk-free asset with the best possible risky asset?**

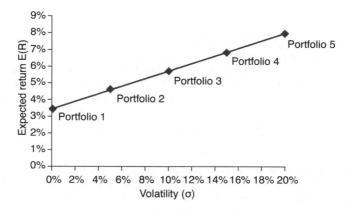

Figure 4.12   Risk-free asset combined with risky asset

All we have to do – easier said than done – is to superimpose the two graphs and test a few simulations. This is what we have done in Figure 4.13 below. We have plotted the curve of optimal portfolios (dotted line) and positioned the risk-free asset (the point on the left, which has zero volatility and a return of 3.5%). We trace a straight line freehand, starting from this risk-free asset, and 'hook' the curve of portfolios. In order to obtain this line of returns in the figure, we just have to combine the risk-free asset with portfolio 1 or portfolio 2.

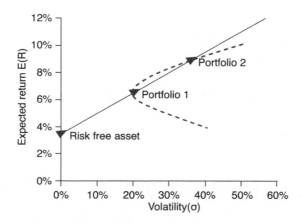

Figure 4.13   Curve of optimal portfolios

DIALOGUE

Capone:	So I take portfolio 2, which I consider as a single asset whose characteristics are $E(R)$ = 8.9% and σ = 35.8%. I combine portfolio 2 with the risk-free asset (for which $E(R)$ = 3.5% and σ = 0%) and I obtain a straight line that represents all possible portfolios, depending on the percentages I invest in the risk-free asset and portfolio 2, respectively.
Luciano:	That's it. You're getting pretty good at this stock market stuff, Al.
Capone:	But I can do better, right?
Luciano:	Sure. We're not calling into question the efficiency of this portfolio – it is located on the efficient frontier. But when we have to trace a straight line from the risk-free asset, what type of risky portfolio should we choose?
Capone:	Logically, the portfolio that is as high and as far to the left as possible. In fact, my line should be as steep as possible, so that it brings me the maximum possible return for each unit of risk.
Luciano:	Don't pull any punches, Al – graphically I mean. And show me the result.
Capone:	Done. Here's my graph (Figure 4.14):

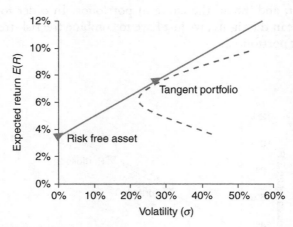

Figure 4.14   Tangent portfolio

Luciano:	I can see you took the steepest line possible; it just grazes the curve of optimal portfolios.
Capone:	Like I said, Lucky, the optimal portfolio is the one that is 'as far to the left and as high as possible'.

126

Luciano:	You're right, Al. It's the portfolio that is tangential to the curve – hence its name. It's the best risky asset to combine with the risk-free asset – the one that will produce the capital allocation line with the best risk–return ratio.
Capone:	I even know what it's called: the **market portfolio**.
Luciano:	Gee, I'd hate to see you become a stock broker, Al.

Conclusion

Let's summarize all the steps that we have followed since the beginning of the chapter. Then we will conclude with a few fundamentals about risky investments.

- We began by explaining how risk is calculated in finance, by calculating the volatility of a risky asset.
- Then we combined a risky asset and a risk-free asset to see the characteristics of such a portfolio.
- Knowing that the risky asset we choose is crucial, we set out in search of optimal risky assets. We built portfolios of various stocks – diversifying the investment – and we ended up with a curve of optimal portfolios.
- Finally, we combined this optimal risky-asset curve with the preceding capital allocation line to determine the optimal portfolio, which we call the tangent portfolio or **market portfolio**.

It is now time to put together what we have learned, which can be outlined in three points:

- The curve of optimal risky portfolios is the same for all investors.
- The optimal portfolio is the same for all investors; it is the **market portfolio**.
- The only personal decision to make is to choose the proportions of market portfolio and risk-free asset.

The curve of optimal risky portfolios is the same for all investors

All professional investors seek an optimal portfolio of risky assets. They spend their days combining stocks to reduce the volatility of their ideal portfolio. That means that as long as there is any possibility of improvement, they continue to buy and sell stocks. The curve of these portfolios is constantly shifting and it is not rigorously the same for all investors. But it is likely that any stock that might improve the portfolio will have been included by all the investors (who are all in competition with each other). So it is not unreasonable to assume that there is a common curve.

The optimal portfolio is the same for all investors; it is the market portfolio

Investors are seeking only one risky portfolio: the tangent portfolio, which is the one that, when combined with the risk-free asset, will obtain the steepest capital allocation line.

In other words, it is a constant process and the best approximation we have of this tangent portfolio at a given time is ... the entire financial market.

For example, when we hear that British Petroleum (BP) represents 4.58% of the UK market, this is not an anecdotal figure. It means that, through their purchases or sales, all investors have achieved what is for them an ideal tangent portfolio and that, on average, 4.58% of this portfolio is BP stock. The same goes for all stocks. This is why the optimal portfolio is called the **market portfolio**; at any given moment, the stock exchange tells us the proportion deemed to be ideal for each stock on the market.

> Capone: What if there is a stock that nobody wants?
>
> Luciano: That's not really possible. If nobody wants it, then everybody will sell it, its price will fall to zero and it will disappear from the market. Or perhaps some cunning devil will spot this devalued stock and realize that it can be used to improve their portfolio of risky assets... Then the stock is back in the game.

The only personal decision to make is to choose the proportions of market portfolio and risk-free asset

Given that all the investors have identified the same ideal portfolio (the market portfolio) as being the best portfolio to combine with the risk-free asset, they are all on the same capital allocation line. The only personal initiative is to choose the proportions to allocate to the risk-free asset and the market portfolio. Let's observe the decisions of a few different investors, plotted on the graph in Figure 4.15.

Wary doesn't want to take any risks, so he has invested 100% of his capital in a risk-free asset. Punter has opted for a 50–50 split; he therefore has a better expected return, at the cost of higher risk.[10] Gambler does not want to bother with any risk-free assets at all. Consequently, his portfolio is 100% stock in the form of the market portfolio. Finally, High Roller

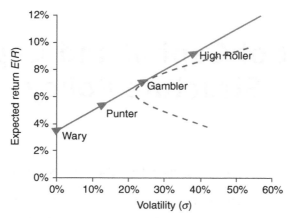

Figure 4.15 Varying the proportions of risky and risk-free assets

wants to take on risk in order to get a higher return. He copies the strategy shown above in Table 4.9 (he borrows money and invests all of it in the risky asset).

Note that there are no ideal proportions here. Each individual chooses the combination that suits him, depending on his aversion to risk and his desire for gain. Wary embodies the proverb 'a bird in the hand is worth two in the bush', while High Roller prefers to follow the maxim 'nothing ventured, nothing gained.'

---

10. Using the portfolio return and volatility formulas, diligent readers can find the figures for each portfolio.

5

Cost of Capital and Capital Structure Policy

If you would know the Value of Money, go and try to borrow some.
Benjamin Franklin (under the pseudonym Richard Saunders)
Poor Richard's Almanack (1754)

Introduction

One of the goals of finance is to choose the right investments. In Chapter 3 we learned how to work through investment decisions. But we had simplified things; the discount rates were already given to us. In this chapter we are going to deal with a fundamental question: How do we set the discount rate for a project? In other words, how do we determine a return expectation? What is the justification for Scrooge McDuck to say: 'I'm willing to invest in the mines of Palo Alto, but I want my investment to give me an annual return of 13%.' Drawing on the knowledge acquired in the preceding chapter, we are going to try to answer all of these questions.

Later, we will expand the discussion to companies and their financial decisions.

The expected return on a stock

Men who don't take risks won't drink champagne.
Russian proverb

The beta of a stock

Let's take a look at Alaskan Wineries stock and observe the monthly fluctuations with respect to those of the global stock market. Figure 5.1 shows this comparison.

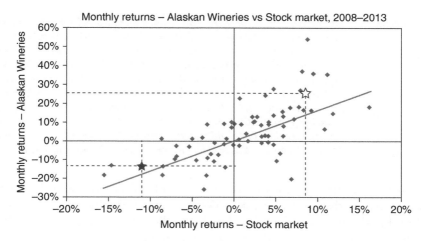

Figure 5.1 Alaskan Wineries vs the stock market

Each small diamond represents a month of stock market returns. We are going to look at the two points represented by stars.[1] Let's suppose that the black star represents the month of March 2009. That means that in March 2009 Alaskan Wineries stock had a return of –13% (vertical axis), while the stock market as a whole had a return of –11% (horizontal axis). Now let's turn to the white star, representing the month of June 2012. The graph tells us that Alaskan Wineries stock had a return of 26% for that month, while the stock market return was 8%.

Look closely at the graph. Each diamond represents a month. We observe a linear trend: when the stock market rises, Alaskan Wineries stock often rises also. When the stock market falls, Alaskan Wineries stock falls most of the time, too. The straight line superimposed over the graph shows the general trend.

DIALOGUE

Ebenezer: I understand the return calculation for Alaskan Wineries. You just have to go back to the calculations in the previous chapter. That means that if I had bought Alaskan Wineries stock on 1 March 2009 and sold it on 31 March 2009, I would have made a loss of 13%. How dreadful! But what does the stock market calculation mean?

---

1. You can meditate on this graph while listening to 'Dark Star' by Crosby, Stills and Nash (*CSN*, 1977 Columbia Records) and 'Loneliest Star' by Seal (*Human Beings*, 2005, Columbia Records).

> Marley: It means that if someone had bought **all the stocks on the market** on 1 March 2009 and sold them all on the 31st, that investor would have made a loss of 11%. Fortunately, there is an easier way to work this out this than buying all the stocks on the market: the trend shown here is the trend of the market index for the period. When we hear that the 'market has closed, down 3%', in fact it is the market index that has fallen by 3% during the day. Most stock market indices (CAC 40, EuroStoxx 50, S&P 500) are very close to the market portfolio (see the end of Chapter 4), which means that we can use the market index to simplify our calculations.[2]

What is even more interesting is the amplitude of the variations. When the stock market rises by 1%, Alaskan Wineries stock rises by 1.9%, on average. But this also works in the other direction: when the stock market falls 10%, Alaskan Wineries stock falls by 19% on average.

DIALOGUE

Ebenezer:	I believe I am beginning to understand: Alaskan Wineries stock moves in the same direction as the market, but amplifies its fluctuations. When the stock market goes up 10%, Alaskan Wineries rises by 1.9 × 10%.
Marley:	And that relationship also works in the opposite direction.
Ebenezer:	But what does this factor of 1.9 really mean?
Marley:	Statistically, I would call it the slope of the line, but in financial terms it indicates that Alaskan Wineries stock is risky. It has returns that are, on average, 1.9 times those of the stock market, which means that its volatility is greater.
Ebenezer:	In other words, it is riskier than the stock market.
Marley:	Correct. This factor is called the **beta (β)** of Alaskan Wineries stock. Every stock — and even every asset — has its own beta.
Ebenezer:	Fine. Alaskan Wineries stock has a beta of 1.9, but what can I compare this with? What are the usual values for betas?
Marley:	Most stocks have a beta of between 0.5 and 1.5, and the extremes are roughly 0 and 2.5. A well diversified portfolio will have a beta of 1, because it will match the market portfolio, that is to say the stock market.[3] It follows, therefore, that a stock with a beta of less than 1 is one that will **absorb** fluctuations in the market. A stock whose beta is greater than 1 will **amplify** market fluctuations and will therefore be riskier.

---

2. We have also included dividends on our graph: these indices therefore provide a good measure of total stock market returns.
3. And when the stock market rises by 10%, the market portfolio naturally rises by $1 \times 10 = 10\%$.

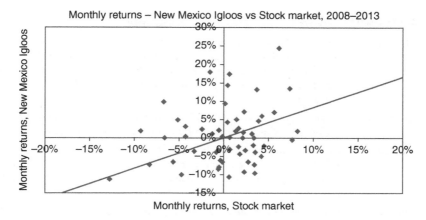

Figure 5.2   New Mexico Igloos vs the stock market

Here is another graph, representing the monthly returns for New Mexico Igloos stock.

The trend shows that New Mexico Igloos stock has a beta of 0.8. It fluctuates less than the stock market. On average, when the stock market rises (or falls) by 10%, this stock rises (or falls) by only $0.8 \times 10\% = 8\%$.

Dialogue	
Ebenezer:	But the points on the graph are scattered around the line. Can we always count on this line and (in this case) the beta of 0.8? Is it dependable?
Marley:	In statistics, we have to measure the 'goodness of fit' of the linear regression. You can't use just any beta simply because it was generated by a spreadsheet. But for many stocks, the fit of the linear regression is good[4] and the beta may be used.
Ebenezer:	Used for what? What is the purpose of this indicator?
Marley:	Let's find out by looking at an example.

The expected return on a stock

> *October. This is one of the peculiarly dangerous months to speculate in stocks. The others are July, January, September, April, November, May, March, June, December, August, and February.*
>
> Mark Twain, *Pudd'nhead Wilson's Calendar for 1894*

---

4. The 'goodness of fit' of the regression is measured using the coefficient of determination (R^2), a function that is found in every spreadsheet program. For the details of these calculations, please visit the book's website.

DIALOGUE	
Marley:	My dear Ebenezer, imagine that I am a spectre from the spirit world and that I can see into the future. I reach in and pull out a few figures. Let's say, for instance, that I can predict next year's inflation rate or interest rates or how much the stock market will pay out.
Ebenezer:	That may be of interest, my dear partner, but don't expect me to invest a single penny in your mangy old circus act.
Marley:	No need, dear friend! If I tell you that the stock market will rise by 7% next year, what can you do with this information — specifically in relation to Alaskan Wineries and New Mexico Igloos stock?
Ebenezer:	Let's see...Historically, Alaskan Wineries' beta was 1.9 and New Mexico Igloos' was 0.8. If I assume that the betas will remain stable over time (which remains to be seen ...) and if the stock market actually does rise by 7% next year, then I should say that Alaskan Wineries stock will rise by 1.9 × 7 = +13.3% and New Mexico Igloos will increase by 0.8 × 7 = +5.6%.
Marley:	That is quite correct, Ebenezer — with all those 'ifs' you employed. Now, what is the significance of these two figures you found: 13.3% and 5.6%? How would you explain them to your new clerk?
Ebenezer:	I would start by saying that Alaskan Wineries stock is riskier than average. Its shareholders are anxious and highly strung, which means that when the stock market rises, they overreact and buy. And so Alaskan Wineries' stock price rises even higher than the market. In contrast, New Mexico Igloos' stock is rather amorphous — also like its shareholders. They endure various turns of fate stoically and they think before they act; in a word, they are calm. Their stock is less risky.
Marley:	Very good. As always, you are perspicacious, Ebenezer. Let's move on. Now, if I tell you that the 13.3% is the exact return **expected** by Alaskan Wineries shareholders, how would you justify that?
Ebenezer:	Quite simple. We have seen that, historically, Alaskan Wineries shareholders demand more than the market return. Whenever the stock market rose by 10%, Alaskan Wineries rose by 19%. But the stock doesn't rise by itself; it rises because of supply and demand. If the stock has regularly settled at 1.9 times the stock market increase, it is because Alaskan Wineries shareholders regularly demand 1.9 times the market return. This is their **return expectation**, given the risk they perceive in the Alaskan Wineries company.

There, that's one thing done and out of the way! There is a formula to determine the return expected by a company's shareholders. But before developing the formula, let's summarize the preceding steps:

- Find the historical market prices of a given stock (for example, Goldbrick stock).
- Compare each monthly return of Goldbrick stock to the monthly return of the stock market and see if there is a linear trend in the relationship between the two.
- Calculate the slope of this line (= the beta of Goldbrick stock).
- Make an estimate of the annual market return for the coming years, which we will call $E(R_m)$ (= expected market return).
- Calculate the expected return for Goldbrick shareholders using the formula: $E(R) = \text{beta} \times E(R_m)$.

The capital asset pricing model (CAPM)

In reality, the return expected by a company's shareholders obeys a slightly classier formula known as the capital asset pricing model (CAPM – pronounced 'cap-em' by those in the know ...). We will write out this formula and then slice it up into bite-sized portions for easier digestion.

The CAPM formula is:

$$E(R_i) \times r_f + \beta_i \times (R_m - r_f)$$

Let's get slicing – don't be afraid; we'll hold your hand.

- $E(R_i)$ represents the historical returns on stock i. Based on these historical returns we will be able to estimate how much of a return shareholders want on this stock.
- r_f represents the **risk-free rate**. This is the return on an asset that has no risk (take another look at the beginning of the previous chapter if you need to). The formula begins with this rate because anyone who invests in a stock wants – at the very least – to get this risk-free rate.
- But of course shareholders want more than the risk-free rate. They demand a **risk premium**. This is what we find in the second part of the formula. The risk premium is also broken down into two parts: a general part that is common to all stocks and a part that depends on each individual stock.

Let's forge ahead:

- The general part is called the **market risk premium** and is written $(R_m - r_f)$. This market risk premium, as you might imagine, is the additional return that the market provides above the risk-free rate. The market risk premium is important because it shows investors' aversion to risk. If the risk-free rate is 4% and the stock market return is 7%, this means that investors want a return of at least 3% more than the risk-free rate to be willing to invest in the stock market. The higher the market risk premium, the greater the risk aversion of investors.[5] The market premium is therefore common to everybody and it is the same in every CAPM formula.

- The part that specifically depends on each stock is represented by the stock's beta (β_i).
- For Curly stock, which has a β_{Curly} of 0.7, the expected return in our example would be $E(R_{Curly}) = 4\% + 0.7 \times (7\% - 4\%) = 6.1\%$.
- Larry stock ($\beta_{Larry} = 1.6$) will have an expected return of $E(RLarry) = 4\% + 1.6 \times (7\% - 4\%) = 8.8\%$.

DIALOGUE	
Ebenezer:	A stock with a beta of 1 ($\beta_{Moe} = 1.0$), will have this expected return: $E(R_{Moe}) = 4\% + 1.0 \times (7\% - 4\%) = 7\%$. This is normal: a stock whose beta is 1 will behave like the stock market as a whole and its return will be the same as the market return: R_m.
Marley:	Exactly. We now have the formula that links risk and return. For a given level of risk (beta) we obtain the corresponding expected return.
Ebenezer:	So for stocks whose beta is >1, shareholders will expect a risk premium that is higher than the market premium. For example, they might expect 1.6 times the general market premium. And for stocks whose beta is <1, they will be willing to accept less than the market premium. For example, 0.7 times the market premium.
Marley:	Precisely.
Ebenezer:	But what if the expected return is not met? What if shareholders don't get their risk premium, what will happen then?
Marley:	They will rant and rave. They'll gnash their teeth, smash the crockery and sell their shares. By selling their shares, they first punish the company, whose share price will drop as a result. It is now at the mercy of a takeover bid by a competitor. But the share price continues to drop and sellers won't find anybody to pick up the stock until it has reached a price where a new investor will get a good return (in other words, the expected risk premium). Thus, a readjustment will have taken place. If the stock does not provide the expected return, shareholders keep selling it until it reaches a price that will allow this return.

---

5. In Europe, the market risk premium ranges from 3% to 6% on average, generally closer to 6% in recent years.

| Ebenezer: | But the former shareholders have taken a loss! Oh what misery – that could have been me! |
| Marley: | We never said stocks were risk-free, did we? On the contrary! That's also why shareholders pay so much attention to companies' financial communications.[6] |

We can now sum up and catch our breath for a minute. Up to now, the discount rate has been a given; our finance department always gave us a return expectation, the minimum required for our investment projects, and we had no choice but to toe the line (see Chapter 3). We have just finished presenting the fundamentals of how returns work. Since Chapter 4 we have understood that there is a linear relationship between the level of risk and the appropriate return expectation for investors, but we now know how to calculate this expected return. If tomorrow we find ourselves hesitating about whether to buy a certain stock, and we wonder whether it is overvalued or if it is a good pony to bet on, we will know how to evaluate a stock (see Chapter 2) by making cash flow forecasts (Chapter 3) and using the right discount rate.

FINANCIALESE —————————————————————

The **expected return** for shareholders is obtained using the CAPM formula. It is what investors want to receive for a given level of risk (measured by the stock's beta). This expected return is also known as the **cost of equity**.

Let's make sure we fully understand this: the expected return is not a monetary cost for companies. When a shareholder demands a 10% return on a stock, the company in question does not take this money out of its bank account. Nevertheless, it is legitimate to speak of cost, because shareholder expectations will put pressure on the company's executives. They will have to find profitable projects, that is, value-creating projects. In Chapter 3 we saw that value creation is measured by the project's net gain, called NPV. Any project that has a positive NPV will contribute to increasing the company's value, and the share price will rise as a result. Not everything is covered in this book, of course. For example, we have cheerfully skipped over the problems involved in determining a stock's beta (statistical accuracy, stability over time) and we hurried through market risk premium

———————————

6. We have omitted shares that are not listed on the stock exchange. But don't forget about them. In the chapters on business valuation (Chapters 6 and 6¾) we will see that we can determine their beta by comparison.

and how to estimate it. These shortcuts have been taken in the interest of simplification. What is important here is not mathematical precision, but understanding the phenomena.

But don't worry: we are going to serve up a second helping of this, to fully illustrate the philosophy of betas.

The economic significance of beta

DIALOGUE BETWEEN TWO BETAS	
Blocker:	I'm having trouble with the notion of beta in relation to market returns. It seems to me that this only concerns financial markets.
Tron:	And yet it can be transposed to the real economy. What CAPM tells us is that certain companies are more sensitive to the current economic situation than others. Take the example of a travel agency. How will its business react to a fast-growing economy or, on the contrary, one that is in recession?
Blocker:	During a period of economic growth everybody has money, families want to do leisure activities and they travel more. When there is a recession, people save their money and they spend their holidays at grandma's house.
Tron:	So, intuitively, the beta of a travel agency is greater than 1, because the amount of business it does depends a lot on the economic situation. It amplifies fluctuations in the general economy. This is also generally true for the consulting industry and some luxury sectors. Conversely, what are the sectors that do not depend so much on the general level of economic activity (sectors that will have the same volume of business regardless of economic circumstances)?
Blocker:	Hmm. Everyday household items and staples: bread, butter, pasta, potatoes, retail banking, running shoes...
Tron:	Exactly! Underlying this ultra-complex formula there is in fact some reasoning about the general economy. A stock's beta is just an indicator of a sector's risks (and the companies operating in that sector).

Table 5.1 Beta by sector

Sectors with a beta <1	Sectors with a beta close to 1	Sectors with a beta >1
Agri-food/retailing	Grocery stores/delicatessens	Gourmet delicatessens
One-star hotels	Three-star hotels	Five-star hotels
Commercial banks	Investment banks	Venture capital
Landline telephone subscriptions	Mobile phone subscriptions	Video games for mobile phones
Microcars, old bangers, mopeds	Family saloons, motorbikes	Minivans, SUVs, sports cars

The cost of capital

First intuition: the cost of capital is a financing cost

Beware of similar sounding terms: the **cost of capital** is not the same as **cost of equity,** which we spoke about earlier. Let's begin our exploration of the cost of capital by studying the balance sheet of Red Inc.

Table 5.2 Red Inc. balance sheet

Assets		Liabilities		
Fixed assets	100	Equity	120	(expected return = 10%)
NWC	50			
Cash and cash equivalents	10	Debt	40	(interest rate = 5%)
Total	160		160	

We observe that in order to finance its business (the 160 invested in assets), the company has asked shareholders for 120 and banks for 40. This financing is expensive: banks require interest payments on their debt and shareholders have an expected return on their investment in these stocks.

The question here is this: 'What should the *minimum* return on assets be so that everyone will be satisfied?'

And the answer goes as follows:

- Shareholders have invested 120 and they expect an annual return of 10%, which is 10% × 120 = 12.
- Banks want an annual interest payment of 5% × 40 = 2.
- In total, the company's assets must generate at least 12 + 2 = 14 to satisfy these financiers. The rate of return is therefore 14/160 = 8.75% annually.

This 8.75% is the minimum return required on the company's assets for all the financiers to be satisfied. This rate is known as the company's **cost of capital**. In fact, it is the average cost of one pound on the liabilities and shareholders' equity side. We could also have obtained this number by calculating the average of financing costs, according to their weight in total financing:

$$\text{Cost of capital} = 10\% \times \frac{120}{(120+40)} + 5\% \times \frac{40}{(120+40)} = 8.75\%$$

This cost of capital will be used as the company's discount rate, because it represents the minimum return that will be required from investment projects.

In reality, this formula is false. The good thing is that it present things simply. However, it overlooks taxes and if there is one thing we should never ignore in finance, it's taxes. So let's take a little trip down taxation lane before we present the real cost of capital.

The impact of taxes

Take two companies: Red Inc. (the one you already know) and Black Inc. The only difference between these companies is that Signor Rossi, CEO of Red Inc., believes in the virtues of debt, while Signor Neri, CEO of Black Inc., won't hear of it. Let's take a look at their balance sheets.

Table 5.3   Balance sheets for Red Inc. and Black Inc.

Red Inc.				Black Inc.			
Assets		**Liabilities**		**Assets**		**Liabilities**	
Fixed assets	100	Equity	120	Fixed assets	100	Equity	160
NWC	50			NWC	50		
Cash and cash equiv.	10	Debt	40	Cash and cash equiv.	10	Debt	0
Total	160		160	Total	160		160

Suppose the two companies are in the same business, in the same sector, and they have the same annual operating profit (EBIT): 14.

Here are their income statements:

Table 5.4   Income statements for Red Inc. and Black Inc.

Red Inc.		Black Inc.	
Operating profit	14.0	Operating profit	14.0
– interest on debt	–2.0	– interest on debt	0.0
Pre-tax profit (EBT)	12.0	Pre-tax profit (EBT)	14.0
– tax (50%)	–6.0	– tax (50%)	–7.0
Net earnings	6.0	Net earnings	7.0

DIALOGUE

Signor Rossi:	*Allora, Signor Neri, what do you think of these figures?*
Signor Neri:	*Bè, Signor Rossi, as you can see, my EBT is bigger than yours!*
Signor Rossi:	*That's true: yours is bigger than mine, but let's calculate the differences in net earnings and interest paid:*

Difference in interest paid on debt –2;
Difference in net earnings –1.

Signor Neri:	That doesn't matter. I still have a bigger EBT than you!
Signor Rossi:	True, but EBT size isn't everything. I paid 2 in interest on debt, which reduced my operating profit, but at the same time I paid less tax than you: −6 compared with −7.
Signor Neri:	Perbacco, è vero! Why is that?
Signor Rossi:	Interest on debt is tax deductible. When we borrow money, we save on taxes. In fact, if I look at the final impact on my earnings, I only paid out 1, which was −2 for the interest expense and +1 for the tax saved = −1 net cost to my company. So in the end my borrowings don't cost me 2/40 = 5%, but rather 1/40 = 2.5% − thanks to the tax saved.
Signor Neri:	Yes, but...
Signor Rossi:	Ok, ok, yours is bigger than mine. Basta, I'm not deaf.

This highly intellectual conversation teaches us that tax savings should be incorporated into finance costs because in effect they allow companies to pay less.[7] In the case of Red Inc., the cost of debt becomes: cost of debt after tax = 5% × (1 − 50%) = 2.5%.

A FOOL AND HIS MONEY ...

While this reasoning works for interest on debt (5% for Red Inc.), it does not work for the cost of equity (10% in our example). Indeed, there is a tax saving only for the costs recorded on the income statement. As interest on debt is part of the income statement, it is a cost that reduces the company's taxable income and so it leads to tax saving. On the contrary, the so-called cost of equity is not an actual monetary cost recorded on the income statement. And so it does not lead to any tax saving.

The weighted average cost of capital (WACC)

We are now going to present the formula for the real cost of capital. Like the preceding one, it is an average of the company's financing costs, weighted according to the proportions of its components. This new formula – and this is the keeper – includes the tax savings due to debt. Here it is:

Weighted average cost of capital =

$$C_{Equity} \times \frac{Equity}{(Equity + Debt)} + C_{Debt} \times (1-T) \times \frac{Debt}{(Equity + Debt)}$$

7. But be careful: first of all, there is a lag between the time the company pays interest and the time it benefits from the tax saving. Furthermore, there can be a reduction in taxes only if EBT (earnings before tax) is positive.

where C_{Equity} represents shareholders' expected return, C_{Debt} is the interest rate on debt, and T is the tax rate.

If we plug in the numbers for Red Inc., we will obtain the following:

$$\text{WACC} = 10\% \times \frac{120}{(120+40)} + 5\% \times (1-50\%) \times \frac{40}{(120+40)} = 8.125\%$$

FINANCIALESE ――――――――――――――――――――――――――――

WACC stands for weighted average cost of capital, so if you hear people in a company saying something that sounds like 'whack', that's probably what it is (unless the 'company' in question is the Mob). It is also known as the **cost of financing.** It will be used as the **discount rate** for investment projects. When the CFO tells you, 'We don't approve any projects unless they have a return of at least 8%', essentially what she is saying is this: 'Our backers demand, on average, an 8% return on the money they entrust to us, otherwise, I can kiss my CFO salary and my fat stock options goodbye.'

DIALOGUE ON BUNKER STREET	
Doctor:	Just to clarify, in Chapter 3, when they said that the discount rate for Le Select Bistrot was 9%, in fact, what they meant was 'the average cost of financing for the bar is 9% annually'.
Detective:	Your logic is flawless, Doctor, but your manicure isn't. The fact that you've been biting your nails suggests to me that you're worried about your investments.
Doctor:	Yes, quite. (coughs nervously) I have two questions, though. The first is: How can I be sure that this WACC will not change over time? After all, we use this measure as a discount rate for the coming years, and it seems odd to think that the cost of financing won't change at all...
Detective:	My dear doctor, we already elucidated that particular mystery in Chapter 2,[8] but let's examine it again. We use today's values because we are raising capital and taking on debt today to finance this investment. Therefore, we contract with shareholders and bankers today, and they express their required returns now for the coming years. Thus the WACC for this project is fixed, shall I say, by contract. Is that clear?
Doctor:	Crystal! But that leads me now to my second question: Doesn't it seem rather peculiar that there would be a single discount rate for all the projects of a firm?

---

8. Please refer to the dialogue between Rocky Beech and Robert Baron on the concept of **opportunity cost** in Chapter 2.

Detective:	You are perfectly right to raise that question, Doctor. Let's examine the formula for WACC: it is the weighted average of the cost of equity and the cost of debt. But we know that the cost of equity is calculated using the CAPM formula and the beta of the stock. Yet, the beta is not the same for different businesses or activities! If a large corporation has an umbrella-manufacturing division and a fountain pen division, there is no reason for the two divisions to have the same risk. Thus, they won't have the same beta, the cost of equity will be different and, lastly, they won't have the same WACC.
Doctor:	To sum up, then, there can be several discount rates within a single firm?
Detective:	Indeed, and it is even an advisable course of action when the firm has several different classes of risk.
Doctor:	That's brilliant!
Detective:	Elementary, my good Doctor.

The purpose of this eloquent exchange is to illustrate the fact that, most of the time, there are several values for WACC within the same company. To see how this is put into practice, we will have to wait until Chapter 6¾.

A few technical points about the WACC calculation

In the interests of pedagogical clarity we set aside certain difficulties in our initial explanations. However, we often begin to ask questions when we come face to face with a task. Here is a list of recommendations for calculating the correct WACC. If these recommendations were to be summed up in a single idea, it would be this: do not forget that what you are calculating will be used as the discount rate for *future* projects. The WACC must therefore be oriented toward the future.

- When entering values in the formula, we must use the market value of equity (or of debt), not the book value recorded on the balance sheet. In order to be able to invest, the company needs to obtain financing. And to obtain this financing, the company will issue securities at their market value, not at their book value. We must therefore use the market values for financing in the formula.[9]
- The interest rate on debt must be a projected rate, not the average of historical rates. And we must take all financial debt into account (both

---

9. For unlisted companies, we will determine the market value by carrying out comparisons. See Chapter 6 on business valuation.

long-term *and short-term* debt) because all these debts contribute to the cost of financing. We should ignore the past debt structure (between long-term and short-term debt), and consider only the expected future debt structure, with corresponding interest rates. It all boils down to the following question: When we seek financing, what is the rate that the bank will be willing to lend at?

- The same goes for the cost of equity. Using a historical beta is fine if that is all you have, but don't forget that you are aiming for the future expected return of shareholders. If you can, adjust the historical beta according to the information you have on the sector and on its future risks (we will talk about this in the next two chapters).
- Finally, for the tax rate, do not use the legal rate. Instead, you should use the actual rate that applies to the company in question. You just have to calculate how much its annual tax is as a percentage of its pre-tax profit. This way you will be taking the company's fiscal specificities into account.
- There is one further detail. We have always included debt in our calculations, but in large companies the notion of **net financial debt** is generally used.[10] We should therefore replace *debt* with *net debt* in the WACC formula.

First and foremost, this list of advice should convince you of the 'rough and ready' nature of these estimates. Finance is not an exact science. What's more, there is a disproportionate number of 'monkeys in business suits' operating in financial circles. Therefore, be rigorous in your reasoning and avoid being too categorical... (Or, at the very least, be able to justify your choices clearly.)

We will now see how a company's WACC may change in relation to its debt financing strategy, and more generally, its capital structure.

Debt financing and WACC

Let's go back to Red Inc.'s balance sheet with the same variables.[11]

Table 5.5   Red Inc. balance sheet

Assets		Liabilities		
Fixed assets	100	Equity	120	(expected return = 10%)
NWC	50			
Cash and cash equivalents	10	Debt	40	(interest rate = 5%)
Total	160		160	

---

10. Reminder: Net debt = debt – cash. See Chapter 1.
11. We assume that the balance sheet is expressed in market values.

The company's WACC is calculated as follows:

$$\text{WACC} = 10\% \times \frac{120}{(120+40)} + 5\% \times (1-50\%) \times \frac{40}{(120+40)} = 8.125\%$$

Question:	Looking at the liabilities side of the balance sheet – the way financing is split between equity and debt – can you think of any way to improve (lower) the company's WACC?

DIALOGUE

Quasimoda:	I have an idea! Red Inc. should take on more debt, because it is less expensive than equity. That way they will lower their WACC and will have a lower financing cost (and a lower discount rate).
Esmeraldo:	Umm…I'd like to see a calculation first.
Quasimoda:	Look, estupido, if we do fifty–fifty financing, there will be 80 of equity and 80 of debt. Then the WACC will be 10% × 0.5 + 5% × (1 – 50%) × 0.5 = 6.25%, instead of 8.125%.
Esmeraldo:	Bravo! And why would shareholders maintain their expected return at 10% when you've just increased the amount of debt and therefore the risk?
Quasimoda:	Ah, well spotted! They'll probably demand a higher return, won't they?
Esmeraldo:	No doubt. That said, it's worth thinking about.

So here is the problem to solve: What is the ideal amount of debt? Is there an optimal amount of debt for a company? One way of thinking about this is to see whether or not increasing the proportion of debt can lower the WACC. After all, if we can lower the company's financing costs, we certainly won't hesitate to do so.

FINANCIALESE ———————————————————————————

These questions relate to a company's **capital structure**. Companies aim to optimize the structure of their financing (equity, debt and other modes of financing), try to reduce costs and understand the consequences of these issues. **Debt financing, dividend policy** and **equity financing** are all part of a company's capital structure policy.

———————————————————————————————————————

In this section, we are going to focus on debt financing and its impact on WACC, taking a progressive approach.

145

What if we lived in a world without taxes...

But if you had been in Utopia with me, and had seen their laws and rules, as I did, for the space of five years, in which I lived among them, and during which time I was so delighted with them that indeed I should never have left them.

Thomas More, *Utopia* (1516) (Burnet translation 1684)

Let's go back to the Red Inc. example. Taking its income statement without the tax element, we'll set up a few calculations to understand better what we could do in terms of capital structure policy. For example, we'll try raising the amount of debt in order to lower the WACC and see if that works.

Table 5.6 Red Inc. income statement without tax

Operating profit	14.0
– interest on debt	–2.0
Pre-tax profit (EBT)	12.0

Table 5.7 Red Inc. balance sheet

Assets			Liabilities		
Fixed assets	100		Equity	120	(10%)
NWC	50				
Cash and cash equivalents	10		Debt	40	(5%)
Total	160			160	

Given that we (momentarily) live in a world without taxes, the entire pre-tax profit of 12 goes into the pockets of the shareholders. Suppose that this company generates the same profit for all future years. Shareholders will get 12 per year and the expected return (= the company's discount rate) is 10%. We can therefore calculate the market value of the company's equity, in the form of a perpetual annuity.[12]

$$\text{Value of equity} = \frac{12}{10\%} = 120$$

And that is exactly what we find on the balance sheet. Marvellous!

---

12. If your memory needs refreshing on the matter of **perpetual annuities (perpetuities)**, head back to Chapter 2 or jump to the index.

Remember that WACC is 8.75% for the moment (without the 50% tax). Now we are going to change the company's debt load and see what happens. Let's take a debt load of 80 (as suggested by Quasimoda) and see what impact that has on the books.

Table 5.8 Red Inc. income statement (increased debt load)

Operating profit	14.0
– interest on debt	–4.0
Profit	10.0

Table 5.9 Red Inc. balance sheet

Assets		Liabilities		
Fixed assets	100	Equity	90.9	(11%)
NWC	50			
Cash and cash equivalents	10	Debt	80	(5%)
Total	160		170.9	

First of all, the interest on debt is now 5% × 80 = 4. This lowers the final profit to 10. But we pay heed to Esmeraldo's remark: given that shareholders now hold stock in a company with a greater debt load, we increase their return expectation to 11%. So we have:

$$\text{Value of equity} = \frac{10}{11\%} = 90.9$$

And if we calculate the WACC, we will get:

$$\text{WACC} = 11\% \times \frac{90.9}{(90.9 + 80)} + 5\% \times \frac{80}{(90.9 + 80)} = 8.19\%$$

That's fantastic: the WACC has effectively been lowered! It's too good to be true!

Indeed, it *is* too good to be true. In fact, it's impossible. Let's give the floor to our two protagonists:

DIALOGUE	
Quasimoda:	But why did that gentleman just say it's not possible?
Esmeraldo:	Look at the balance sheet, Quasimoda. How much is the asset side worth?
Quasimoda:	160.
Esmeraldo:	Right! And how much is the liabilities side worth?
Quasimoda:	90.9 + 80 = 170.9. Oh, that's odd, the liabilities are not equal to the assets.
Esmeraldo:	You see the problem? How can increasing the debt change the value of the company? The assets are still only worth 160...so liabilities should remain at 160.
Quasimoda:	Yes, of course, my darling. But your idea sounds very woolly. How can the liabilities side stay at 160?
Esmeraldo:	There are two ways to show this. Let's see...

Demonstration 1 (the more complicated one)

Suppose that there are two identical companies that exist in parallel universes. The first, before we change the debt load (equity = 120, debt = 40), will be called RedOne. The second, after we change the debt load (equity = 90.9, debt = 80) will be called RedTwo. We are going to compare the values of these two companies, since the only difference between them is the proportion of debt to equity (capital structure policy).

To do so, we will sell 50% of RedTwo's shares.

DIALOGUE	
Quasimoda:	Why do we sell 50% of the shares?
Esmeraldo:	To get the money, of course. So, have you worked it out – how much is it?
Quasimoda:	Well, it's 50% × 90.9 = 45.45. Now what?
Esmeraldo:	Now we borrow 40 (at 5% interest). So how much do we have altogether in cash?
Quasimoda:	45.45 + 40 = 85.45. What are we going to do with all this dough?
Esmeraldo:	Invest the whole lot in RedOne shares!
Quasimoda:	What? The other company? Why?
Esmeraldo:	Uh, you'll see. Ok, have you done it? Then let's look at the results.

Table 5.10 Capital from sale of RedTwo shares and borrowing

Sale of 50% of RedTwo shares	45.45
+ debt at 5%	40
= Total to invest	85.45
RedOne equity	120
With 85.45 we can buy	71.21% of RedOne's capital

Let's compute the gains from this operation. As shareholders of RedOne, we are going to receive dividends. But we have to subtract the interest payment on the debt of 40. The results of the calculation are:

Table 5.11 Net gain from RedOne investment

Dividends from RedOne	12
of which we get	71.21%
Equals a dividend of	8.55
− interest on debt of 40	−2
Equals a net gain of	6.55

DIALOGUE

Quasimoda: We went through all that just to get 6.55?

Esmeraldo: No, we went through all that for a demonstration. I remind you that we only sold 50% of RedTwo; we hung on to the other 50%. Now we are going to compare the gains from the 50% we sold (the 6.55 gain that we received above) with the gains from the 50% we kept.

Table 5.12 Net gain from RedTwo investment

Dividends from RedTwo	10
of which we get	50%
Equals a net gain of	5

DIALOGUE

Esmeraldo: Now, which would you rather have: the 50% that returned 6.55 or the 50% that returned 5?

Quasimoda: Is this a trick question? I'm no fool, I want the one that pays more, obviously.

Esmeraldo: And since everybody is going to think like you, what are all the other investors going to do?

Quasimoda:	They're going to sell their RedTwo shares, take out a personal loan and invest all the money in RedOne shares.
Esmeraldo:	What will the consequence be?
Quasimoda:	The share price of RedTwo will fall (since everybody is selling them) and that of RedOne will rise (because everybody is buying them). This movement will continue as long as there is a difference in the gains.
Esmeraldo:	And there will be a difference in gains as long as the values of the two companies are not the same. Only when the two companies have the same value will the speculation cease.

We have just reproduced the Modigliani–Miller demonstration which, in 1958, made its authors very famous (and probably earned them a little money into the bargain).

The **Modigliani–Miller theorem** says this: In a world without taxes, there is no point in changing a company's debt load, because it won't alter anything: neither the value of the company, nor its WACC will change.

This demonstration was a little long, but we can offer you another, more intuitive version.

Demonstration 2 (the simpler one)

There is no point in trying to change the value of a company by varying its debt load, because a company's value is the value of its assets. In our example, it is worth 160 whether or not we make its debt go up and down like a yoyo. Think about this: the value of your house won't change whether you finance it with a mortgage or through personal savings.

In fact, our initial reasoning – which led to a decrease in WACC – was based on a false assumption. We assumed that shareholders would adjust their expected return to 11%, but in fact they will adjust their expected return to the additional risk they face. In our example, the expected return actually increases to 12.5%. Now we have:

$$\text{Value of equity} = \frac{10}{12.5\%} = 80$$

And if we calculate the WACC, we find:

$$\text{WACC} = 12.5\% \times \frac{80}{(80+80)} + 5\% \times \frac{80}{(80+80)} = 8.75\%$$

This is, of course, the initial WACC. Changing the debt load has therefore changed nothing – neither the total value of the company (160), nor the WACC (8.75%).[13]

DIALOGUE	
Quasimoda:	But that means that there is no point in taking on debt...
Esmeraldo:	In a world without taxes, indeed, debt financing does not provide any additional value. But we don't live in a world without taxes. What's more, Modigliani and Miller's theorem is based on a very simplified world where everyone can borrow money at the same rate, where there are no conflicts of interest, where there are no transaction costs, etc. In other words, it's time to return to the real world.

Unfortunately, we *do* live in a world with taxes... though sometimes that's a good thing. For example, interest payments on debt can be deducted from corporate income tax; and we are going to see that this *does* lower the WACC. Let's take two formulas: the WACC formula that we already know and the one for expected return on assets $E(R_{\text{Assets}})$, which is the formula for WACC without taxes:

$$E\left(R_{\text{Assets}}\right) = C_{\text{Equity}} \times \frac{\text{Equity}}{(\text{Equity} + \text{Debt})} + C_{\text{Debt}} \times \frac{\text{Debt}}{(\text{Equity} + \text{Debt})}$$

Weighted average cost of capital =

$$C_{\text{Equity}} \times \frac{\text{Equity}}{(\text{Equity} + \text{Debt})} + C_{\text{Debt}} \times (1-T) \times \frac{\text{Debt}}{(\text{Equity} + \text{Debt})}$$

Now let's see what these indicators give for Red Inc., depending on the debt load.

Table 5.13 Effects of varying the debt load

Debt	0	20	40	60	80	100	120	140
Equity	160	140	120	100	80	60	40	20
Interest rate on debt	5.00%	5.00%	5.00%	5.00%	5.00%	5.00%	5.00%	5.00%
Expected return on equity	8.75%	9.29%	10.00%	11.00%	12.50%	15.00%	20.00%	35.00%
$E(R_{\text{Assets}})$	8.75%	8.75%	8.75%	8.75%	8.75%	8.75%	8.75%	8.75%
WACC	8.75%	8.44%	8.13%	7.81%	7.50%	7.19%	6.88%	6.56%

13. NB: if we used an expected return other than 12.5%, the company's total worth would no longer be 160 and that would favour the strategy indicated in the first demonstration – at least until we returned to the equilibrium value of 160.

The shareholders' expected return grows with the amount of debt, in keeping with the Modigliani–Miller theorem. Similarly, as there are no taxes, the expected return on assets, $E(R_{\text{Assets}})$, remains at 8.75% regardless of the amount of debt. We do observe, however, that the WACC declines.

DIALOGUE	
Quasimoda:	Where might the decrease in WACC come from?
Esmeraldo:	Knowing that the pre-tax indicator, $E(R_{\text{Assets}})$, remains stable and that the after-tax indicator, WACC, falls, we infer from this that the tax is what lowers the cost of financing.
Quasimoda:	So it's because debt financing costs are tax deductible and that costs the company less. But won't the shareholders compensate for this by demanding a higher return?
Esmeraldo:	No, because the shareholders do not base their expectations on the real cost of debt. They increase their expectations in relation to the amount of debt and that's what they have done in this table. The tax deduction for borrowing costs comes as a bonus, like a fiscal gift from the government which helps lower the after-tax cost of financing.

Thus, in a world with taxes (yours, and incidentally – sigh – that of the authors), it is possible to reduce a company's cost of capital by increasing the amount of debt financing.

There are however two limitations that prevent us from reaching 100% debt financing:

- The interest rate will not remain at 5%. The bank will take the growing risk into account and will gradually increase the bank's own expected return.
- In order for interest payments to be tax deductible, the company must have some taxable income. As soon as the company makes a loss, it no longer pays taxes. In that case, continuing to increase the debt load will not produce any additional tax savings.

There are also bankruptcy costs

The world of finance is a mysterious world in which, incredible as the fact may appear, evaporation precedes liquidation. First the capital evaporates, and then the company goes into liquidation.

Joseph Conrad, *Victory* (1915)

When you begin to borrow money, you get caught up in a spiral: you make a commitment to honour your obligations: interest payments and repayment of the principal. With a small amount of debt, the burden is not too heavy and the company can cope with it. But as the amount of debt increases, difficulties begin to appear: a payment that cannot be made on time, or interest payments that cause the company to run an overdraft. These complications also have costly implications:

- If the company delays its payments to the bank, it will have to face the wrath of lawyers and bailiffs – people who charge for their services.
- If the company makes its payments on time but runs an overdraft, it will have to pay overdraft fees. Or, if it delays payments to suppliers and employees, it will have to pay compensation as well as various fees, and it will suffer loss of confidence, which itself is costly.

Costs that are incurred as a result of an excessive debt burden, are known as **the costs of financial distress** or **bankruptcy costs**. As you might imagine, the greater the amount of debt, the greater the bankruptcy costs.

There comes a time when the game is no longer worth the candle. At first, the tax saving from debt financing was lowering the WACC, but beyond a certain debt load, financial distress costs cause it to go back up. If we plot the WACC in relation to the amount of debt, the curve we get has the following shape:

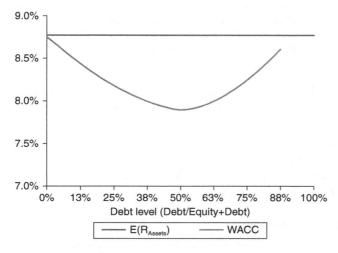

Figure 5.3 WACC and expected return on assets depending on debt load

In the beginning, debt financing brings about tax savings and lowers the cost of financing (WACC). But the bank starts to increase its interest rates and financial distress costs begin to appear. Beyond a certain point, the disadvantages outweigh the advantages and the WACC starts to rise.

DIALOGUE	
Quasimoda:	Does this mean that there is an optimum level of debt? We observe a point on the graph where the cost of financing the company bottoms out.
Esmeraldo:	Yes. That's when the tax savings are still greater than the costs of financial distress.
Quasimoda:	But how do we determine this ideal level of debt for a given company? Is there a formula?
Esmeraldo:	Unfortunately not. We know that there is an optimum and we know why, but we cannot determine it precisely.
Quasimoda:	Why?
Esmeraldo:	Because a company is not a laboratory where you can modify one variable with 'all else being equal'. Inflation, productivity and risk aversion change every day. What's more, the costs of financial distress are difficult to measure – the tax savings too, for that matter.
Quasimoda:	So what can we do?
Esmeraldo:	We can test different levels of debt to see how the company reacts over time. We can observe other companies in the same sector. They regularly post what they call their targeted level of debt. Companies in a given sector often have a similar debt level. That will give us some idea of the optimal debt load – though without any certainty.

We do not, therefore, have a hard and fast position on debt financing policy, especially given that there are alternative theories, which also have their supporters.

Indeed, we have focused here on reducing the WACC, but for some companies, reducing the cost of financing is not the most important thing because they have other priorities. We will now take a look at two alternative theories before concluding.

Pecking order theory

So far we have sought to optimize the debt/equity ratio, because we considered that these two types of financing were easy to find. The **pecking**

order theory postulates, however, that some types of financing are easier to obtain than others. A company will therefore finance its business through the types of financing that are easiest to obtain. The pecking order of capital sources is as follows:

- Priority is placed on internal financing. This is the money the company has on hand and can be used quite freely without having to provide justifications.
- Only when internal funds are depleted does the company move on to debt financing. The company has to prove itself to the bank by submitting forecasts and other documents, so it is more time consuming, but once the loan has been approved they are all set – until it has to be repaid.
- Finally, if the company needs additional financing, it can issue securities. The company's executives have to put on a pair of comfortable shoes and travel around the country making presentations to potential investors and analysts (these trips are known as 'road shows'). They distribute information brochures, comply with regulations, issue regular financial communications, answer questions, pay out reassuring dividends – basically, they have to pamper the shareholders. Moreover, when a company decides to issue new equity, the question that must be asked is: 'At what price?' The price has to be sufficiently attractive to new investors but must not adversely affect current shareholders, who do not want the company to have a fire sale on shares. It can be quite a dilemma.

In this theory, the approach to capital structure policy is not as simple as choosing between debt and equity. Instead of optimizing interchangeable sources of financing (to lower the WACC), the company seeks out the least costly sources of financing in terms of time and energy. Issuing new equity is only done as a last resort. And in the real world we observe that some companies do indeed follow this approach.

Agency theory and free cash flow theory

This theory of capital structure policy is based on the principle that certain people are productive only when under pressure. Imagine a CEO who sleeps on a mattress full of cash. This executive doesn't have to get up at the crack of dawn and race to work, but can sleep in, listening to the sweet rustling of dollar bills. Now imagine a CEO who sleeps on a bed of damp straw in a draughty cabin. This hungry executive won't have any choice but to get up early to go out and find value-creating projects. According to this theory, (too much) free cash flow[14] leads to managerial laziness or, worse, executives who dip their hand in the till to pay for private golf lessons (because important contracts are signed at the 19th hole, so they say ...). The shareholders' strategy will therefore be to drain the company of its free cash. And a good way to do that is to load the company up to the hilt with debt: having to make interest payments and pay back capital will push the CEO to seek out projects that will bring in the money the company needs... if only to justify his or her salary. Debt financing thus becomes a disciplinary mechanism that helps to bring the CEO's interests in line with those of shareholders. Note that this 'free cash flow theory' is in fact a subsection of agency theory, which we will look at in more detail in Chapter 7.

Conclusion

> *[She] has been here twenty-seven times to ask for twenty francs. She did not know that we never have twenty francs. One has a thousand francs, or one sends to one's notary for five hundred; but twenty francs I have never had in my life. My cook and my maid may, perhaps, have so much between them; but for my own part, I have nothing but credit, and I should lose that if I took to borrowing small sums. If I were to ask for twenty francs, I should have nothing to distinguish me from my colleagues that walk the boulevard.*
>
> Honoré de Balzac, *A Man of Business* (1844, English translation 1895–98)

We have seen that the cost of financing a company (its WACC) defines its minimum return threshold; investment projects have to return more than the cost of financing. This justifies using the WACC as the discount rate when calculating a project's value. Indeed, a project that earns more than its cost of financing is a project that will provide investors with a decent return: the bank will get the desired interest rate and shareholders will get their expected return. The excess return – the amount by which the project's return exceeds the WACC (known as **value creation**) – will go

---

14. Free cash flow is defined here as 'the cash that remains in the company once all profitable projects (those with a positive NPV) have been launched'. In other words, free cash flow here is cash that the company doesn't currently need. The greater the free cash flow, the greater the risk of managerial laziness.

into the pockets of the shareholders. Now we see why companies seek to reduce the cost of financing: the lower the cost of financing, the greater the excess return on projects.

We can summarize these ideas in the form of a Holy Trinity of financial management. To create value in finance, a company must:

1. invest in projects that return more than the cost of financing (this is the area of capital budgeting);
2. try to reduce the cost of financing (this is the area of capital structure policy);
3. not adhere blindly to rule no. 1: the intrinsic risk of each project must be taken into account.

Indeed, we have seen that there is not just one, but several WACCs – depending on the company's various business activities and their respective risk levels (betas). We will put these notions into practice in Chapter 6¾.

6

Business Valuation

No, Mr. Brewster, it is absolutely genuine. Here is a telegram from the Probate Court in Sedgwick's home county, received in response to a query from us. It says that the will is to be filed for probate and that Mr. Sedgwick was many times a millionaire. This statement, which he calls an inventory, enumerates his holdings and their value, and the footing shows $6,345,000 in round numbers. The investments, you see, are gilt-edged. There is not a bad penny in all those millions.

George Barr McCutcheon, *Brewster's Millions* (1902)

Introduction

Knowing how to value a business serves multiple purposes. First of all, this knowledge is used when selling a company, either wholly (outright sale) or partly (selling shares, issuing new shares). It is also useful when buying a company from your friends, in order to fine-tune your price negotiations. The value of your own company can also be used as collateral when taking out a large loan. Finally, to do a business valuation properly you have to ask some fundamental questions: Where does the company's performance come from? Is it long lasting? What is the level of risk in its various business activities? How much would a financier's expected return be?

In this chapter we will put into practice all the concepts we have introduced in the previous chapters. In particular, we will need to refresh our knowledge of the following:

- cash flows – calculating (Chapter 1), discounting (Chapter 2) and forecasting (Chapter 3);
- WACC and beta (Chapter 5);
- perpetual annuities (Chapter 2).

What, are you still here? *Please*, go back and have a look through those chapters to refresh your memory before jumping into this one.

The value of a business[1]

Value and price

The *value* of a business is something you ascertain all on your own, sitting in front of your computer. The *price* is determined by two parties hashing it out in a negotiating room that reeks of cigars and sweat. Only the price matters. In real life, in a face-to-face between Mr Tek Nishun, 'the human calculator', and Sam 'gift of the gab' Sharpshooter, the negotiator, it's Sam who wins every time. So what is the point of knowing the value of a business or conducting a business valuation?

Answers:

- to provide arguments to be used in the negotiations in order to obtain a better price;
- to better understand the strengths and weaknesses of the company;
- to assess the quality of future scenarios.

Never forget this, however: a good business valuation combined with bad negotiating will always result in a bad price. A valuation scribbled on the back of an envelope coupled with good negotiating skills may result in a good price.

Enterprise value and market value

When we hear that the Mexican Peyote Company has been sold for 100 million pesos, what value are they talking about? The value of the company's assets or the value of its equity?

In fact, there are two values: market value (MV), which corresponds to equity, and enterprise value (EV), which corresponds to assets. The **market value** is what we look for in a business valuation (this is also called **equity value** or, for listed companies, **market capitalization**, often abbreviated to **market cap**). Indeed, to acquire a company all you need to do is buy up all the shares – in other words, all of its equity. Actually, you don't have to buy 100% of the shares to acquire the com-

---

1. Business valuation is not an exact science – it's often a bit like cooking where the recipe is only a guide. So while reading this chapter, music lovers may wish to listen to the soundtrack to *Chicken Run* or *Ratatouille*.

pany; you just need to hold a majority of them in order to gain control of voting. Nevertheless, when we speak of a company's market value, we mean 100% of its equity. This is the value we usually talk about in a valuation.

However, there is also another important metric called **enterprise value** (EV), which corresponds to the market value of the company's assets.

$$\text{Enterprise value (EV)} = \text{Market value of equity (MV)} + \text{Debt (D)}$$

Table 6.1 Balance sheet for Wacky Tacky Co. (market value)

Assets		Liabilities	
Assets	150	Equity	100
		Debt	50
Total	150	Total	150

Note: The balance sheet in market values is different from the balance sheet published with the annual report, which shows book values. Typically, companies publish their balance sheets only in book values (this is in fact what we used throughout Chapter 1). This table just shows what a company would look like after a valuation has been done, to illustrate the concepts of EV and MV.

The market value (MV) of Wacky Tacky is £100 and its enterprise value (EV) is £150.[2] You may wonder what enterprise value (EV) is used for, given that we are interested only in equity (market) value. In fact, we will see that in most business valuations it is easier to start with enterprise value and then work back from there to calculate market value. It takes a little longer, but it's easier.

We will now look at the three main types of business valuation: the asset valuation method, the market approach using multiples, and finally the biggie, the income approach using discounted cash flows (DCF).

2. From now on, we will use only token units: when we talk about a value of, say, £100, feel free to add millions, billions or zillions to your taste (and serve hot).

The asset valuation approach

To come to business, Good and I took the diamonds to Streeter's to be valued, as we arranged, and really I am afraid to tell you what they put them at, it seems so enormous. They say that of course it is more or less guess-work, as such stones have never to their knowledge been put on the market in anything like such quantities. It appears that (with the exception of one or two of the largest) they are of the finest water, and equal in every way to the best Brazilian stones.

H. Rider Haggard, *King Solomon's Mines* (1885)

Although the most intuitive, this method is comparatively little used, because it often results in companies being undervalued. The asset-based approach is static. It involves adjusting the value of assets on the balance sheet and then deducting the value of outstanding debt. We obtain the adjusted net asset value (adjusted NAV), which corresponds to the company's market value. Let's illustrate this method using the balance sheet of Layla Co.

In Figure 6.1(a) we see the company's accounting balance sheet. These are book values that do not necessarily correspond to market values. They have been recorded at historical value, then amortized, and some changes in their value have not been recorded. In Figure 6.1(b) we see the adjusted balance sheet: experts have audited the accounts and appraised

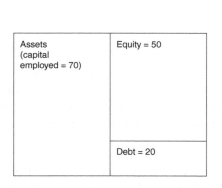
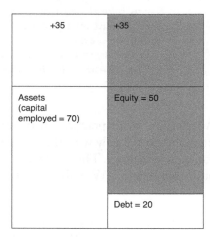

Figure 6.1 (a) Accounting balance sheet   (b) Adjusted balance sheet

the machines, land and inventories, brands and patents. They conclude that assets can be adjusted by £35. The total value of the **adjusted assets**[3] is therefore 70 + 35 = £105. This is what we can expect to get as a selling price for the assets. But if we sell the assets, we will have to pay back the debt of £20. What remains will be the **adjusted net asset value**:

Adjusted net asset value = Adjusted asset value − Debt = 105 − 20 = £85

The adjusted net asset value is represented by the total grey area on the right. This adjusted NAV therefore corresponds to the market value of the company's equity, which is £85.

DIALOGUE	
William:	Why don't they just adjust the equity directly by +£35?
Kate:	Because the value is in the assets and it does not depend on the type of financing used (see Chapter 5 for more on capital structure). Pragmatically, it is easier to audit real assets and check their price (for example on the second-hand market) than it is to adjust shareholders' equity. This is one example of using asset valuation in order to ascertain the value of equity.
William:	OK, so it's easier to adjust the assets. By the way, how did they come up with an adjustment of +£35?
Kate:	There are two possibilities: either the assets were recorded on the balance sheet and they had to be adjusted (land and machines, for example) or there are intangible assets that were not on the balance sheet (patents, brands and so on). For the first category, you can take the cost of a new asset and adjust it with a depreciation coefficient or adjust the balance sheet values using an annual rate. For the second category, you have to do an independent valuation of the asset in question, then add it to the adjusted asset value. That's easier said than done.

Apart from these practical difficulties, there is a major drawback to this method: it deals only with the balance sheet, which means that it ignores the company's earnings. This is why we cannot confine ourselves to this method of business valuation. We will now take a look at a method based on earnings.

---

3. The adjusted net asset value is therefore synonymous with enterprise value (EV). The distinction stems from the calculation method. *Adjusted assets* is computed by adjusting the book value of assets, while EV is obtained by discounting future cash flows, as we will see shortly.

Valuation using multiples

In Northern and Central Africa, wedding gifts may amount to twenty camels, or sixty cows, or several hundred goats, or more than one thousand chickens. So what's a camel worth in chickens?

VIGNETTE ⅢⅢⅢⅢⅢⅢⅢⅢⅢⅢⅢⅢⅢⅢⅢⅢⅢⅢⅢⅢⅢⅢⅢⅢⅢⅢⅢⅢⅢⅢⅢⅢⅢⅢⅢⅢ
Kentigern wants to buy a small property in Glasgow. At one estate agent's he finds a wee flat measuring 500 square feet advertised at £100,000. He investigates the price of small properties in the area by looking at past transactions, and he determines that the average price is £160 per square foot. Kentigern returns to the agent and negotiates a price of £140/sq. ft. He tells the owner: 'You know, the other flats are selling for £160/sq. ft., but they all have a lift and yours doesn't.'

Kentigern ends up getting the flat at his price
ⅢⅢⅢⅢⅢⅢⅢⅢⅢⅢⅢⅢⅢⅢⅢⅢⅢⅢⅢⅢⅢⅢⅢⅢⅢⅢⅢⅢⅢⅢⅢⅢⅢⅢⅢ

FINANCIALESE

Kentigern has constituted a sample of **comparable assets** (a peer group); that is to say, he has chosen transactions involving assets similar to what he wants to buy (an estate in Bath would not be deemed comparable). He has thus obtained an **average valuation multiple** (£160/sq. ft), which he adjusts to the specificities of the apartment he wants. This **adjusted valuation multiple** (£140/sq. ft) is what he applies in his valuation.

Companies are not valued on the basis of their surface area in square feet, however (except perhaps warehouse companies and farms), but on their capacity to generate earnings. The multiples used will therefore be multiples of earnings.

Different types of multiple

Let's say that we want to value Layla Co., which is in the business of manufacturing broken hearts. In the broken heart industry, we observe that four companies have been sold in recent months, as shown in the table below. In Table 6.2, the selling price will be the market value of equity (MV). The other indicators have been taken from the companies' financial statements.[4]

---

4. Except for EV, which has been calculated as EV = MV + debt.

Table 6.2 Market value and other indicators for four companies

Company	MV	Debt	EV	Sales	EBITDA	EBIT	Net earnings	Cash flow
Roxanne	100	20	120	150	21	12	6	7.5
Susanna	120	60	180	200	30	20	16	22
Angie	130	15	145	200	34	24	10	16
Gloria	90	10	100	110	22	16.5	11	16.5
Average	110	26.25	136.25	165	26.75	18.13	10.75	15.5

MV: market value of equity; EV: enterprise value; EBITDA: earnings before interest, tax, depreciation and amortization; EBIT: earnings before interest and tax. All of these indicators have been covered thoroughly in Chapter 1 and in its appendix on IFRS.

These four companies are not the same size and have not been sold at the same price. Although we have calculated the averages, this has been done deliberately (*argumentum ad absurdum*) to show that it is meaningless to calculate the average of their selling price (MV).

Saying that, 'In the broken heart industry, on average, a company sells for £110' would be a bit like telling a bespoke tailor that 'the average man is 5'9" tall'. Instead, on the basis of the companies' earnings indicators, we have calculated some multiples, which are presented in Table 6.3.

Table 6.3 Multiples for four companies

Company	EV/Sales	EV/EBITDA	EV/EBIT	MV/Net earnings	MV/Cash flow
Roxanne	0.8	5.7	10.0	16.7	13.3
Susanna	0.9	6.0	9.0	7.5	5.5
Angie	0.7	4.3	6.0	13.0	8.1
Gloria	0.9	4.5	6.1	8.2	5.5
Average	0.8	5.1	7.8	11.3	8.1

DIALOGUE

Cassidy: Why did they calculate certain multiples based on enterprise value (EV) and others based on the market value of equity (MV)?

Sundance: It depends whether you take earnings **before interest expense** or **after interest expense**. If you consider net earnings or cash flow, these are earnings **after** interest expense. That means that these earnings are for the shareholders because the bank has already been paid. These earnings are therefore compared to the company's value relevant to shareholders: MV. On the other hand, the

Let's take look at the multiples in Table 6.3. The sales multiples (first column) seem to be quite close, so we could say that, on average, companies in this industry sell for 0.8 times their annual sales. For the other multiples we observe greater variation between the companies. We will begin our valuation by taking the averages of all these multiples and using them to appraise Layla. For this step, we have taken Layla's financial data from the company's annual report and made Table 6.4.

Table 6.4 Financial data for Layla Co.

Company	MV	Debt	EV	Sales	EBITDA	EBIT	Net earnings	Cash flow
Layla	?	50	?	180	36	27	18	47

We take the average of each multiple and apply it to Layla. The results are given in Table 6.5.

Table 6.5 Values for Layla Co. obtained using market multiples

Value of Layla Co.	EV/Sales	EV/EBITDA	EV/EBIT	MV/Net earnings	MV/Cash flow
Enterprise value	150	185	210		
– Debt	–50	–50	–50		
= Market value	100	135	160	204	380

Let's explain the calculation carried out in the first column. We have seen that, on average, the companies in this sector sell for 0.8 times their annual sales (0.83 in fact: the figures shown in the tables have been rounded off, but we use the full numbers for our calculations). We apply that to Layla's sales and we obtain EV = 0.83 × 180 = £150. Given that Layla is carrying £50 in debt, we compute MV = EV – D = 150 – 50 = £100. We proceed the same way for the other columns. The last two columns are simpler, because they give us MV directly.

DIALOGUE

Cassidy: What is striking when we look at the values obtained is their amplitude: the average MV is £196, but they range from £100 to £380 (a factor of 4)!

Sundance: That teaches us two things. First, business valuation is not an exact science: an amplitude of ±30% is not rare (in our example it is much more). Second, it underlines the importance of selecting comparable companies, the point of which is to reduce the amplitude. We are going to look at this in detail.

What constitutes a comparable company?

ADMIRATION, n. Our polite recognition of another's resemblance to ourselves.

Ambrose Bierce, *The Devil's Dictionary* (1911)

A comparable company is one that can be used as a reference for business valuation. At the very least, it must be in the same sector and it is even better if it is in the same business as the target company. If it is roughly the same size (because size has an impact on multiples), that is better still. Finally, it must have similar risk and growth characteristics.

By following these criteria scrupulously, we are certain of just one thing: the only company that is truly comparable to Layla is Layla! But there is no reason why we can't take other companies and adjust their multiples, just as Kentigern did for his small flat. Let's take the four companies we have already seen, add Layla, and use several indicators for comparison.

Table 6.6 Comparison of five companies

Company	EV/EBIT	MV/Cash flow	Sales	EBIT/Sales	Debt/Cash flow
Roxanne	10.0	13.3	150	8.0%	2.7
Susanna	9.0	5.5	200	10.0%	2.7
Angie	6.0	8.1	200	12.0%	0.9
Gloria	6.1	5.5	110	15.0%	0.6
Average	7.8	8.1	165	11.3%	1.7
Layla			180	15.0%	1.1

We observe that, on average, companies sell for 7.8 times their EBIT, but with some variation: Angie went for 6 times its EBIT, while Roxanne got

10 times. In fact, these companies do not have the same operating margins. Gloria has the highest ratio (EBIT/sales = 15%) and Roxanne the lowest (8%). If we reason only in terms of operating margin, the company most comparable to Layla is Gloria (15% margin in both cases), followed by Angie (12%).

Now let's look at the debt-to-cash flow ratio, which indicates the size of each company's debt load relative to its cash flow. Gloria and Angie are carrying the least debt and Layla is situated just above these values (1.1 compared with 0.6 and 0.9, respectively), while Roxanne and Susanna are carrying much more debt.

We conclude that the two companies that are truly comparable to Layla are Angie and Gloria. We must therefore use an EV of 6.05 times EBIT (the average of Angie and Gloria) or an MV of between 5.5 and 8.1 times the cash flow.

Using all these multiples[5] we generate Table 6.7:

Table 6.7 Multiples from comparable companies applied to Layla Co.

Company	EV/Sales	EV/EBITDA	EV/EBIT	MV/Net earnings	MV/Cash flow
Angie	0.7	4.3	6.0	13.0	8.1
Gloria	0.9	4.5	6.1	8.2	5.5
Average	0.8	4.4	6.1	10.6	6.8
Value of Layla					
EV	147	159	163		
– D	–50	–50	–50		
= MV	97	109	113	191	319

We observe that the EV multiples for the two comparable companies are very close. In this case we would rather use valuations based on EV, which give us a market value for Layla between £97 and £113.

DIALOGUE

Cassidy: Are these five the only possible multiples?
Sundance: No, we can use any multiple we want; it could be a function of sales by volume, surface area, average customer purchase and so on. The only condition is that the multiple must be representative of the business. Valuing a bookstore according to the number of books, for

---

5. This approach is typically what an investment bank would be doing in the course of its mergers and acquisitions (M&A) business. Those multiples (often called **M&A comparables**) are by far the most frequently used indicators in company valuations.

> example, may be valid because the margins are relatively stable. On the other hand, valuing an antique book seller using a multiple of the number of books sold would not be.
>
> Cassidy: So ultimately you have to analyse the target very carefully to be sure you understand its business.
>
> Sundance: Always. The few hours spent carrying out a diagnostic analysis and investigation will be well spent because they allow you to rule out the non-comparable companies. In the case of Layla, our first estimate (the average of five multiples using five companies) gave us an average MV of 196. Our final result (the average of three EV multiples using two companies) gave us a market value of 106, which is 45% less than the first estimate. If you are buying a company, it's worth taking the time to do a little investigation...

We have almost finished with multiples. But there is still one point to discuss. What if no comparable company has been sold in recent years? What do we do then?

This brings us to the next topic: **stock market multiples**.

Stock market multiples

> *If everyone is thinking alike then somebody isn't thinking.*
> General George S. Patton, Jr (1885–1945)

We no longer need to be on the lookout for companies being sold, nor do we need to calculate multiples for these transactions: the financial markets will provide us with share prices, which are the market values of listed companies. Better still, most of the stock market websites and business newspapers give a few valuation multiples directly, company by company. Let's take our previous example, Layla, the company that produces broken hearts. In this sector there are three listed companies: Lou Easy Ann, Magnolia and Crazy Mama. Here is their latest stock market data:

Table 6.8 Stock market data for three companies

Company	Share price	Number of shares	MV	Debt	EV	Sales	EBIT	Net earnings	Cash flow
Lou Easy Ann	£70.00	4	280	120	400	200	56	28	32
Magnolia	£49.00	10	490	50	540	300	70	35	30
Crazy Mama	£17.00	50	850	120	970	1,000	214	74	140

MV: market value of equity; EV: enterprise value; EBIT: earnings before interest and taxes. Apart from the first column, all the amounts are in millions.

In Table 6.9 we have calculated a few common market multiples:

Table 6.9 Market multiples for three companies

Company	EPS	P/E ratio	PCF	EV/EBIT
Lou Easy Ann	£7.00	10	8.8	7.1
Magnolia	£3.50	14	16.3	7.7
Crazy Mama	£1.48	11.5	6.1	4.5
Average		11.8	10.4	6.5

EPS: earnings per share; P/E ratio: price/earnings ratio; PCF: price cash flow.

Earnings per share (EPS) is obtained by taking the company's net earnings and dividing by the total number of shares. For Lou Easy Ann, for example, EPS = 28 million pounds/4 million shares = £7. This figure means that each share is 'entitled' to a profit of £7.[6] On the one hand, we have the share price and on the other we have earnings per share. We can combine these two indicators to obtain a valuation multiple: the **price/earnings ratio** (P/E ratio). The P/E ratio compares what the market is willing to pay (the share price) with the return produced by one share in a year (earnings per share). For Lou Easy Ann the P/E ratio = share price/EPS = £70/£7 = 10.

DIALOGUE	
Frankie:	This P/E ratio means that the stock market investor buys Lou Easy Ann stock at ten times its earnings per share. So this is an indicator that tells us whether a stock is in great demand or not: the higher the P/E ratio, the higher the price investors are willing to pay, right?
Johnny:	That's right. In fact, in this case we could say that investors are paying £70 for a share that earns £7 of profit a year, so in a sense they are willing to wait ten years to make a profit on their investment. A high P/E ratio is a sign of confidence in the durability of the company.
Frankie:	But there is no guarantee that profit will remain at £7 per year. We actually hope that profit will increase over time…in which case it will take less than ten years for the investment to turn a profit.
Johnny:	Indeed. The P/E ratio also captures the company's projected growth. A high P/E ratio indicates a high earnings growth forecast.

---

6. Part of this profit will be paid out as dividends and the rest will be retained and reinvested in the company.

To sum up, the P/E ratio gives us an idea of how attractive a given stock is to investors. The higher the P/E ratio, the more attractive the stock, either because investors have confidence in the soundness of the company or because they think that it has growth potential.

Using the P/E ratio in business valuation

From the previous table we observe that, on average, the share price of the companies in this sector is 11.8 times their earnings per share. This means that the financial market values these companies at 11.8 times their earnings. We can therefore apply this multiple to Layla, as it belongs to the same sector. Since Layla's net earnings are 18, we obtain MV = average P/E × earnings = 11.8 × 18 = £212.

DIALOGUE	
Frankie:	I see that they've calculated an average of three companies without worrying about whether or not these companies are comparable.
Johnny:	You're right, but this is just an early stage in the valuation; it's not perfect. Magnolia has a P/E of 14, while Lou Easy Ann's is 10. This difference may suggest a lack of comparability.
Frankie:	So how do we proceed?
Johnny:	We must remember that the P/E ratio is an indicator of confidence and expected growth. We have to take companies that are similar to Layla in terms of size, risk (which is linked to confidence) and expected growth.
Frankie:	But we'll never find identical companies with the same debt load, the same growth…Matching the size alone is a tall order! Listed companies tend to be large, but Layla is small (you just have to compare the amount of sales). Where is the comparability?
Frankie:	Size is indeed a problem, because listed companies are generally larger than the companies we want to value, and are often leaders in their market. But – as with the other indicators (risk, growth) – the goal is not to find an elusive 'carbon-copy' company. We will have to make adjustments.

Let's take a few figures to illustrate this idea:

Table 6.10 Comparison of four companies

Company	P/E ratio	Sales	Growth	Debt
Lou Easy Ann	10	200	5.00%	0.8
Magnolia	14	300	8.70%	0.5
Crazy Mama	11.5	1,000	4.00%	0.3
Layla	?	180	6.00%	0.4

Growth: annual future growth outlook; Debt: debt/equity (book value).

We observe several things:

- Crazy Mama is too big to be compared with Layla (comparison of sales).
- Lou Easy Ann's expected future growth is similar to Layla's, so we will head toward a reference P/E ratio of 10.
- But in terms of risk (or confidence), Lou Easy Ann is carrying more debt than Layla, so Magnolia is more comparable.

We end up with a rough-hewn figure and will settle on a P/E ratio of 11. It is higher than Lou Easy Ann's P/E ratio (because Layla has lower debt risk), but lower than Magnolia's (weaker growth outlook) and lower than Crazy Mama's (smaller size, greater debt load, but better growth).

So we have MV = reference P/E ratio × Layla's earnings = 11 × 18 = £198.

DIALOGUE

Frankie: All that work for this! We do all these pseudo-scientific calculations and then at the last minute we just decree a P/E ratio of 11! That's a bit of hocus-pocus, isn't it!

Johnny: Indeed. Once again, our added value is not to be found in a precise figure, but in the reasoning process.

Frankie: But are there any precise formulas for adjusting the P/E ratio?

Johnny: No. Just as Kentigern adjusted his square foot price 'using ball-park figures', we will proceed by approximations. Some people use the **price/earnings to growth** indicator (PEG). It's equal to the P/E ratio divided by the company's expected growth, which is a little more accurate than a valuation using just the P/E ratio. We're going to calculate the PEG for these companies, using the information that we have for each of them.

Table 6.11 Price/earnings to growth (PEG)

Company	P/E ratio	Growth	PEG
Lou Easy Ann	10	5.00%	2
Magnolia	14	8.70%	1.61
Crazy Mama	11.5	4.00%	2.88
Average			2.16
For Layla	13.0	6.00%	

Growth: annual future growth outlook; PEG: price/earnings to growth = P/E ratio/expected growth (in percentage points).

For example, Lou Easy Ann's PEG = P/E ratio/growth = 10/5 = 2.

DIALOGUE

Johnny: We observe that in this sector the P/E ratio 'minus growth', which we call PEG, is 2.16 on average. This means that for Layla, we have an estimated P/E ratio equal to PEG × expected growth = 2.16 × 6 (%) = 13. This gives us a reference MV of P/E ratio × Layla's earnings = 13 × 18 = £234.

Frankie: Whaddaya know – another new value for Layla!

Johnny: What did you expect, Frankie? That all the methods were just going to spit out the same final value? Let's hear what Dirty Henry has to say...

VIGNETTE

Inspector Dirty Henry conducts gruelling interrogations. When he has several witnesses, he questions them one by one for hours, watching for tiny discrepancies in their testimonies. And when he doesn't find any differences between their stories, he books them all and throws them in the holding cell!

Because in real police work you never have **exactly** the same testimonies; people make mistakes about the time or the colour of someone's hair. So if three witnesses do tell exactly the same version of the events, they are probably accomplices who have rehearsed their story together.

The same goes for business valuation. An investment bank that gives you seven valuation methods with seven final values ranging from £99 to £101 has most likely 'twisted' some of the indicators to arrive at a closely grouped result. But it is precisely **because** there are differences between the values that we begin to think about the reasons behind these differences and we get down to the real work of valuation.

Other stock market multiples

The reasoning we have followed for the P/E ratio can also be applied to other stock market multiples: you have to choose comparable companies and then adjust the multiple according to the differences with the target company.

Before we move on, we are just going to talk about two other multiples that are often used and give our opinion of each: the price/cash flow ratio and the price-to-book ratio.

Price/cash flow (P/CF) is the ratio of share price to cash flow. It is therefore very similar to the P/E ratio. Net earnings has simply been replaced by cash flow in the calculation. P/CF is not used as much as the P/E ratio and it's a shame. For several chapters now we have been emphasizing the importance of cash flow in finance (the flow of money the business generates). This is notably the case in business valuation: what we are trying to value is the company's ability to generate sums of money in the future. It is therefore rather surprising that the P/E ratio is used much more often than the P/CF ratio. There is one possible explanation for this: while the notion of net earnings is clearly defined in the accounting standards and has a precise value, the concept of 'cash flow' covers several different metrics. What exactly are we talking about: cash flow, operating cash flow, free cash flow? So when a financial website posts a company's P/E ratio we generally know how it has been calculated. On the other hand, when we see P/CF we need to know exactly which cash flow formula has been used. This may explain the reluctance to use this metric even though, intrinsically, it is to be preferred for a valuation.

The **price-to-book ratio** (P/B ratio or market-to-book ratio) compares the share price to the book value of the share. It is therefore the relation between the market value (MV) observed on the stock market and the accounting value of equity found on the balance sheet. Let's see what this ratio gives for our companies. In Table 6.12 we have gathered their equity values and calculated their P/B ratio.

Table 6.12 Price-to-book ratio

Company	MV	Equity	P/B ratio
Lou Easy Ann	280	150	1.87
Magnolia	490	100	4.90
Crazy Mama	850	400	2.13

MV: market value of equity; Equity: book value of equity; P/B: price-to-book ratio = MV/equity.

We observe that our three companies are valued by the market at 1.8–4.9 times the book value of their equity. The explanation for this is very simple: the market takes into account not only what is on the balance sheet but revaluations too, and most importantly the company's potential. In other words, they are less concerned about the past than the future. Some business valuators and analysts use this indicator to revalue the book value of a company's equity, saying that MV = P/B ratio × book value of equity. It is therefore an alternative to the P/E ratio. Instead of using a multiple of net earnings, they use an equity multiple. We feel that this is dangerous or even downright fallacious. What is certain is that for these three listed companies, there is a difference between what is recorded on the balance sheet and what is valued by the market. What is less sure is that this difference can be applied to another company – an unlisted one to boot!

DIALOGUE

Frankie:	And yet we use the same procedure as for the P/E ratio, so why this reluctance?
Johnny:	Because you have to make a mental leap. Let's take the basic idea and apply it to the three multiples we've already seen. The basic idea is that a company is worth the cash flows that it can generate, just as a house is worth the present value of its future rent. It is quite logical therefore to postulate the market value (MV) as a function of the cash flow generated. This is what the price/cash flow ratio does and that is the indicator that we prefer. Then, doing a little mental gymnastics, we can say that the company's net earnings will pay dividends that are monetary and, in terms of calculation, net earnings are not so different from cash flow, so we can compute MV as a function of the net earnings generated. This is the method using the P/E ratio that we have already described in detail. However, we would need to make a gigantic mental leap to say that 'past net earnings, accumulated in the company's equity that is recorded on the balance sheet, are linked to future cash flows and that there is a link between the book value of equity and MV.' Hence our reluctance.

Valuation using discounted cash flows (DCF)

For anything worth having one must pay the price;
and the price is always work, patience, love, self-sacrifice –
no paper currency, no promises to pay, but the gold of real service.

John Burroughs (1837–1921)

Discounted cash flow (DCF) is familiar to us. We used it in Chapter 2 when we were doing financial calculations, then again in Chapter 3 to make capital investment decisions. Buying a company is, of course, nothing more than an investment decision. It is a matter of paying a certain price (the initial investment) in exchange for the promise of future cash flows. There are only two differences between the two:

- In an investment decision, we know the amount of the initial investment and we seek to determine the project's NPV; in a business valuation, on the other hand, we determine the amount that should be paid for an NPV of zero. We know that if we pay less than this amount, the NPV will be positive.
- For investment projects, the time horizon is often finite. The construction project ends, the machine is scrapped, the market dries up (but a store remains). On the contrary, when doing a business valuation we never aim at less than infinity. We will therefore savour the pleasure of making calculations to infinity – which is always good for the ego!

Two general formulas for business valuation using discounted cash flows

Remember that there are two values: the market value of equity (MV), which is what we are seeking to establish (because that is what is being bought or sold), and the enterprise value (EV), which represents the economic value of the company's assets.

We have this equation:

Enterprise value (EV) = Market value of equity (MV) + Debt (D)

We need to find either MV or EV by discounting the future cash flows. The general discounting formula is as follows:

$$V_0 = \frac{CF_1}{(1+i)} + \frac{CF_2}{(1+i)^2} + \frac{CF_3}{(1+i)^3} + \cdots + \frac{CF_\infty}{(1+i)^\infty}$$

Thus we will determine the value of a business by discounting its future cash flows in the same way as we valued a bond at the end of Chapter 2. It should be noted, however, that the indicators are not the same for MV and EV: the cash flows used will be different, as will the discount rates.

Let's take the most direct approach first: determining MV.

$$MV_0 = \frac{FCFE_1}{(1+C_E)} + \frac{FCFE_2}{(1+C_E)^2} + \frac{FCFE_3}{(1+C_E)^3} + \cdots + \frac{FCFE_\infty}{(1+C_E)^\infty}$$

where MV: market value of equity in year 0; FCFE: free cash-flow to equity; C_E: cost of equity.

In the indirect approach, we begin by calculating EV:

$$EV_0 = \frac{FCFF_1}{(1+WACC)} + \frac{FCFF_2}{(1+WACC)^2} + \frac{FCFF_3}{(1+WACC)^3} + \cdots + \frac{FCFF_\infty}{(1+WACC)^\infty}$$

where EV: the value of assets in year 0; FCFF: free cash-flow to the firm; WACC: weighted average cost of capital.

Once EV has been calculated, we have to subtract debt:

Market value of equity (MV) = Enterprise value (EV) − Debt (D)

We will now describe these two valuation formulas in detail, dealing with the following three points in order: how to make cash flow forecasts, how to determine the discount rate, and how to take it to infinity. In fact, we will follow the same procedure each time, represented by these arrows in Figure 6.2:

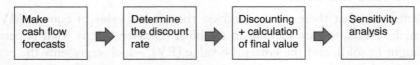

Figure 6.2 Procedure for company valuation using DCF

Making cash flow forecasts[7]

To determine the future cash flows of a company we are going to use the example of Blue Steel Co., the leading Welsh steel producer, whose past financial statements we have reproduced in Table 6.13.

---

7. The first chapters of this book familiarized us with several cash flow calculations: past cash flows for financial analysis (see Chapter 1) and cash flow forecasts for investment decisions (see Chapter 3). Make sure that all of these ideas are running like clockwork in your head; we're not going to go through them all again!

Table 6.13 Blue Steel financials (balance sheet)

Balance sheet

Assets	2011	2012	2013	2014	2015
Gross fixed assets	484.2	513.3	550.2	616.8	647.6
– cumulative depreciation	−267.5	−295.3	−356.2	−389.6	−413.0
Net fixed assets	216.8	218.0	194.0	227.2	234.7
Net financial assets	71.7	71.7	71.7	71.7	71.7
Net assets	288.5	289.7	265.7	298.9	306.4
Net working capital (NWC)	196.7	244.2	310.4	393.8	411.5
Cash and cash equivalents	88.8	25.5	50.9	16.7	31.2
Capital employed	573.9	559.4	627.0	709.3	749.0
Liabilities	**2011**	**2012**	**2013**	**2014**	**2015**
Equity	305.6	318.1	292.7	301.9	307.3
Long-term debt	258.8	218.0	297.1	348.8	408.0
Short-term debt	9.6	23.4	37.2	58.6	33.8
Capital employed	573.9	559.4	627.0	709.3	749.0

From this balance sheet, which we have presented in a financial way (direct calculation of working capital and capital employed), we can quickly glean some useful information: assets have depreciated by ⅔, equity is stagnant, the level of debt is high and growing. In a word, things are not so rosy among the Welsh steelmakers. Let's take a look at their income statement.[8]

Table 6.14 Blue Steel financials (income statement)

Income statement	2011	2012	2013	2014	2015
Sales	1,477.8	1,566.5	1,679.3	1,882.4	1,976.6
Sales growth		6.0%	7.2%	12.1%	5.0%
– production costs	−1,332.8	−1,408.1	−1,507.8	−1,727.9	−1,790.0
Gross profit	145.0	158.4	171.5	154.5	186.6
as % of sales	9.8%	10.1%	10.2%	8.2%	9.4%
– SG&A expenses	−75.8	−86.4	−89.1	−82.1	−80.7
Growth in these expenses		14.0%	3.1%	−7.9%	−1.7%

Continued

---

8. Reminder: the way the income statement is presented differs according to whether we follow local accounting standards or IFRS rules. In this chapter we have followed international (IFRS) standards. Local accounting standards may follow a different framework. The two frameworks and their differences are described in the appendix to Chapter 1.

Table 6.14 Continued

Income statement	2011	2012	2013	2014	2015
EBITDA	69.2	72.0	82.3	72.5	105.9
– depreciation, amortization and provisions	–9.8	–39.6	–86.7	–53.1	–33.2
EBIT	59.4	32.4	–4.4	19.4	72.7
– interest expense	–17.3	–13.8	–18.1	–26.3	–28.6
+ financial revenues or interest income	1.4	2.2	0.6	1.8	–1.5
Earnings before tax	43.5	20.8	–21.8	–5.1	42.6
Extraordinary items	0.0	0.0	–3.6	20.5	–33.6
– tax	–17.4	–8.3	0.0	–6.1	–3.6
Net earnings	26.1	12.5	–25.4	9.2	5.4

Sales are growing steadily and profit margins are stable, even though there have been some erratic jumps in depreciation and/or provisions. The interest expense siphoned off nearly a third of earnings last year. It's not a pretty picture. Let's see what we can do in forecasting.

Based on our audit of this company, we are going to give a few projected indicators (growth, profit margin) and simulate a few future decisions (investments).

Table 6.15 Projected income statement

	2015	2016	2017	2018	2019	2020	Note
Sales	1,976.6	2,055.7	2,137.9	2,223.4	2,312.3	2,404.8	
Sales growth	+5.0%	+4.0%	+4.0%	+4.0%	+4.0%	+4.0%	a
– production costs	–1,790.0						
Gross profit	186.6	209.7	218.1	226.8	235.9	245.3	
% of sales	9.4%	10.2%	10.2%	10.2%	10.2%	10.2%	b
– SG&A expenses	–80.7	–80.7	–80.7	–80.7	–80.7	–80.7	c
Growth in these expenses	–1.7%	+0.0%	+0.0%	+0.0%	+0.0%	+0.0%	
EBITDA	105.9	129.0	137.4	146.1	155.2	164.6	
– depreciation, amortization and provisions	–33.2	–35.0	–40.0	–45.0	–45.0	–45.0	d
EBIT	72.7	94.0	97.4	101.1	110.2	119.6	
– interest expense	–28.6	–31.6	–28.7	–27.2	–25.0	–22.0	e
+ financial revenues or interest income	–1.5	0.0	0.0	0.0	0.0	0.0	f

Continued

Table 6.15 Continued

	2015	2016	2017	2018	2019	2020	Note
Earnings before tax	42.6	62.4	68.6	73.9	85.2	97.6	
Extraordinary items	–33.6	0.0	0.0	0.0	0.0	0.0	g
– tax	–3.6	–25.0	–27.5	–29.5	–34.1	–39.0	h
Net earnings	5.4	37.4	41.2	44.3	51.1	58.6	

Notes and comments:

– For the purpose of comparison, we have included the data from the year that is already finished (2015) as the first column, shaded grey. The forecast really starts in 2016.

(a) An analysis of the sector shows that future growth will be limited. We therefore use a growth rate of 4% per year over the next five years.

(b) Rather than simulate production costs, we have directly calculated the margin on production. Given the latent gains in productivity and future investments, the company should be able to achieve a margin of 10.2%. In practice, a more detailed analysis of costs would be necessary.

(c) Selling, general and administrative expenses tend to be fixed costs and so we have kept them at the same level. We might postulate that increases in these overheads will be offset by gains in productivity.

(d) Depreciation is linked to the company's future investment strategy. Given the age of the machines, we have projected an investment of £45 per year. Depreciation (currently £33.2) will increase gradually to reach £45 per year.

(e) It is rather difficult to predict interest payments on debt. Not only do you have to predict the interest rates for the next five years, but you also have to predict the amount of future debt. For the moment we have made simplified assumptions: an interest rate of 7.5% per year (it was 6.5% on debt in 2015) to reflect the company's financial problems and debt that is gradually being paid off as cash is generated. We will come back to the sticky problem of forecasting the interest expense.

(f) It is just as difficult to forecast financial income, although generally speaking the amounts are smaller. To err on the side of caution, we have decided that there will be no financial income.

(g) How can you predict extraordinary items? Out of prudence (and ignorance) we assume that there will be no extraordinary items.[9]

(h) In 2015, the company paid £3.6 in tax, leaving net earnings of £5.4 We calculate the effective tax rate like this: $T = 3.6/(5.4 + 3.6) = 40\%$. As the rate was the same for all the previous years, we will use it in the forecast.

DIALOGUE

Ginger:	You get the feeling that most of these assumptions are made rather hastily. But these are decisions that will influence the cash flows and ultimately the valuation of the company!
Rocky:	Don't you forget it, sister; that is a key point! A valuation model is like a recipe for fried chicken: it's not enough to follow the directions, you also need to start with a good quality chicken and use the right sort of spices. Here, the key ingredients are the sales and the profit margins and they will determine the quality of the final result.

---

9. In fact, we cannot predict that these items will be zero. Instead, we assume that, over the years, extraordinary income will offset extraordinary losses.

Ginger:	Then why make such simplistic assumptions?
Rocky:	First of all, they are not so simplistic. A truly simplistic assumption would have been to say: 'we suppose that net earnings will be 3% of sales.' Second, the publisher of this book would have a conniption if we used up too much ink, so we had to simplify things with respect to reality. In any case, assumptions are always debatable. We will refine our reasoning when we do the sensitivity analysis.[10]

We can now start the cash flow calculations. We are going to begin with *free cash flow to equity* (FCFE) and then move on to *free cash flow to the firm* (FCFF).

Free cash flow to equity

We are going to apply the calculations from the end of Chapter 1 to the letter when we speak of operating cash flow and free cash flow.

Table 6.16 Cash flow

Year	2016	2017	2018	2019	2020
Net earnings	37.4	41.2	44.3	51.1	58.6
+ add back depreciation and provisions	35.0	40.0	45.0	45.0	45.0
= Cash flow	72.4	81.2	89.3	96.1	103.6

We arrive at an initial figure for cash flow. Now we need to deduct the growth in working capital and capital expenditure. Working capital was given in the company's past balance sheets and we remember (Chapters 1 and 3) that it is correlated to sales. We can therefore estimate projected working capital based on that of year N, by applying the sales growth rate.

Table 6.17 Increase in working capital

	2015	2016	2017	2018	2019	2020
Sales growth		+4.0%	+4.0%	+4.0%	+4.0%	+4.0%
Net working capital (NWC)	411.5	427.9	445.1	463.0	481.5	500.7
Increase in working capital		+16.5	+17.2	+17.8	+18.5	+19.3

---

10. And for those who want to play, the spreadsheet is available on the book's website.

In addition, we have hypothesized a capital expenditure (Capex) of £45 per year over the next five years. We can therefore calculate the free cash flow to equity:

Table 6.18   Free cash flow to equity

	2016	2017	2018	2019	2020
Cash flow	72.4	81.2	89.3	96.1	103.6
– increase in working capital	−16.5	−17.2	−17.8	−18.5	−19.3
– Capex	−45.0	−45.0	−45.0	−45.0	−45.0
= Free cash flow to equity	11.0	19.0	26.5	32.6	39.3

Well that's one thing done. Let's keep this value for cash flow handy.

Free cash flow to the firm

Now we will turn to the question of the indirect method. We have mentioned that, in certain cases, we calculate the value of assets first (EV), then subtract debt to get the market value (MV). Why make things so complicated? Because of comment *e* on our projected income statement (Table 6.15), about forecasting the interest expense.

Indeed, it is rather laborious to forecast an industrial strategy for five years with investments, margins, working capital and depreciation – so many hypotheses can be made. But on top of that, we have to forecast the interest expense, which means postulating a future interest rate on debt and a future debt load. And all of this for five years. In others words, we are sure of nothing.

An elegant solution would be to calculate the cash flow without the interest expense, which would avoid the complexity of forecasting financial policy.

Since this cash flow is calculated without taking the interest expense into account, it is not intended only for shareholders: it will be shared between shareholders and lenders (banks). We call this **free cash flow to the firm** (FCFF) because it comes from assets and is unaffected by the company's capital structure. Figure 6.3 illustrates this idea.

What these two companies have in common is that their assets generate an FCFF of £20. The capital structure does not matter: if shareholders have invested a lot (company on left) they will get most of the FCFF in the form of free cash flow to equity (FCFE); if banks have contributed a lot to the company's financing (company on right), the split will be different, but the FCFF will still be £20.

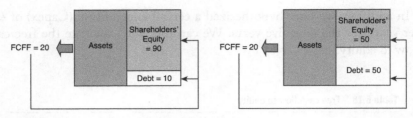

Figure 6.3 FCFF is unaffected by capital structure

Thus, by excluding the interest expense from the cash flow calculation, we get an FCFF that does not depend on the company's capital structure and that can be used to value the assets independently of the structure of the company's liabilities.

Let's calculate this cash flow for Blue Steel.

Given that we want a cash flow without the interest expense, we will start with EBIT (earnings before interest and tax) from the income statement (Table 6.15 above). But the EBIT must be taxed. We therefore tax it at 40% as though there were no interest expense and we get the income before interest expense but after tax (usually called 'net operating profit after taxes' or NOPAT), shown in Table 6.19.

Table 6.19 Net operating profit after taxes (NOPAT)

	2016	2017	2018	2019	2020
EBIT	94.0	97.4	101.1	110.2	119.6
– theoretical income tax	–37.6	–38.9	–40.4	–44.1	–47.8
Net operating profit after taxes (NOPAT)	56.4	58.4	60.7	66.1	71.8

Now we just have to calculate the cash flow as we did before and we get free cash flow to the firm (FCFF), shown in Table 6.20.

Table 6.20 Free cash flow to the firm

	2016	2017	2018	2019	2020
NOPAT	56.4	58.4	60.7	66.1	71.8
+ add back depreciation and provisions	35.0	40.0	45.0	45.0	45.0
= cash flow to the firm	91.4	98.4	105.7	111.1	116.8
– increase in working capital	–16.5	–17.1	–17.8	–18.5	–19.3
– Capex	–45.0	–45.0	–45.0	–45.0	–45.0
= Free cash flow to the firm	29.9	36.3	42.9	47.6	52.5

There, that's done. Now we have two types of cash flow: free cash flow to equity (direct method) and free cash flow to the firm (indirect method).

FINANCIALESE ⎯⎯⎯⎯⎯⎯⎯⎯⎯⎯⎯⎯⎯⎯⎯⎯⎯⎯⎯⎯⎯⎯⎯⎯⎯⎯⎯

The names of these cash flows are a mouthful! **Free cash flow to equity** (FCFE) is cash flows that go exclusively to the shareholders. It represents what is left after deducting all projected expenses. We often speak of net FCFE, where 'net' indicates that we have taken everything into account.

Finally, given that these cash flows represent the balance left over for shareholders after taking all needs into account, some practitioners call them **dividends**. Well, why not? But beware: the real dividends are a percentage of net income, whereas net FCFE is the amount that *could* be paid out as dividends, should the company wish to do so.

Free cash flow to the firm (FCFF) is the cash flow left after deducting all operating expenses, but which has not yet been shared among shareholders and lenders.

Having come to the end of this rather long section, we can now turn to the calculation of the various discount rates.

Determining the discount rates for a valuation

In the direct method, we determine the cash flows for shareholders. It is therefore logical to discount them at a rate that represents shareholders' return expectations. We dealt with the question of shareholders' return expectations extensively in Chapter 5. This is the **cost of equity**, which we determine using the capital asset pricing model (CAPM) and the stock's beta.

The indirect method, on the other hand, entails discounting the operating cash flows generated by assets. What is the expected return on assets? It is the weighted average cost of capital (WACC), which was presented in Chapter 5. We will therefore apply what we saw in the previous chapter to Blue Steel Co.

DIALOGUE

Al Dente: Yo, Pepe, there's something that's tickling my brain. Blue Steel Co. is up for sale, right, so that means it's an investment. But what discount rate should I use: the buyer's discount rate or the seller's?

Pepe Roni: What does your intuition tell you, Al?

Al Dente:	Well, I would say that we should use the buyer's discount rate. They are the ones who are going to have to finance the acquisition and they'll have their own shareholders and bankers on their back with return expectations. And yet, I have this niggling feeling that there's a trap here...
Pepe Roni:	You're right, there is a trap. We're going to use the seller's discount rate.
Al Dente:	And why is that?
Pepe Roni:	There are several reasons: some incidental, others more fundamental. One incidental reason is that we don't always know who the potential buyers are and therefore we can't possibly know their cost of capital.
Al Dente:	And the fundamental reasons?
Pepe Roni:	Let me ask you a question first. At the beginning of Chapter 2, even before we learned how to determine a discount rate, we still knew how to define the characteristics of such a rate. What was the rule again?
Al Dente:	'The discount rate must match the project's risk. The riskier the project, the higher the discount rate.'
Pepe Roni:	Right! Now let's return to Blue Steel. What is the project's risk and how do we determine the discount rate?
Al Dente:	The project's risk is the intrinsic risk of the Blue Steel company and the discount rate to use is the rate demanded by Blue Steel's capital providers – the people who finance the company's assets. So we'll use Blue Steel's cost of equity and its WACC. That means we are going to use the seller's rate.[11]

Calculating the cost of equity for Blue Steel

We need to collect some information about Welsh financial markets in order to apply the CAPM formula. After conducting this research, we decide to use the following information: the risk-free rate r_f is currently 4%; the market risk premium $(R_M - r_f)$ is estimated at 5%; finally, the beta of steel industry stocks is usually $\beta = 1.5$, but Blue Steel is heavily in debt, so we will use $\beta = 2.0$.

Applying the CAPM formula described in Chapter 4, we obtain Blue Steel's cost of equity:

$$\text{Cost of equity } (C_E) = r_f + \beta \times (R_M - r_f) = 4\% + 2.0 \times 5\% = 14\%$$

---

11. Let's split a few hairs (after all, that's the purpose of footnotes). A heckler (I see one at the back of the room) might say: 'the real discount rate to use is the cost of financing for the future entity, the sum of the acquiring firm and the acquired firm.' That's incorrect. In Chapter 4 we saw that companies have several discount rates depending on their various business activities. If Blue Steel becomes a subsidiary of a nappy conglomerate, its discount rate will remain linked to the risks of the steel industry and not to those inherent in the bottoms of babies, the incontinent and astronauts.

That done, let's move on to WACC.

Calculating Blue Steel's WACC

Out of the goodness of our hearts we will reproduce the WACC formula for you here, but slackers should go back and refresh their memory of how we arrived at it by leafing through Chapter 5 again.

Weighted average cost of capital =

$$C_{Equity} \times \frac{Equity}{(Equity+Debt)} + C_{Debt} \times (1-T) \times \frac{Debt}{(Equity+Debt)}$$

We already have the cost of equity. We have estimated the cost of future debt at 7.5% and we have a corporate tax rate of 40%. We still need the values for equity and debt. Remember that the WACC formula must be calculated using market values.

And there's the catch. We are trying to value Blue Steel, which means that we are trying to establish the market value of its equity. But in order to determine the discount rate … we need to know the market value of its equity! It's a classic Catch-22. So how can we find a way out of this Escheresque conundrum?

We are going to proceed by making an approximation, thanks to our knowledge of multiples. A brief incursion into Welsh financial markets reveals that steel companies with a similar level of risk have a P/E ratio of 7. If we posit that this indicator is valid for Blue Steel, then we can determine a reasonable approximation of the market value of its equity. As the projected net earnings for 2016 were £37.4, we obtain:

Approximate value of equity = P/E ratio × Net earnings = 7 × 37.4 = £262

DIALOGUE	
Al Dente:	Whoa, not so fast! With your little sleight-of-hand trick you've just given us the market value of Blue Steel, so why not just stop there?
Pepe Roni:	Because we are no longer reasoning with multiples; we are trying to make a more precise valuation – with cash flows and all that jazz.
Al Dente:	What if we discount the cash flows and end up with an MV of, let's say, £600 – what would that say about the validity of the £262 that we just plugged into the WACC?

Pepe Roni: If that happens, it will mean that the P/E ratio of 7 wasn't right. We will change the £262 in the WACC formula to £600 and we'll redo the discounting with the new rate.[12]

Al Dente: Another question: you used the net earnings from 2016, not 2015. Why?

Pepe Roni: Two reasons. The more important is that we are oriented toward the future value of equity, so we have to use projected earnings. The other is that the net earnings in year 2015 are weighed down by negative extraordinary items, which means that the 2015 figure is not representative of Blue Steel's average earning potential.

We have almost everything now; we just need to find the market value of Blue Steel's debt. But on this point we are going to disappoint those readers who admire meticulous workmanship. Following the lead of most business valuators, we are going to settle for the balance sheet value: £442.[13]

We now have all the elements we need to apply the WACC formula:

$$\text{WACC for Blue Steel} =$$

$$14\% \times \frac{262}{(262 + 442)} + 7.5\% \times (1 - 40\%) \times \frac{442}{(262 + 442)} = 8.04\%$$

Here we have the perfect ending to this section on discount rates.

Now we just have to take it to infinity – which is a stroll in the park.

To infinity and beyond!

Eternity is long, especially toward the end.

attributed to Franz Kafka (1883–1924)

Both of our valuation formulas end with this little sign – what are we saying – this unnerving, mind-boggling symbol: ∞ aka infinity. Because, contrary to the investment in a special machine to drill the holes in Swiss cheese, an investment in a company is never supposed to end. There are countless

---

12. This is called an iteration and this type of iteration always moves toward more stable rates.

13. Although it would be more accurate to use the market value of debt, calculating it would require us to collect the company's debt repayment schedules and discount them according to the rate curve, as we did at the end of Chapter 2. The additional accuracy gained by applying this method is rarely worth the time and effort spent on it.

examples of companies that have celebrated their bicentennial and others are even older.[14]

This means that in order to value Blue Steel we need to estimate its cash flows not only for the next five years, but for the ten years after that and another fifty beyond those, and so on until the Day of Judgement when cyborgs come from the future to reformat our RAM.

How are we to simulate this sequence of cash flows to infinity? We cannot rely on the spreadsheet function of 'adding columns to the right', because spreadsheets only have a few hundred columns and, if you think about it, a few hundred years is still a very long way from infinity.

In fact, we have to turn to an old friend: the **present value of a growing perpetuity** (see the dialogue between Humphrey and Ingrid in Chapter 2).

Let's return to the Blue Steel case, using the general discounting formula for the moment:

$$V_0 = \frac{CF_1}{(1+i)} + \frac{CF_2}{(1+i)^2} + \frac{CF_3}{(1+i)^3} + \cdots + \frac{CF_5}{(1+i)^5} + \left[\frac{CF_6}{(1+i)^6} + \cdots + \frac{CF_\infty}{(1+i)^\infty} \right]$$

We have split the formula into two parts. The left side, without brackets, represents the first five projected cash flows, which does not cause us any trouble. The right side, in square brackets, represents an infinite series. The first way to go about this is to remove the awkward side: we get rid of the company before the end by selling it in year 5, just after receiving the fifth cash flow. The formula becomes:

$$V_0 = \frac{CF_1}{(1+i)} + \frac{CF_2}{(1+i)^2} + \frac{CF_3}{(1+i)^3} + \cdots + \frac{CF_5}{(1+i)^5} + \frac{V_5}{(1+i)^5}$$

Apparently, doing that does not help: we still have to find the value for V_5 and we end up with another series of cash flows discounted to infinity:[15]

$$V_5 = \frac{CF_6}{(1+i)} + \frac{CF_7}{(1+i)^2} + \frac{CF_8}{(1+i)^3} + \cdots + \frac{CF_\infty}{(1+i)^\infty}$$

14. The Japanese construction company, Kongo Gumi, said to be the oldest company in the world, was in operation for 1,428 years, until it went bankrupt in 2006.
15. Be careful with the first terms and the exponents; we are now in year 5 and we discount from year 5 onward.

Actually, as explained in Chapter 2, we can simplify this infinite series by making just one hypothesis: we will say that starting in year 5 the subsequent cash flows will grow steadily by g % annually. That means that all the cash flows after year 5 can be expressed as a function of CF5.

Thanks to the **Gordon–Shapiro formula,** this becomes:

$$V_5 = \frac{CF_6}{(i-g)} \text{ or } V_5 = \frac{CF_5 \times (1+g)}{(i-g)}$$

Basically, to value a business we need the following two formulas:

$$V_0 = \frac{CF_1}{(1+i)} + \frac{CF_2}{(1+i)^2} + \frac{CF_3}{(1+i)^3} + \cdots + \frac{CF_5}{(1+i)^5} + \frac{V_5}{(1+i)^5}$$

and

$$V_5 = \frac{CF_6}{(i-g)} \text{ or } V_5 = \frac{CF_5 \times (1+g)}{(i-g)}$$

DIALOGUE

Al Dente: Do we always carry out a valuation over five years?

Pepe Roni: No, it's just a practical convention. In fact, we value over n years, where n represents the horizon of a reasonable projection, let's say between three and ten years. It's just that, most of the time, it's hard to make a forecast beyond five years.

Al Dente: How do we find the value for g, the growth rate of cash flows to infinity?

Pepe Roni: Humphrey and Ingrid talked about that in Chapter 2. It is primarily a rate for a mature company. The growth rate g should be a value between 0% and 3% depending on the (very long-term) growth outlook.[16]

Valuation of Blue Steel using the two methods

We now have all the indicators and formulas needed to perform the valuation of Blue Steel's market value of equity. Let's get down to it!

---

16. FYI: the average annual growth rate for the world economy was 2.21% between 1820 and 1998. Source: OECD, 2001.

The direct method (discounting cash flows to shareholders' equity)

Table 6.21 recalls FCFE from our calculations.

Table 6.21 FCFE

	2016	2017	2018	2019	2020
Free cash flow to equity (FCFE)	11.0	19.0	26.5	32.6	39.3

Cost of equity: 14%. We still have to determine g. As the steel industry can be said to have reached maturity, more or less, we will use a value of $g = 1\%$. The market value (MV) will therefore be:

$$MV_0 = \frac{11.0}{(1.14)} + \frac{19.0}{(1.14)^2} + \frac{26.5}{(1.14)^3} + \frac{32.6}{(1.14)^4} + \frac{39.3}{(1.14)^5} + \frac{MV_5}{(1.14)^5}$$

and

$$MV_5 = \frac{39.3 \times (1 + 1\%)}{(14\% - 1\%)}$$

Table 6.22 shows the detail of all the calculations leading up to the final value for MV.

Table 6.22 MV of equity (direct method)

	2016	2017	2018	2019	2020
Free cash flow to equity (FCFE)	11.0	19.0	26.5	32.6	39.3
Cost of equity	14%				
Present value of cash flows	9.6	14.6	17.9	19.3	20.4
Growth rate to infinity (g)	1%				
Estimated cash flow (FCFE) for year 6	39.7				
Estimated final MV (MV₅)	305.4				
Sum of present values of first five cash flows	81.83				
+ present value of the final MV	158.6				

= Market value (MV) of equity	240.5

The indirect method (discounting free cash flows to the firm)

Table 6.23 recalls the values for FCFF previously calculated:

Table 6.23   FCFF

	2016	2017	2018	2019	2020
Free cash flow to the firm (FCFF)	29.9	36.3	42.9	47.6	52.5

We recall that the WACC is 8.04%. And we continue to use the same value for growth (g = 1%).

The table below shows the detail of all the calculations up to the final value for MV.

Table 6.24   MV of equity (indirect method)

	2016	2017	2018	2019	2020
Free cash flow to the firm (FCFF)	29.9	36.2	42.8	47.6	52.5
WACC	8.04%				
Present value of cash flows	27.7	31.0	34.0	34.9	35.7
Growth rate to infinity	1%				
Free cash flow to the firm (FCFF) for year 6	53.0				
Estimated final value (EV5)	753.4				
Present value of the first five cash flows	163.3				
+ present value of the final value	511.9				
= Enterprise value of assets (EV)	675.2				
− current net debt	−410.6				
= Market value of equity (MV)	264.6				

DIALOGUE

Al Dente: Still…one of the methods says £240, the other says £264. If we really had to choose between them, which value would we go for?

Pepe Roni: I'll get to your question in a minute, but first I just want to say that we don't give a damn about these values. The only thing that counts in the real world is the selling price – and that will be decided in an arena that's a whole lot tougher than these spreadsheet columns! Now, if we have to choose between the two, I prefer the indirect method (FCFF discounted to WACC). In the direct method we have to estimate the future interest expense, which means we have to make projected balance sheets for five years and decide on the company's financial policy. It's not mentioned in the tables here,[17] but we assumed that the company would pay back its debt gradually. These assumptions have an impact on future interest expenses and therefore on the cash flows to shareholders' equity. And there's no guarantee that our assumptions are right. So I prefer to stick with cash flows that don't include finance costs.

Al Dente: So, depending on its financial policy decisions, the value of the company will change?

Pepe Roni: Actually, the value will change depending on all the assumptions we make. That's why we have to carry out a sensitivity analysis.

Summary of the two methods and the values obtained

Using the first method (FCFE), we obtained a valuation of £240.5 The second method (FCFF) gave us an MV of £264.6: a difference of 10%, which is quite reasonable.

Don't forget that we needed to assume a market value of equity in order to determine the WACC. We set it at £262, which is close to the two values obtained.

Sensitivity analysis

The only sure thing about luck is that it will change.

Wilson Mizner (1876–1933)

We already practised doing this kind of analysis on a capital budgeting decision at the end of Chapter 3. It is a matter of varying the hypotheses to see what impact this will have on the value calculated. To simplify the

---

17. But the spreadsheet available online contains EVERYTHING you could possibly think of … and more.

DIALOGUE	
Topsy:	It looks as though sales are set to grow by 3% annually for five years, instead of 4%. So the market value (MV) of the company will be £260 (-1.8%) – not worth crying over.
Turvy:	Then let's leave sales growth at +4%. What would happen if we lost a percentage point on the profit margin?
Topsy:	If the profit margin declines from 10.2 to 9.2%, the company's MV will plummet to £140 – that's -88%! This means that it's more important to keep an eye on our margins than it is to worry about growth in sales. A tiny drop in margins causes the value to nose-dive...
Turvy:	Let's keep the initial figures then. What about working capital? Should it remain correlated to sales?
Topsy:	Normally, working capital is correlated to sales because any increase in sales volume causes an increase in operating expenses. But when we look at previous years at Blue Steel, we observe that working capital has not always been a fixed proportion of sales. In past years, working capital went from 48 days of sales to 76, which is worse for the company. Imagine if Blue Steel's operations were rationalized over two years and we once again achieved a level of working capital equal to 48 days of sales, starting in year 2018. The company's MV would increase to £473 (+79%)!
Turvy:	Yes, but at the same time, reducing working capital by that much is going to be tricky. Customers will start to complain.
Topsy:	That's the whole point of doing a sensitivity analysis! It shows us which indicators really influence the value of the company. Knowing that sales growth has little impact on the value of this company, but that profit margins and working capital are very sensitive variables, what do you think we should do?
Turvy:	We might decide to sell a little less – by cutting off the customers who usually pay very late, for example.
Topsy:	Exactly. Because sales growth has little impact on MV, eight days of working capital saved in the first year would have a greater impact on company value than if sales were to remain stagnant (0% growth for five years). This tells us what our priorities should be.
Turvy:	So we should always focus on working capital rather than sales!
Topsy:	Not so fast! That's not an absolute rule. It's the conclusion that we happen to draw in this case from our valuation of Blue Steel. But another valuation in another industry would lead to different conclusions. Hence the importance of conducting a sensitivity analysis for each valuation.

presentation of results, we are only going to use the indirect method (based on FCFF). We obtained a value of £264 using the following variables:

- annual sales growth of 4%;
- profit margin of 10.2%;
- working capital that increases proportionally with sales.

We are going to apply a few variations to these figures and see what impact this has on the valuation.

Sum of the parts (SOTP) – or what about mixing recipes?

We have presented the three valuation methods as being complementary, if not opposed: asset valuation focuses only on the present balance sheet; comparables (or multiples) express value as a multiple of next year's profit, so they are focused on the income statement of one year; and finally, DCF deals with all the future years of profit, up to the ineffable infinity. But what if we want to have a smorgasbord of the different methods in one company valuation? This is called **sum of the parts** (SOTP). Let's take an example.

T-Rex-Mex is a company specialized in the 'cretacean diet' (raw meat, uncooked vegetables, unwashed fruit) and the founder, Captain Flint, wants to value his business. The problem is this: there are three lines of business (meat, vegetables, fruit), whose characteristics are quite different. The meat business is the biggest chunk, and forecasts in that sector are fairly easy to do. In the vegetables business unit, the future is less clear and there are many competitors. Finally, the fruit business is very unpredictable, so a good forecast is out of the question. With your help, Captain Flint decides to do a sum of the parts:

- The meat business unit will be valued using DCF. There is plenty of information, so Captain Flint feels confident he can run his forecasts up to infinity, and discount the cash flows using a properly determined discount rate.
- The vegetables business will be valued with an M&A multiple of EBIT. There is enough competition to build a sample of comparable companies, and even if the future is blurred, Captain Flint feels confident that he can at least forecast the EBIT of the vegetables business unit for next year.

- Finally, due to the lack of available data, the fruit business unit will be valued using the asset valuation method (the value of fields and orchards being adjusted using market real estate data).

Now, Captain Flint just has to sum up these three values to get the total value of the company's assets: the enterprise value (EV) of T-Rex-Mex. In short, the sum of the parts method (SOTP) consists in evaluating the different lines of business using the best method available for each business unit, and then adding up all the values to get the value of the whole. This is particularly handy whenever (a) information is scarce in some business lines and abundant in others, or (b) business units differ dramatically in their characteristics (growth, margins, risk and so on).[18]

Conclusion

We have seen several business valuation methods, ranging from the simplest (and least accurate) to the most complicated (which is also the most accurate). At one extreme we have the asset-based approach (which uses only the current balance sheet) and, at the other extreme, discounted cash flows (with all its hypotheses, projections and determination of the discount rate). In the middle we find the various methods using multiples (transaction multiples and stock market multiples). These are intuitive and fairly easy to perform, but they require you to think about the comparability of companies.

In sum, a business valuation – whatever the method – is an intellectual process that seeks to understand value and risk. When you try to model the future of a company you are necessarily trying to understand that company. It is only under these conditions that you will be able to reach – in a negotiation room that reeks of smoke and sweat – a satisfactory selling price.

---

18. If there had been enough information, Captain Flint could have calculated three DCFs for the different business units. This would then have required three different discount rates. The issue of multiple discount rates within a single company will be covered in Chapter 6¾.

6¾

Revenge of the Betas: A Bonus Chapter for Insomniacs

Introduction

The concept of beta has been used extensively in the last two chapters. We first presented this risk metric in Chapter 5 from a stock market perspective: a stock's beta is a measure of its volatility. But we very quickly started using it to determine discount rates (expected returns). At the end of Chapter 5, we looked at a company's financial policy and its impact on the cost of financing. Finally, in Chapter 6 we used beta in the CAPM formula to value Blue Steel Co. To spare the reader's flagging neurons we did not take it any further at that time. But there is indeed more to say on the matter – and that is what we are going to do in this bonus chapter.

By the way, it will not have escaped the attention of alert readers that we skated rather quickly over the determination of Blue Steel's beta. Hey presto, I pull it out of my hat and nobody even blinks. That's all well and good, but it is after all the beta that determines the discount rate we used to value the company. So it's worth learning a little more about it, isn't it?

This bonus chapter (modelled on the bonus tracks you sometimes get on DVDs) is aimed at those who want to know more. But it requires curiosity and a willingness to delve deeper into the concepts already presented. In other words, those who are not presently in such a frame of mind can jump ahead to Chapter 7, where we will talk about the stock market – that's always good for a giggle.

Ontological exploration of beta

Every asset has a beta. Every stock listed on the exchange has a beta. Unlisted stocks also have a beta, although it is harder to observe. An SME has a beta. Copper, rice, plantains – anything that may be bought or sold has a beta.

DIALOGUE	
Barbara:	Even noodles have a beta?
Kenneth:	Let's deal with a better known example first, before we tackle the delicate subject of noodles. What does the beta of a stock represent?
Barbara:	The volatility of its return. The more the value fluctuates, the higher the beta.
Kenneth:	And what makes the value fluctuate so much?
Barbara:	Market fluctuations, which are amplified or dampened by the beta of the stock in question.
Kenneth:	Now we're getting somewhere! A stock's beta represents its dependence on the economic context. If the market rises, the price of stocks with a high beta will rise by more than stocks with a low beta and vice versa. Now let's talk about noodles. Intuitively, does the price of noodles depend on the economic context?
Barbara:	Uh, no, not so much. Whether the economy is booming or just shuffling along in the most depressing depression, people continue to eat the same amount of noodles. That said, wheat production (and therefore noodles) does depend on climatic variations.
Kenneth:	So even though it's not perfectly stable, the value of noodles (= the selling price) depends very little on the economic context. The price of noodles is not very volatile, which tells us that noodles have a low beta. On the other hand, luxury wristwatches probably have a high beta because the demand for them will depend on whether the economy is good (I just got my bonus!) or bad (time to tighten your belt).[1]

---

1. Very very rich people may be able to ignore fluctuations in the economy, so ultra luxury watches will have a low beta.

> Barbara: OK, to sum up then, we can estimate the beta of an asset by answering the following question: In the event of a recession (or strong economic growth), how will the value of this asset change? If the asset is hardly affected, then its beta is probably less than 1. If its price starts to go like a yo-yo then its beta is certainly greater than 1. Riveting stuff, but how does this help us?
>
> Kenneth: It show us that companies do not all have the same risk and it helps us understand the basis of their risk. Let's read what the authors have to say about it.

Asset beta

A ship in harbor is safe – but that is not what ships are for.

John A. Shedd, *Salt from My Attic* (1928)

Some industries are riskier than others and within these industries some companies are riskier than others. The indicator for this risk is called **asset beta** (or *unlevered beta*). Although not necessarily very accurate, this indicator is based on common sense. You have to ask yourself: 'If there is a recession (or economic growth), what will happen to this company's earnings or cash flows?'

Roughly speaking, any increases or decreases in earnings (or cash flows) are caused either by sales or by costs.

- Industries with high betas are those whose sales are relatively sensitive to the economic context and whose costs are relatively insensitive to the economic context. This is the case, for example, with the steel industry, which has enormous fixed costs whereas the price of steel fluctuates a great deal.
- Industries with low betas are those whose costs adjust to the economic context (variable costs) or those whose sales are not greatly affected by the economic context (haircuts, toilet paper, umbrellas).[2]

The beta of a stock

A company's shareholders face two types of risk:

- **Business risk,** which depends on the industry risk and the positioning of the company within that sector. The business risk is indicated by the company's asset beta.

---

2. We presented an initial approach to this concept along with other examples in Chapter 5 in the section entitled 'The economic significance of beta'.

- **Financial risk**, which depends on the company's debt load and which is therefore particular to each company.

The sum of these two components will be the 'total corporate risk' faced by shareholders. Thus when we measure a stock's beta using linear regression, as we did for the graphs at the beginning of Chapter 5, the beta captures both risks: business and financial. This means that in a single sector two companies can have very different betas:

- In terms of business risk, although it is the same industry, the two companies may differ in their market positioning and their cost structure, which makes one company more sensitive to the economic context than the other.
- As for financial risk, the two companies will probably not have the same debt load.

FINANCIALESE —————————————————————————

Asset beta is also called **unlevered beta**. This must not be confused with the **beta of the company's stock**, which is also known as **equity beta** or **levered beta**.

To avoid any confusion, we will use terms from the balance sheet as much as possible:

- We will use the term **asset beta**, because it is the company's assets that bear the business risk.
- Instead of stock beta, we will use the term **equity beta**.

Thus we can say: equity beta = asset beta + an 'adjustment' due to debt.

Finally, as long as we are on the topic of financial jargon, when we hear people talking about a company's 'beta', they mean equity beta (the beta of the company's stock).

Toward a better understanding of financial policy

> *I know that two and two make four – and should be glad to prove it too if I could – though I must say if by any sort of process I could convert two and two into five it would give me much greater pleasure.*
>
> George Gordon Byron (1788–1824)

In our presentation of betas we started with asset beta. And indeed the first question that a potential investor will ask is: Should I invest in this sector or not? The answer will depend on the company's risk, the business risk, which is indicated by its asset beta.

Then comes the second question: If I invest, how much should I borrow?

The second beta, equity beta, starts with the business risk and is the consequence of two choices: which industry and how much debt. We will illustrate this with a few arithmetic examples.

Cecilia & Co. is considering getting into the broken hearts business. This is a sector that has its highs and lows but does not depend too much on the economic context. The business risk beta for the sector is 0.8, which means for example that a 10% rise in the economy (GDP for instance) will produce a corresponding rise in returns for this sector of 0.8 × 10% = +8%.

Cecilia & Co.'s asset beta is therefore 0.8. However, the company is currently reconsidering its financial policy, so they ask their bank to run a few simulations, varying the company's debt/equity ratio. These simulations are presented in Table 6.25 below.

Table 6.25 Capital structure of Cecilia & Co.

	Equity	Debt	Interest rate
Cecilia 1	100	0	4.00%
Cecilia 2	80	20	4.50%
Cecilia 3	50	50	6.00%

NB: the risk-free rate is $r_f = 3.5\%$; the stock market return here is $R_m = 8.5\%$.

As we can see, the more debt Cecilia & Co. takes on, the higher the interest rate required by the bank to offset the increased risk. But what is more interesting here is that we can calculate the **beta of debt**.

The beta of debt

We have seen that every asset has a beta. Here we see that the bank does not apply the same interest rate to the three debt levels because the risk is not the same. And what is the metric for this risk? Beta. After all, a company's debts are its bank's assets, so debts do have a beta. We can therefore calculate the beta of the three debt levels. For this, we will need to recall the formula for CAPM (Chapter 5).

$$\beta = \frac{E(R_i) - r_f}{}$$

which can be rearranged like this:

$$\beta_i = \frac{E(R_i) - r_f}{R_m - r_f}$$

The interest rates given in Table 6.25 are the bank's expected return, $E(R)$. Running the formula with the given values, we find the beta for the three different debt levels.

Table 6.26 Beta of debt

	Equity	Debt	Interest rate	Beta of debt
Cecilia 1	100	0	4.00%	0.1
Cecilia 2	80	20	4.50%	0.2
Cecilia 3	50	50	6.00%	0.5

Sample calculation: for the first line, beta = (4.0% − 3.5%)/(8.5% − 3.5%) = 0.1.

DIALOGUE

Devils:	I'm having trouble with this concept of the beta of debt. I can understand that a stock fluctuates with variations in the market, but surely an interest rate is stable; it doesn't vary.
Dust:	If the interest rate were stable, that is to say not sensitive to the economic context, then the beta of debt would be 0. If that were true – which would be awesome! – then we would compute the CAPM formula and get E(R) = r_f + 0 × (R_m − r_f) = r_f, which means that everyone could borrow at the risk-free rate. But in the real world that's not the case...
Devils:	Uh, time out! Can you explain it a different way?
Dust:	All right. The way CAPM works is that when there is a risk you have to pay a risk premium on top of the risk-free rate. This reasoning works for debt too. The riskier the debt, the higher the risk premium. That's what the beta of debt represents.
Devils:	One last question: when Cecilia is not in debt, why is the beta of debt 0.1 (and not 0)?
Dust:	Because there is already a risk. The sector itself is risky, the company may go bankrupt, and so the bank requires a risk premium!

Calculating the beta of equity

Remember that asset beta comes first and that it is our debt financing decision that introduces an additional layer of risk for shareholders. Let's suppose that Cecilia & Co. decides not to take on any debt. This is shown in the 'Cecilia 1' line of Table 6.26.

Figure 6.4   Cecilia 1 and Cecilia 2

Devils:	And how do you do the calculation in practice?
Dust:	The asset beta should correspond to the average of the betas on the liabilities side, so that the risk on each side will be the same. This is what we will get:

$$\beta_{asset} = \beta_{equity} \times \frac{equity}{equity + debt} + \beta_{debt} \times \frac{debt}{equity + debt}$$

For Cecilia 2, if we calculate the weighted average of betas:

$$0.95 \times \frac{80}{80 + 20} + 0.2 \times \frac{20}{80 + 20} = 0.8$$

we arrive at the asset beta again.

In fact, the 0.95 is found by reversing the previous formula:

$$\beta_{equity} = \beta_{asset} + [\beta_{asset} - \beta_{debt}] \times \frac{Debt}{Equity}$$

We apply this formula to Cecilia 2 and sure enough we get: 0.8 + (0.8 – 0.2) × (20/80) = 0.95.

DIALOGUE

Devils:	So we don't calculate the 0.15 adjustment directly? Instead we calculate the equity beta using that unsightly formula above?
Dust:	Right, because we are trying to find equity beta. And that unsightly formula, as you call it, has the benefit of clearly showing that equity beta is equal to asset beta plus an adjustment whose amount depends on the level of debt.

Let's take a look at the final table (6.27) for Cecilia.

Table 6.27 Equity beta depending on capital structure

	Asset beta	Equity	Debt	Beta of debt	Equity beta
Cecilia 1	0.8	100	0	0.1	0.80
Cecilia 2	0.8	80	20	0.2	0.95
Cecilia 3	0.8	50	50	0.5	1.10

We observe three things in Table 6.27:

- First, in keeping with what we have already said, the business risk does not change. The corresponding asset beta is always 0.8.
- Second, the betas of debt and equity increase with the level of debt, but the average of the two betas is always 0.8. These results reflect Modigliani–Miller's findings on financial policy: shareholders adjust their return expectations very precisely to compensate for additional risk (see Chapter 5).
- Thus the beta of equity (the beta of listed stocks), is in fact a two-stage rocket: it includes the business risk of the sector (0.8) and an adjustment due to debt (+0.3 in the case of Cecilia 3).

This last remark is important because, let's not forget, there is only one Cecilia & Co. Yet we found three different betas for its equity depending on the company's debt load. This means that when you are doing a business valuation you have to be extremely careful about determining the beta. Nice timing – that is the subject of the next section.

How to determine the beta of an unlisted company

And as the evening twilight fades away
The sky is filled with stars, invisible by day.
Henry Wadsworth Longfellow, *Morituri salutamus* (1874)

To determine the beta of a stock in Chapter 5, we performed a linear regression between that stock's returns and market returns. But how do you determine beta if the company is not listed on the stock market?

We are going to describe a procedure that allows us to determine the beta for any company or indeed any type of investment project. The procedure is as follows:

- Identify comparable listed companies (same sector, same line of business).
- Calculate the betas for each of these listed stocks.
- Eliminate the bias due to the various debt levels of these companies.
- Retain the beta obtained.

This will be much clearer with an example. Let's continue with the broken heart industry. Lonelyhearts Co. is a small, joint-stock company – it has shareholders – but is not listed on the stock exchange. We would like to determine its beta, which will allow us to calculate its WACC and the expected return for its shareholders – all of which is very useful. The only information we have on Lonelyhearts Co. is the following:

Table 6.28   Lonelyhearts Co. financials

	Equity	Debt	Interest rate
Lonelyhearts Co.	100	80	4.60%

Where the risk-free rate r_f = 3.5% and the stock market return R_m = 8.5%.

We want to know the equity beta of Lonelyhearts Co., but since the company is unlisted we will need to find comparable listed companies and then calculate the beta of their stock. In the broken heart industry, we find four comparable companies whose information is provided in Table 6.29:

Table 6.29   Comparable listed companies

	Equity beta	Equity	Debt	Interest rate
Billie Jean	0.8	100	20	3.80%
Solea	0.87	100	40	4.00%
Pocahontas	0.95	100	60	4.50%
Sara	1.05	100	100	5.00%
Average	0.92			

Where the risk-free rate r_f = 3.5% and the stock market return R_m = 8.5%. The equity betas were determined by linear regression of market returns, as explained at the beginning of Chapter 5.

DIALOGUE

Devils: Oh yeah, easy-peasy-lemon-squeezy! We have four equity betas from four companies, the average is 0.92, so we just use 0.92 as the equity beta for Lonelyhearts Co. and we can pack up and go home!

Dust: You think so? Can you remind me of our conclusions from the previous section?

Devils (rereads his notes laboriously):   Hmm, it says here that the value for equity beta depends on the level of debt.

Dust: So, in this case, do you think that we can just calculate the average of the betas in the first column?

Devils:	I guess not, because these companies won't have the same debt level. But I do remember this: equity beta = asset beta + an adjustment due to debt. So we have to correct the equity beta by 'removing' this adjustment in order to obtain the bare asset beta for each company.
Dust:	That's exactly right! We'll show the calculation in detail for Billie Jean and then give the four results.

Based on the interest rate for Billie Jean, we can calculate the beta of its debt by applying the formula derived from CAPM:

$$\beta_i = \frac{E(R_i) - r_f}{(R_m - r_f)}$$

For Billie Jean we get:

$$\beta_{\text{Debt}} = \frac{3.80\% - 3.5\%}{(8.5\% - 3.5\%)} = 0.06$$

Unlevering equity beta

The formula for calculating asset beta is:

$$\beta_{\text{asset}} = \beta_{\text{equity}} \times \frac{\text{equity}}{\text{equity} + \text{debt}} + \beta_{\text{debt}} \times \frac{\text{debt}}{\text{equity} + \text{debt}}$$

When we apply this to Billie Jean, we get:

$$\beta_{\text{asset}} = 0.80 \times \frac{100}{100 + 20} + 0.06 \times \frac{20}{100 + 20} = 0.68$$

DIALOGUE	
Devils:	For once I actually understand! Billie Jean is in an industry with little risk, so its asset beta is 0.68. But the company is in debt, which increases the risk for shareholders. Ultimately, what shareholders want is a beta of 0.80, which we can break down into an asset beta of 0.68 and an adjustment due to debt of 0.12 (0.80 - 0.68).
Dust:	Well done! Now let's take a look at the results for the four companies.

Table 6.30 Asset beta for comparable companies

	Equity beta	Equity	Debt	Interest rate	Beta of debt	Asset beta
Billie Jean	0.80	100	20	3.80%	0.06	0.68
Solea	0.87	100	40	4.00%	0.1	0.65
Pocahontas	0.95	100	60	4.50%	0.2	0.67
Sara	1.05	100	100	5.00%	0.3	0.68
Average	0.92					0.67

N.B. the risk-free rate r_f = 3.5% and the stock market return R_m = 8.5%. We obtained the asset betas using the above formula for unlevering equity beta.

DIALOGUE

Devils:	Hey, that's odd, the four companies have almost the same asset beta.
Dust:	Not so odd – they're in the same industry and they face the same business risk. Asset beta is a much more stable and more reliable metric than equity beta.
Devils:	Does that mean that instead of calculating the average of the equity betas (0.92), we should 'unlever' them to arrive at their asset betas?
Dust:	Yes, that metric will be more reliable. After all, what we are mainly interested in is the business risk.

Now we have the average asset beta for the four comparable companies (0.67). This is the beta that corresponds to the business risk of that industry. We are going to assume that Lonelyhearts Co. has the same asset beta. After all, it is in the same industry and faces the same business risks, so it is not such a wild assumption.

We therefore set the asset beta of Lonelyhearts Co. to this value: β_{asset} = 0.67.

DIALOGUE

Devils:	That's it, we finally have our equ...oh no, it's the asset beta!
Dust:	So, my dear sparring partner, what do you think we should do now?
Devils:	Think it through! Say, for example, Lonelyhearts Co. faces a business risk (asset beta = 0.67) and on top of that the company is in debt! We have to factor in the adjustment caused by Lonelyhearts' debt. Am I right?
Dust:	Yes. Well done. We are going to lever (add the debt) the asset beta.

Levering asset beta

The formula for levering asset beta is the one we used for Cecilia 1, 2 and 3:

$$\beta_{\text{equity}} = \beta_{\text{asset}} + [\beta_{\text{asset}} - \beta_{\text{debt}}] \times \frac{\text{Debt}}{\text{Equity}}$$

In order to apply this to Lonelyhearts Co. we need to know the beta of its debt.

Here is the company's financial data again:

Table 6.31   Lonelyhearts Co. financials

	Equity	Debt	Interest rate
Lonelyhearts Co.	100	80	4.60%

Where the risk-free rate r_f = 3.5% and the stock market return R_m = 8.5%.

Now we apply the formula derived from CAPM again:

$$\beta_i = \frac{E(R_i) - r_f}{(R_m - r_f)}$$

and plug in the values for Lonelyhearts Co.:

$$\beta_{\text{debt}} = \frac{4.60\% - 3.5\%}{(8.5\% - 3.5\%)} = 0.22$$

Here is the final step: determining Lonelyhearts Co.'s equity beta.

$$\beta_{\text{equity}} = \beta_{\text{asset}} + \left[\beta_{\text{asset}} - \beta_{\text{debt}}\right] \times \frac{\text{Debt}}{\text{Equity}}$$

$$= 0.67 + [0.67 - 0.22] \times \frac{80}{100} = 1.03$$

Voilà! We have determined the equity beta of an unlisted company – knowledge that can be used for many things:

- It allows us to calculate the cost of equity and the WACC of any company, whether listed or not.
- It allows us to determine the discount rates for any kind of company, for example when doing a business valuation (Chapter 6) or capital budgeting (Chapter 3).

DIALOGUE

Devils:	Can we summarize the whole procedure?
Dust:	Of course. We've made a diagram of it (Figure 6.5).
Devils:	Just one question about the vocabulary: why do we speak of 'unlevering' and 'levering' the betas?
Dust:	(sighs) Because finance people get a kick out of five-dollar buzzwords.

FINANCIALESE

We say '**unlevering**' equity beta, but in the formula we add the debt, which is counter-intuitive. What we are doing, in fact, is taking the risk back to ground zero. By calculating the average, we shift from the liabilities side (capital structure) to the assets side (business risk, independent of financing). As we are isolating the business risk, it might make sense to say 'stripping' the beta.

Similarly, when we **lever** (or re-lever) the beta afterwards, we are introducing a risk premium to the beta. We might say 'fattening' the beta (to include the effect of debt financing).

A few useful applications for these formulas

We have already seen that we can use these formulas for an unlisted company. But they have other fun applications as well.

Understanding a listed company

Even when a company is listed it can be interesting to see how it fares with respect to its competitors in terms of business risk. Breaking down the risks helps us to understand the company's business strategies.

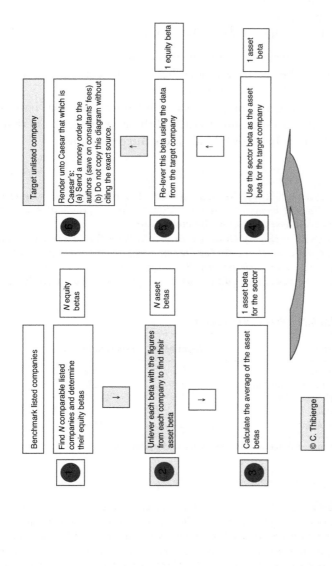

Figure 6.5 Determining the equity beta of an unlisted company

Calculating the different risks for company divisions

Let's imagine a listed company called Ghouls Inc. (equity beta = 1.1) that has three distinct lines of business:

- frightening small children;
- selling earplugs to parents;
- manufacturing prescription glasses for Cyclops.

Of course, we could always 'strip' (unlever) the equity beta to get asset beta (0.9), but that would be the overall asset beta for the company as a whole and not the beta of each line of business.

What we need to do is to find pure-play companies (ones that have only one line of business) corresponding to each of these three sectors so that we can determine the asset betas of Ghouls Inc.'s three divisions.

DIALOGUE

Mummy: Aren't we splitting the hairs a little too fine here? Why put the three lines of business under the microscope when we already have the overall asset beta for the company?

Deady: Let's answer that with an example. We look for benchmark companies in those three sectors (each company being a pure-play – only one line of business) and then we determine those three asset betas. The results of our research are summarized in Table 6.32.

Table 6.32   Pure-play companies

Sector	Asset beta	Expected return
Scare Kids Inc.	0.6	6.5%
The Earplug Company	1.0	8.5%
Cycl-Optical Ltd	1.5	11.0%
Reminder:		
Ghouls Inc.	0.9	8.0%

Where the risk-free rate r_f = 3.5% and the stock market return R_m = 8.5%.

DIALOGUE

Deady: Imagine that Ghouls Inc. is thinking about investing in a new earplug machine. The company's financial controller has estimated the project's return at 8.2% annually. Is this a worthwhile investment?

Mummy: Well, if we take Ghouls Inc.'s overall asset beta of 0.9, the expected return on projects will be 8%. Since this particular project is supposed to return 8.2%, it will be approved. But I have a funny feeling that would be a mistake!

Deady:	You're dead right. The project is to be undertaken by the Earplug division of Ghouls Inc. The minimum return needed is therefore 8.5%, because that's the return expected by shareholders of The Earplug Company (a benchmark company in the same sector).
Mummy:	So the project should be rejected.
Deady:	Exactly. If we don't look at the betas of the three divisions separately, mistakes will be made. For example, looking only at its overall beta, Ghouls Inc. would approve a project in the Cyclops division with a projected return of 10% (but it should be rejected since 10% < 11%) and it would reject a project with an expected return of 7.5% for the 'Children Frightening' division when it should be approved (7.5% > 6.5%). All of this may end up costing Ghouls an arm and a leg.

Determining the beta for investment projects

In the previous example, we spoke of divisions in a large company. In fact, we have shown indirectly how this reasoning might be useful in making capital budgeting decisions. Indeed, we have gradually zoomed in from a broad view (the company as a whole, with an overall asset beta) to a component view (the company is made up of three divisions each with a distinct beta). We can now move in to an even more detailed view: a company made up of several divisions, each of them handling many investment projects. And each investment project has its own beta.

DIALOGUE	
Mummy:	As I live and breathe! That means we are going to have to calculate an asset beta and a discount rate for each investment project now?
Deady:	No, fortunately we don't have to do that. A company that makes yogurt (asset beta = 0.5) does not have to determine the beta of an investment in a yogurt machine; it is 0.5. We can use the company's asset beta for all projects that come under the company's core business.
Mummy:	Whew! I was afraid this would keep me up all night!

Conclusion

This is a short chapter, but it has been rather heavy-going due to the number of connections made between the various concepts. Congratulations to all those who made it this far and who feel they are up to the challenge of reproducing this approach in the real world. Investing time in this chapter will generate a truly positive NPV (in the long run).

7

The Stock Market

Stock Market Prices
Helium was up. Feathers were down. Paper was stationary. Knives were up sharply. Pencils lost a few points. Hiking equipment was trailing. Elevators rose, while escalators continued a slow decline. Light switches were off. Mining equipment hit rock bottom. Diapers remained unchanged. Shipping lines stayed on an even keel. Balloon prices were inflated. And batteries exploded in an attempt to recharge the market.

Anonymous

Introduction

The stock market crystallizes many dreams, but it is also the focus of fantasies and numerous ideological discourses. Let's navigate these troubled waters together and try to improve our understanding in the following areas:

- the purpose of the stock market;
- the main types of transaction that are carried out on stock exchanges;
- the mechanisms for making money – or losing it, as so often happens – on the stock market.

Unlike the other chapters, this one is essentially literary. Instead of calculations – only a few here – there will be discussions and commonsense explanations. We might say that this chapter is the philosophical and conceptual counterpart to Chapters 4, 6 and 6¾, which dealt with portfolio management and asset valuation in a very concrete, applied fashion.

Purpose of the stock market

Countries do not necessarily need to have a stock market. People can live very happily without a daily stock ticker. That said, it must be acknowledged that the stock market does fulfil three important needs for finance in particular and for the economy in general:

- raise funds;
- facilitate trading;
- put a price on things.

We are going to treat these three topics in order.

Raise funds

Nemo is morose. His ship, the Nautilus, is falling apart at the seams. The argon conduits are leaking into the cabins and the graphic display hardware is so underpowered you can't even play the holographic version of Pong on it. Nemo would like to invest in a new ship. The problem is that his cash reserves have sunk to -10 degrees Kelvin. Jesse James Bank is willing to lend him 100 tera, but a new ship would cost 1,000 tera.[1] Where will he ever find the money? His neighbour, Ned, comes to see Nemo and shares the following proverb:

'Little streams make great rivers.'

(silence)

'Your heart's in the right place, Ned, but I've got work to do here ...'

'I would add that the more numerous the little streams, the greater the final river. Tell me, how many households are there in the submarine city of Atlantis?'

'Nearly 20 million. Why?'

'Imagine if each household gave you 50 meg. How much would that make?'

'20 million × 50 = 1 billion meg, or 1,000 tera. Exactly the price of a new ship!'

What Ned is showing Nemo is the principle of collective funding: bringing common interests together. This is not a new principle. In the 15th century, bourgeois European families would pool their money to outfit a ship and send it to India. The wealth of a single family would never have sufficed, but by combining the contributions of 100 families they could build a very fine ship.

Today, the stock market makes this possible. Like Nemo, companies need large amounts of money to finance major investments. As they rarely have this much cash on hand, they issue securities; that is, they create and

---

1. The local currency in Atlantis is the KB. A meg is worth 1,000 KB. A gig is worth 1,000 meg and a tera is worth 1,000 gig.

sell shares to the general public. For example, 20 million British households each contributing £10 will enable a company to raise £200M of capital.

DIALOGUE	
Nemo:	But what's stopping me from raising the money like that without going through the stock market?
Ned:	Nothing, but it would probably be more costly and less efficient. More costly because you would have to contact each of those 20 million households and less efficient because not all of them would be persuaded by a ragged old man to part with their money.
Nemo:	So it has to be the stock market?
Ned:	The stock market was designed for exactly this type of operation. There are traders and communication channels that facilitate the flow of information, so anyone who is interested in investing will be kept up to date about it. In addition, the stock market is regulated, with a set of rules and constraints. That means that any company that wishes to raise funds on the market has to provide a certain number of guarantees and financial information, which reassures potential investors.

Note that it is not only businesses that raise capital by issuing securities; national governments also regularly issue bonds, underwritten by the general public, to finance major economic projects. Occasionally these governments are responsible enough to remain solvent and pay back their debts.

Facilitate trading

The stock market is a place that makes it possible to gather savings from multiple sources in order to finance big projects. But the stock market is like a prison: it is simple enough to get into it but quite another matter to get out again. The stock market must therefore ensure the fluidity of trading, allowing individuals to buy securities (or dispose of them) and companies to get out of the stock market entirely by going private. **Market liquidity** is ensured by several mechanisms.

The primary market and the secondary market

The **primary market** handles the issue of new securities, while the **secondary market** deals with existing securities – rather like the market for new cars and the market for used cars. In reality, the distinction is not very important: buying a 'new' Aronnax security during a new stock issue is equivalent to buying an existing one, because the two have exactly the same characteristics. This is due to the principle of the fungibility of securities, which we will now describe.

The fungibility of securities

VIGNETTE |||||||||||||||||||||||||||||||||||||||||||||||||||||||||||||||||||||||||||||||||||||||||||||||||||||||||||||||||||||||||||||||||||||||||||||||||
When a car is first placed on the market, it is new (primary market). Later, it is sold as a used car on the secondary market. Even when it is new, though, it is unique and cannot be confused with another new car of the same make and model.[2] Cars are not fungible. A piece of music in MP3 format, on the other hand, is digital and therefore undegradable. It can be sold and resold without any loss of value (it can even be multiplied like the loaves and fishes in the New Testament).

A security is midway between a car and an MP3 track. It is undegradable (but cannot be multiplied by the shareholder) and it is fungible: one Aronnax share can be substituted for another Aronnax share.
|||||||||||||||||||||||||||||||||||||||||||||||||||||||||||||||||||||||||||||||||||||||||||||||||||||||||||||||||||||||||||||||||||||||||||||||||||||||||||||||||

The principle of fungibility is important because it means that securities are perfectly standardized. Take the example of coffee. We can buy 'medium quality' or 'high quality' coffee in bulk. But we cannot guarantee that two lots of 'high quality' coffee, one bought in Tegucigalpa and the other stolen in Ulan Bator, will have exactly the same composition, down to the last bean. Consequently, the two lots may not have the same price. On the other hand, two Aronnax shares are exactly the same and will have the same intrinsic value, which facilitates trading.[3]

Liquidity

Securities cannot be sold if there are no buyers present. This situation can occur, but market regulators (the SEC in the US, FCA in the UK, AMF in France, and so on) operate several systems to ensure that investors are present.

There are two concerns that need to be addressed:

- Buyers need to be present alongside sellers so that transactions will take place.

---

2. Because it has a serial number and a number plate. Imagine that you lend your car to a friend, and a few days later she returns a car of the same make and model, but it's not yours ...
3. It is true that there may be several types of stock (ordinary, preferential, without voting rights and so on), but within each category the securities are perfectly substitutable.

- There have to be enough buyers and sellers present so that transactions will be carried out at a representative price.

Companies and traders are there to ensure that there is a minimal level of liquidity on the markets and alert mechanisms are in place to detect insufficient trading.

Put a price on things

A market where all the assets are standardized and which has sufficient liquidity is one where satisfactory prices will generally be reached; that is to say, prices that correctly reflect supply and demand. We won't worry too much about market efficiency for the moment. We are not concerned about whether prices are fair; it is enough to know that they exist.

The stock market is like a gigantic laboratory for observation.

SLICE OF LIFE . . . .
Russell Sprout wants to buy a small hat business in Ghent. He hires some well dressed consultants to do a business valuation. They estimate the future cash flows, determine the discount rate, establish an end value and finally, after a few days, give him a range of values (and a very precise invoice).

To save himself time and money, Russell could have gone online himself and checked stock market websites to see the share price of hat businesses with respect to their earnings (this is the principle of multiples, particularly the P/E ratio, that we saw in Chapter 6).
. . . .

It is true that the value observed by Russell would be less accurate and not as closely tuned to the specificities of his target company, but at least it would be very fast.

Just as we use square foot prices to assess the price of a flat, we can use the prices set by the financial markets as references for the value of assets. Quotations exist for many things: stocks, debt securities (in the form of bonds), raw materials, currencies and so on. And these quotations are updated every minute.

Thus the stock market[4] makes an entire set of market prices available very quickly and we don't have to obtain the prices of private transactions. In this regard, it provides extremely useful economic information.[5]

---

4. We use the term 'stock market' specifically for stocks; 'financial markets' is more general.
5. The value may differ from the price listed. Nevertheless, knowing the price gives investors a starting point.

The main types of stock market operation

Initial public offerings

Let's take the example of a chain of restaurants, Thai Tanic LLC, which is held by private shareholders.

For the moment the share capital is distributed as follows:

- Brock O'Lea: 51 shares (51% of the capital);
- Sal A. Mander: 30 shares (30% of the capital);
- Tom A. Toe: 19 shares (19% of the capital).

In order to begin trading publicly, they have two options: either each shareholder sells some of his existing shares (the total capital remains the same) or they decide to create new shares (there is an increase in capital). Most often, the second option is chosen. But in either case the shareholders' stake in the capital will be diluted. For example, Brock O'Lea will lose his majority, unless he buys most of the newly issued shares.

FINANCIALESE ─────────────────────────────

If 70% of a company's capital is held by private shareholders, it can offer only 30% of its shares to the public. This 30% is called the **float**. The 100% is known as the company's **market capitalization** (even though public trading involves only 30% of the capital).[6]

The first offer of a company's shares on the market is called an **initial public offering** (IPO). This is known as **going public** or **taking a company public**.

Most of the time, the terms 'stock' and 'share' are synonymous (stock price, share price, stockholder, shareholder and so on).

'Going public' is synonymous with 'joining the big leagues'. There can be many reasons for a company to want to take this step:

- To finance investment on a larger scale than is possible by calling on private shareholders, whose resources are necessarily limited. Going public is often justified by a high growth strategy.
- To benefit from the way the stock market works, which facilitates trading. Imagine what would happen if Thai Tanic LLC did not go public and Tom A. Toe wanted to sell his shares. Who could he sell them to? It's hard to find someone who would be willing to buy 19% of an unlisted company,

---

6. Market capitalization is equal to the total number of shares × the share price. This corresponds to the market value of equity (MV) discussed in Chapter 6.

given that a minority shareholder has no real influence over management decisions, nor over dividend distribution policy. Going public makes it easier for the founders to sell their stake in the future should they so desire.[7] What's more, if a company is listed on a liquid market, its shareholders can sell exactly the number of shares they want, whereas a stake in an unlisted company must often be sold as a whole.

- To be recognized as a major player. The stock market offers advantages, but it also imposes rules. To be listed on the stock exchange, a company must comply with certain regulations concerning information quality and standards. At the same time, this allows them to obtain better financing terms from banks and even to benefit from media exposure. Consequently, going public is often accompanied by a strategy of enhanced corporate communication.

It should be noted, however, that these regulatory constraints can be very costly. In the wake of recent financial scandals and the toughening of compliance requirements concerning financial information, the game is no longer worth the candle for companies below a certain size. Mid-size companies may even choose to go private (leave the stock market) when they realize that the advantages offered by the stock market no longer offset the extra work required. They prefer to do without the access to capital markets in order to spend more time on their business and less time on financial communication. The private equity market has developed to help mid-size companies raise funds without the constraints of an initial public offering.

Equity issuance/follow-on offering

Growing companies need to invest regularly (Chapter 3) and therefore need to raise capital (Chapter 5). In pursuing their financial policy and balancing their capital structure (debt-to-equity ratio), companies will sometimes decide to increase shareholders' equity.

As we have already explained, an equity issuance is when a company creates new shares and sells them on the stock market in exchange for fresh money, which will first be deposited in the company's bank account (**current assets**) before being invested in **fixed assets** or working capital.

The fundamental question that comes up is the following: what price should the new shares be issued at?

---

7. Going public or selling their stake is often the final goal of company founders.

DIALOGUE	
Me:	Well, since the company is already listed on the stock market, we will issue new stock at the current share price.
Mrs Jones:	Yes, but there is a paradox here: if we issue shares at **exactly** the market price, what would be the incentive for new investors to buy them? They might as well buy shares that are already in circulation, if they are the same price. The new share offering could end up being a flop.
Me:	Well, in that case, we'll issue them at a price that is lower than the market to attract buyers.
Mrs Jones:	If we do that, the current shareholders will be unhappy because they will think that we are cheapening the stock by letting new buyers in at a lower price. That's the paradox: we can't issue the new shares either at the market price or at a lower price – and most definitely not higher!

In fact, there is a way to resolve this paradox:

* First, we never issue shares at the 'current' market price. Imagine that Octopus Sushi stock is currently trading at £100. The investment bank that is underwriting the share issue sets the price at £100. But by the time the prospectus is released and the formalities have been taken care of, the share price of Octopus Sushi has fallen to, say, £97. And now the company's executives are asking £100 for shares whose twin sisters are worth £97 on the market. It is reasonable therefore to reduce the price of the new shares to buffer against market fluctuations. That said, this reduction may be quite small.
* Second, if the new shares are being issued much below the market price, existing shareholders will be given a **pre-emptive right** (also known as **subscription right** or **subscription privilege**) offering them exclusivity in buying the new stock. This way, they are the only ones to benefit from the windfall.

DIALOGUE	
Me	But what if they don't want to plough more money into the company? Then there's nothing to be gained from having a pre-emptive right.

Mrs Jones:	In that case, they could sell their subscription rights to someone else [reminder: these rights are needed to buy the new shares]. Subscription rights allow you to buy shares at a specified price that's good for a specified amount of time. Thanks to the law of supply and demand, the sellers will come away with exactly the difference in value that they were offered.
Me:	I would like to believe you, but an example would definitely help here.
Mrs Jones:	Read on...

Octopus Sushi's capital stock is made up of one million shares. These shares are currently trading at £100. The firm's executives want to raise £8M through a stock issue. To buffer against market fluctuations in the share price they set the price of the new stock at £80. The current shareholders shriek like scalded cats ('Wretched capitalists are bleeding us dry! What about our rights that we worked so hard for? We demand justice!'). But the executives announce these rules:

- One subscription right will be given for each existing share. A total of one million subscription rights will therefore be distributed to current shareholders (and only to them).
- Ten subscription rights are needed to buy one new share. There are one million rights and 100,000 new shares (£8M/£80) – a proportion of ten rights to each new share.
- Current shareholders can use their rights to buy new shares if they want to take part in the stock issue or they can sell their rights if they do not wish to participate. The subscription rights are to be listed on the stock exchange.

DIALOGUE	
Me:	How much will it cost existing shareholders to subscribe to the new stock issue?
Mrs Jones:	For every ten existing shares, they will receive ten subscription rights free of charge, which they can then use to buy one new share for £80. Since they only have to pay £80 for something that is trading at just under £100, they're happy.
Me:	Why 'just under £100'? I thought the market price of the share was exactly £100.

Mrs Jones:	That's right. But for £100 today, they would be buying one of the 'old' shares, which is now made up of one share + one subscription right. So a new 'bare' share is worth a little less. To find out how much, we have to subtract the value of the subscription right that is attached to the old shares.
Me:	And how do we work out the value of a subscription right?
Mrs Jones:	Since the subscription rights are listed on the stock market, the price depends on supply and demand.
Me:	Go on...
Mrs Jones:	There are two possibilities for new investors to buy this company's stock. Either they buy an existing share on the secondary market at the current share price (£100), in which case they will get a share and a subscription right. Or they buy ten subscription rights from a current shareholder and exercise them to buy a new share for £80. So the price of the right will settle where either option will cost the new investor exactly the same amount; in other words, a price where £100 – 1 right = £80 + 10 rights. According to our calculations, the equilibrium price of one subscription right will be £1.818.

Thus if current shareholders exercise their subscription rights, they will buy new shares at a preferential price (£80). If they don't exercise them, they will sell them and get 10 × 1.818 = £18.18 in cash (assuming they sell them in lots of ten). They will be happy in either case. As for new investors, either they will buy an existing share (£100) and sell the attached right for £1.82[8] or they will buy ten rights for £18.18 and then buy a new share for £80. In either case, they will end up paying the same amount:

$$100 - 1.82 = 80 + 18.18 = £98.18.$$

DIALOGUE	
Me:	But what if the share price drops to £90? Then it would be better to buy existing shares at £90!
Mrs Jones:	No, because the subscription rights are also listed, and they will fall to a price slightly below £1 each.
Me:	And what if the share price falls below £80?

---

8. We have rounded off the pence.

> Mrs Jones: Then the subscription rights will be worthless and the equity issuance will be a failure. Why pay £80 for new shares when the old ones are trading for less? But such a situation would mean that the share price had plummeted by 20% in a few days. That's not impossible, but it's extremely rare.

Finally, without getting into too much theory, let's look at two amusing points about equity issuances.

If it's for sale, it's too expensive

Shareholders are obsessed with the value of their capital. They scrutinize the CEO's every effort as he or she strives to push up the stock price. CEOs are 'indentured' to their shareholders insofar as their salary, their bonuses and even their job depend on shareholder satisfaction.

Given these circumstances, it follows from **signalling theory** that an equity issuance will be carried out only when the shares are overvalued on the stock market.

Why? Because if the shares are overvalued, current shareholders will push for new shares to be sold in order to bring in new investors at top dollar. On the other hand, if the shares are undervalued, the current shareholders will not want to devalue their capital by allowing new investors to get in at a cut-rate price. Thus an equity issuance will occur only if it serves the interests of the current shareholders; that is, if the share price is high. Otherwise, the company will raise capital through other means (debt, cash reserves, selling assets and so on).

Like a (money) serpent eating its own tail

One does not carry out an equity issuance just for the fun of it. This type of operation is done only when a company has a serious need for financing. This is the case, for example, when an important investment project is being considered. Studying an investment project involves capital budgeting and the calculation of the project's net present value (NPV, seen in Chapter 3).

We are now faced with the following paradox:

- A company will carry out an equity issuance only when it wants to invest.
- A company will invest only if the projected investment will create value.
- This future value creation increases the present value of the company.

- Therefore, a company that wants to invest has already incorporated the future gains from the investment in its stock price (that is to say, in an efficient market – see discussion below).

Thus, the new shares will be issued at a price (offering price) that already incorporates the future gains from the investment. New investors who buy these shares are in fact paying for the value of the company plus the net gains of the future investment... which their money helps to finance.

Payment of dividends

When a company is a cash cow, you have to milk it regularly. That's what dividends are for: they take earnings out of the company in the form of cash for shareholders. But dividends are not the only gain for shareholders. Shareholder compensation is made up of two things: capital gains (share price appreciation) and dividends (a share of net earnings paid in cash).

$$\text{Total shareholder return} = \text{Appreciation} + \text{Yield}$$

$$\text{Total shareholder return} = \frac{\left(\text{Share price}_{\text{final}} - \text{Share price}_{\text{initial}}\right)}{\text{Share price}_{\text{initial}}} + \frac{\text{Dividend}}{\text{Share price}_{\text{initial}}}$$

Let's look at La-Fing stock. It was trading at £40 on 1 January in the Year of the Dragon and at £42 on 31 December the same year. The Year of the Dragon being particularly bountiful, La-Fing stock paid a dividend of £1 per share. We obtain the following return:

$$\text{Total shareholder return} = \frac{\left(£42 - £40\right) + £1}{£40} = \frac{£2}{£40} + \frac{£1}{£40} = 5\% + 2.5\% = 7.5\%$$

On the contrary, shares that pay large dividends are called **value stocks**. These are often shares in companies operating in a mature sector or in an economy without growth.[9]

Johnny:	But we don't have to buy on 1 January and sell on 31 December, do we?
Mary:	No, it's just a convention so that we can calculate the return over a calendar year. The real return calculation will use the actual purchase and resale dates.
Johnny:	Looking at the return formula, we realize that it doesn't matter whether there's a 5% share price appreciation and a 2.5% dividend yield or a 1% share price appreciation and a 6.5% dividend yield; the result is still 7.5% for the shareholder.
Mary:	That's true mathematically speaking. But it doesn't mean that shareholders are indifferent to the breakdown of their revenues. Some of them prefer capital gains; others prefer dividends.
Johnny:	Why?
Mary:	There are several reasons, which we will read about next.

Differences between capital gains and dividends:

- First of all, there is a fiscal difference in many countries. Capital gains are taxed at a fixed rate, whereas dividends are considered as additional income and are taxed at the shareholder's marginal tax rate. Thus, a shareholder with a high income will be taxed more on dividends than a shareholder with less income, but both of them will pay capital gains tax at the same rate.[10]
- Second, we have to consider liquidity. A dividend is money paid in cash (usually once a year) – in other words, a regular cash flow. On the other hand, a capital gain is made only at the end of the investment, when the shareholder sells the stock.
- Finally, there is the matter of uncertainty. Dividends are certain because they are paid in cash. On the other hand, a capital gain (based on current stock prices) is only the *expectation* of a return. The share price fluctuates

---

9. These points were covered briefly in Chapter 4, in the section on risky assets.

10. In the UK, capital gains are taxed (as of 2014) at a fixed rate of 18% or 28%, depending on the total income of the individual (and under a certain threshold of capital gains, no tax is due). Dividends are taxed at another fixed rate, either 25% or 30.5%, depending again on the total income. Therefore, in the case of the UK, dividends and capital gains are taxed at different (but fixed) rates.

every day and until the shares are actually sold, the investor is not sure to receive this money.

DIALOGUE

Johnny: So, depending on the type of shareholder and the tax system in each country, there will be a preference for dividends or for capital gains, right? For example, people who want a regular annual income and are not in a high tax bracket will prefer stocks that pay large dividends.

Mary: That's the general idea, but in fact it's more complicated than that for two reasons. First, because an investor's goal is not necessarily the maximization of gains, but very often the diversification of risk. Second, because investors can set up their own 'customized' dividend policy, as we will see.

Dividend policy

> Whoever sows sparingly will also reap sparingly, and whoever sows generously will also reap generously.
>
> The Bible, 2 Corinthians 9:6

Some companies pay gushing dividends. Others abstain, hold all their liquid assets and pour them back into the company. But this won't necessarily attract thirsty investors to the former and abstemious ones to the latter. Indeed, whatever the dividend paid by a company, each shareholder can construct their own dividend policy as they like. Let's take the case of Arlecchino, who leads a lavish, extravagant lifestyle, and Pantalone, who is something of a tightwad. Imagine that Arlecchino holds Camelidae stock, which does not pay dividends (fate is sometimes cruel), while Pantalone has been afflicted with stock in Geyser Co., which regularly distributes its earnings. How will each of them handle their situation?

- Arlecchino needs money on a regular basis, but the stock he holds does not pay any dividends. (On the other hand, the stock price grows constantly, because no dividends are leaving the company.) No dividends, no problem: Arlecchino will regularly sell off a few shares to get the cash he needs.
- Pantalone has no use for the gurgling dividends of Geyser Co. He takes the money and buys more shares in the company.

Thus each of them uses the dividend policy to their advantage. Arlecchino transforms the growth in his shares into liquid assets and Pantalone reinvests his liquid assets in growth!

225

DIALOGUE

Johnny:	Wouldn't it be easier for Arlecchino to buy Geyser Co. stock and for Pantalone to invest in Camelidae stock?
Mary:	As we saw earlier, the decision to invest in a given stock is shaped primarily by the need to diversify risk.[11] Since investors can adjust the amount of their liquid assets at any time, they are not going to change the composition of their portfolio as a function of dividend payments.
Johnny:	But there are transaction costs, taxation...
Mary:	That's true, but that's always the case in finance. Nothing is free and (very) few things are exempt from taxes.

If we keep this idea of adjustment in mind, we can more easily understand certain stock market terms. A **stock dividend** is a dividend payment in the form of shares instead of cash.[12] The shareholders are free to sell these shares to get the cash or keep them for future growth. A **share repurchase** (or **buyback**) is when a company buys its own shares back from shareholders (those who are willing to sell) and cancels them (destroys them) so that it no longer has to pay dividends on those shares in the future.

DIALOGUE

Johnny:	In conclusion, a company's dividend policy doesn't matter very much...
Mary:	In large part, that is true, because everyone can reshape their liquid assets (though they must pay certain transaction fees). But it does not mean that companies act randomly. Quite simply, it's just like debt financing policy: there are several theories that explain why a company pays dividends (or borrows money), and what works for one company may be inappropriate for another.

How to earn money on the stock market

What between tipping the man who had brought us home, and paying for the broken sculls, and for having been out four hours and a half, it cost us a pretty considerable number of weeks' pocket-money, that sail. But we learned experience, and they say that is always cheap at any price.

Jerome K. Jerome, *Three Men in a Boat* (1889)

---

11. For a detailed discussion of diversification, jump in your time machine and travel back to Chapter 4.
12. The inland revenue service does not fall for this ruse and taxes these 'free' shares as income.

The stock market – more particularly, investments in the stock market – is a topic of conversation that interests everybody at fancy dinner parties. Just as in an action film, there are mouth-watering promises, bad guys in expensive suits, a lot of cut and thrust and a treasure at the end – for someone. But, like an action film, it is all too good to be true. Everything that we are going to say in this section has already been examined and demonstrated in thousands of research papers. But, just as there are still people around who refuse to believe that Elvis is dead (long live the King!), there will always be sceptics on these topics, too. They will no doubt make their brokers and their bankers rich, and perhaps that will trickle down to the economy.

We are going to begin with the highly controversial topic of market efficiency; then we will discuss human nature – particularly its most woeful flaws – and we will conclude with a few ideas that we hope will take the edge off these harsh realities.

The efficiency of financial markets – the concept and its avatars

The efficient market hypothesis has probably caused more ink to flow than the Shroud of Turin and the Dead Sea Scrolls combined. This is probably due to an incorrect use of the word 'efficiency'. Just as the word 'awful' has strayed from its original meaning (inspiring awe), 'efficiency' is today wrongly considered to be synonymous with perfection. And financial markets are far from perfect (otherwise, we would have heard about it). Let's first take a look at what economists mean by the notion of 'efficient markets'.

VIGNETTE |||||||||||||||||||||||||||||||||||||||||||||||||||||||||||||||||||||||||||||||||||||||||||||||||||||||||||||||||||||||||||||||||

Eddie plays the ponies. Sinclair does not. Eddie doesn't like Sinclair's highfalutin manners and Sinclair thinks Eddie is a little greasy: ideal conditions for a duel down at the track. Eddie draws first: 'Let's bet $100 on three races over at Belmont. Whoever loses has to shine the other guy's shoes for a year.'[13] Eddie follows a scientific approach: he has gathered all the past statistics on all the races, he knows every thoroughbred down to its hooves and his decisions are based on the analysis of all this information. Sinclair is a poet at heart, who follows his inspiration: he won't bet on Hoof Hearted; he favours Fleet-O'-Foot.

But despite Eddie's diligence and Sinclair's nonchalance, in an efficient market, Eddie won't win more than Sinclair. It's not a matter of good luck or bad luck. Information[14] spreads very fast in an efficient market, it is digested by hundreds of punters, and they place their bets on the basis of

---

13. This is an image, of course. Throughout this vignette, readers can replace 'punter' with stock market investor, 'horse' (and thoroughbred, nag, etc.) with stock, and 'bet' with market order (buy or sell).
14. The results of past races, articles in the racing news, tips and rumours about dodgy bookmakers. In short, everything that is published, said or implied is market information.

this information. As a result, the odds (market prices) already reflect all of this past information. Knowing that Blue Sky is actually a despondent nag is no longer useful because the information has already been incorporated in the current odds, which are long.

Three forms of efficiency

> *As a general rule, the most successful man in life is the man who has the best information.*
>
> Benjamin Disraeli (1804–81)

The term 'efficiency' refers here to the speed and efficiency with which information spreads. In an efficient market, investors are always on the lookout for new information and they immediately adjust the price they are willing to pay in relation to the news.

We can distinguish three types of efficiency:

- **Weak-form efficiency.** In this type of market, current stock prices already include all the history of past market prices. So if the 'horse racing' market is characterized by weak-form efficiency, there is no point in acquiring past results: they have already been incorporated into the punters' decisions, and hence in the current odds. This information will not therefore provide a decisive advantage in finding the right horse to bet on.

In a nutshell: in a market with weak-form efficiency, there is no point in 'betting' on the future change in a stock price based on past performance by doing what is known as a 'technical analysis', because all the information that past prices might contain is already reflected in the current stock prices.

- **Semi-strong-form efficiency.** When efficiency takes a semi-strong form, stock prices not only reflect the history of past prices, but also all public information. This means that as soon as the screens announce that 'Manure Melody (from Super Stud Stables) has just won the 4th', all the odds are instantly adjusted, raising the value of Super Stud's other horses, for example. If at that precise moment a punter says, 'hey, here's an interesting bit of news, I'm going to amble over to the track and place a bet on Glue Factory, from Super Stud Stables', he or she will already be too late: this information has already been incorporated into the odds on Glue Factory.

In a nutshell: in a market with semi-strong efficiency there is no point in making buy or sell decisions on the basis of corporate announcements published in the press, because all this public information has already been included in stock prices the moment it appears on screens.

- **Strong-form efficiency.** In a market with strong efficiency, stock prices reflect not only past prices and all public information, but also all hidden or insider information (not yet published). This means that the instant Joker the Jockey whispers in his horse's ear, 'I put some ground chilli pepper in your feed to pep you up,' all the punters rush to the betting windows to readjust the odds on Fire-in-the-Hole.

In a nutshell: in a strong efficiency market, there is no such thing as insider trading; as soon as confidential information comes into existence, it is automatically included in the stock prices.

This last form of efficiency – where all existing information is instantly included in stock prices – does not exist but represents an ideal objective to attain. After all, the objective of an efficient market is to have information circulating fluidly so that nobody can take advantage of it before anybody else.

But let's forget about strong efficiency as an objective. What is even more important is the current state of finance research. According to the vast majority of research studies, the major financial markets are now situated between the semi-strong and strong forms, which sets the bar very high if you are seeking market performance.

The impact of efficiency on investors

From the description of the three forms of efficiency, you get the impression that there is no point in reading the press; no sooner is a piece of information published (or conceived in somebody's mind) than 'poof!' the stock prices instantly adjust. In reality, a few paradoxes are necessary for this to work.

- **It is precisely because investors believe that markets are not efficient...that they contribute to their efficiency.** Indeed, given that Tweedledum thinks he can do better than Tweedledee, he reads the press, meditates at the bottom of the rabbit hole while listening to the business news on the BBC World Service and finally decides to buy a certain stock, telling himself, 'given what I've heard on the news, the stock price should rise.' But at the same time, with the same information and the same certainty, Tweedledee arrives at the opposite conclusion: the stock price will drop. Through their strategy of searching for information before deciding to buy or sell, Tweedledum and Tweedledee contribute to the process whereby this information is incorporated into the stock price. The greater the number of active stock market investors, the faster the information will be reflected in stock prices. In other words, because everyone thinks they are cleverer than everyone else, nobody is able to earn more than anyone else.

- **Anticipating the future ... turns it into the present**. We have seen that published information is instantly reflected in stock prices. The only way to earn money, then, is to find information that has not been published yet. As soon as the information is published, it will be too late, so it is better to act before everybody knows about it. Once again, Tweedledum and Tweedledee will be trying to find out what the next published result will be. And they will buy or sell stock on the basis of their forecasts. The action they take will thus affect stock prices even before the publication of the news, making the market even more efficient. We arrive at the following paradox: when a company publishes its results, the stock price may not even quiver because the information – even though it was not public – has already been anticipated and incorporated into the stock price.

DIALOGUE

Bull: But down at the racetrack, Eddie knows his stuff better than Sinclair! So why doesn't he win more than Sinclair?

Bear: He does win more often than Sinclair, but he doesn't benefit all that much from it for two reasons: costs and risk. Eddie may achieve better performance than Sinclair, but he will have extra costs (subscriptions, calculation time, multiplication of transactions, taxes, antidepressants) that will cancel out some of his winnings. And Eddie is not alone; thousands of punters do the same analyses with the same past information and so competition is extremely tough. Performance should therefore be measured after subtracting all the costs that have been incurred.

Bull: And the risk?

Bear: Let's take an example. Eddie's (net) gains are +9% on average, with a volatility of ±45%, while Sinclair earns +5% on average, with a volatility of ±15%.[15] Using these two figures we can calculate a risk/return ratio (RRR) for each of the two investors. For Eddie, RRR = 9/45 = 0.2 whereas for Sinclair, RRR = 5/15 = 0.3.

Bull: So?

---

15. Those with a porous memory are advised to take a trip back to Chapter 4.

Bear: *Comparatively, for one point of risk, Eddie earns a return of 0.2 points, whereas Sinclair earns 0.3 points. Using this indicator we calculate a **risk-adjusted return** and we find that Sinclair's relative performance is better than Eddie's in this case.*[16]

How to deal with an annoying relative

Families are like fudge – mostly sweet with a few nuts.

Anonymous

We all have a brother-in-law[17] who starts blowing his own trumpet at the end of a family dinner: 'I've made 12% a year on the stock market – that's even better than the FTSE 100! Aren't I clever!'

Here are three questions that will bring this pompous bore down a notch or two:

- 'Is the period of this investment greater than five years?' (If not, his performance may be down to sheer luck.)
- 'Is the performance you're bragging about calculated after deducting all costs and does it cover all the transactions?' (He might be 'overlooking' that disastrous investment in the Poco-Poco mines that put a dent in the overall performance of his portfolio.)
- 'Are your investments in the same risk category as an investment in the FTSE 100?' (If not, or if he's in doubt, he needs to calculate a risk-adjusted return before coming to any conclusions.)

If your brother-in-law answers 'yes' to these three questions (without lying), then either (1) he was lucky or (2) he belongs in the category of a statistical exception, like one in a million (you wouldn't think it to look at him, though, would you?). And in neither case is there anything to suggest that he will be able to pull off the same feat in the coming years.

---

16. There are other indicators that can be used to calculate the risk-adjusted return more accurately, but they are more complex to present, so let's stick with this one, if you don't mind.
17. Or a long-winded mother-in-law, a tiresome neighbour, a smarmy colleague …

DIALOGUE

Bull: So the market is perfect?

Bear: No, not really. The fact that everyone adjusts their bets does not mean that they all adjust them the same way. What we observe is that there is no single individual who wins every time.

Bull: Why isn't this very rapid adjustment that we observe (called **efficiency**) synonymous with perfection?

Bear: Because we were talking about an information market. What punters (or investors) look at is published information. But racing odds and stock prices are not the real value of horses and shares, they are **opinions on the value** of horses and shares. That is the very principle of a wager.

Bull: But these opinions are based on real phenomena, published results, dividend payment announcements. The opinion of the value should therefore be close to the real value, shouldn't it?

Bear: Normally there shouldn't be any difference between the two. But that's not always the case, for a number of reasons: information may not be circulating fluidly, there are also speculative bubbles, there are conflicts of interest and the human brain can make errors of judgement – for example, by deliberately ignoring certain information or by focusing too much on certain news items.[18]

Bull: So what does 'an efficient market' mean in economic terms?

Bear: It means that nobody will be better off than anybody else.

To conclude this section, **a market is said to be efficient when no individual is able, over the long term, to achieve a risk-adjusted performance that is better than the average of the other investors**. This notion of efficiency is therefore not synonymous with fair value. The fact that there are periodic **speculative bubbles** in the property market (everybody agrees that prices are too high and yet prices do not decrease) means that the assets are not correctly valued. This does not mean, however, that one individual can gain more than everyone else (at the same risk level). In this case, the market is considered efficient, in the economic sense of the term.

The phenomenon of speculative bubbles leads us to a new section – in which we will discuss the human factor.

---

18. This even happens to apparently rational people; in fact it happens especially to apparently rational people: since they have a high opinion of their own abilities, they feel confident in the efficacy of what they are doing.

Ode to human frailty

PIBCAK: Problem Is Between Chair And Keyboard

(Common acronym for user error in computing)

In this section we are going to discuss two typically human pitfalls. The first (agency conflicts) concerns delegation and the confidence that you may have in someone to whom you entrust your interests. The second (behavioural finance) concerns judgement and the errors that are commonly observed in human beings (yes, even you – no don't look at the person sitting beside you).

Agency conflicts

But to enable a prince to form an opinion of his servant there is one test which never fails; when you see the servant thinking more of his own interests than of yours, and seeking inwardly his own profit in everything, such a man will never make a good servant, nor will you ever be able to trust him.

Niccolo Machiavelli, *The Prince* (1532), chapter XXII

Most investors entrust the investment of their assets to an asset manager. Company treasurers solicit the advice of analysts and fund managers. Private individuals often ask a broker to recommend good investments. In these agency relationships, the question of the agent's compensation is crucial, for two reasons:

- First, the agent's compensation is a cost and this cost is taken out of the investment's performance.
- Second, the way agents are compensated will have an impact on their behaviour.

VIGNETTE ||||||||||||||||||||||||||||||||||||||||||||||||||||||||||||||||||||||||||||||||||||||||||||||||||||||||||||||||||||||||||||||||||||||||||||||||

Ophelia Damp is the owner of a two-bedroom semi in Bye-on-Tyme. She hires an estate agent to sell this 'outstanding, original property' by any means necessary. Their interests are ostensibly aligned: the estate agent gets a percentage of the selling price, so it would seem to be in her interest to sell the property for as much as possible, which is also Ophelia's objective.

Alas, there may be a number of imperfections in this agency relationship. For example, the agent might rather sell a lot of properties quickly (even at low prices) than sell fewer at higher prices (but slowly).[19] Or perhaps the agent's

---

19. Here we find the ratio of profit margin to asset turnover that was illustrated in Chapter 1.

income does not depend solely on the selling price, but also on other related services (getting exclusive agency listings, referring contractors and various building specialists). In short, Ophelia may end up taking a bath in this deal.

Agency theory explains the conflicts of interest between shareholders and CEOs, between bankers and shareholders, and, more generally, whenever a property owner mandates and pays an agent to act in his/her name. The agent will often attend to his/her own interests before looking after the interests of the mandating party.

SLICE OF LIFE

Christian Thibaut, a finance professor, entrusts his money to an asset manager. This manager invests it in securities that perform well: bionic opto-electronic companies — a growth sector if ever there was one! Two months later, the manager sell the shares (+1.3% gain) and shifts to cloning technology companies. Unfortunately, these shares do not perform well enough (+0.2%) and so, out of an abundance of caution, the manager sells them after a month and invests in property in Corsica. Three months later, he gets out of Corsican real estate (+0.5%) and puts the whole lot on explosives manufacturers, and so on.

You see what's happening here: the investor thinks that the individual performances are added together (1.3 + 0.2 + 0.5 = +2%), whereas in fact they are being amputated each time by commissions on buying and selling. Let's say the commission is 0.1% on each transaction: both sales and purchases. The investor therefore pays a commission of 2 x 0.1% = 0.2% each time the portfolio is shifted to a different stock. In our example there were three such adjustments, so the performance is only +2% – (3 x 0.2%) = +1.4% in five months.

And while the investor is shaking his head in sorrow at the dismal performance of his portfolio, the asset manager is cracking open the champagne to celebrate his six commissions.

Some asset managers are in the habit of 'turning over' portfolios quickly, which maximizes their interests as portfolio managers (getting commissions). But hopping from one stock to another amputates the final return earned by the investor.

The only reasonable way to ensure that the asset manager's interests are aligned with those of the investor is to index the manager's compensation to performance. Not only will asset managers be more motivated to ensure good performance, but in the event of a loss they will not be paid or they may even have to reimburse, from their own funds, part of the loss they have caused the client to bear.

We are not suggesting that asset managers are all a bunch of crooks. Our aim here is to urge readers to think about their own agency relationships. What is the compensation of your agents based on? Is this aligned with your own interests or, on the contrary, is there a possible conflict of interests?[20] And, in the event of the latter, which party is likely to lose out in this relationship?

Behavioural finance

> *I can calculate the movement of the stars, but not the madness of men.*
>
> Sir Isaac Newton (1642–1727), allegedly commenting on his heavy losses in the South Sea Company investment bubble

For centuries finance has been seen as a world of rational minds. While sociologists were working on crowd panic behaviour and psychologists were exploring the human mind, finance researchers developed scientific models based solely on reason – no fooling around for them! For a long time these financial models were taught, applied and used under a sacrosanct law: human beings are rational and they make decisions that optimize their satisfaction. You just have to run the model, said the finance researchers, and it will show us which direction to take. And then suddenly, in the latter half of the 20th century, there was a bolt from the blue: human beings are not entirely rational, sometimes they make decisions that are not entirely based on pure logic.

In this new field of study, known as **behavioural finance**, researchers have identified a number of psychological or cognitive biases that lead to decisions that are not perfectly rational. We will list a few examples and applications.

Availability heuristic

Behind this inelegant term lurks a mechanism of the human brain: we attribute much more importance to the things that we have heard a lot about. This causes us to pay too much attention to certain pieces of information in our decision-making process.

---

20. Your employees, your subordinates, your plumber, your banker – these are all agents that you have mandated.

In the stock market, a lot of investors are victims of the availability heuristic.
For example, investors hear much more about their own country than they
do about other countries. This prompts British investors, for example, to hold
a lot more British stocks than necessary. In so doing, they obviously fail to
benefit from the effects of international diversification – which is not optimal
for their portfolio. The human mind believes that the more visible it is, the
more important it is (or the more probable), which is not always the case.[21]

Overconfidence and confirmation bias

*With money in your pocket, you are wise, and you are handsome,
and you sing well too.*

Yiddish proverb

When the Cincinnati Kid wins several times in a row (on the stock market,
at poker, at the races) he starts to believe that he is smarter than the other
gamblers. This overconfidence will influence his risk-taking and his decision-making, usually in an adverse way. He thinks he can do no wrong.
The Kid will invest more and more and take bigger and bigger risks. He
will even go into debt in order to have more capital to invest. This overconfidence is often combined with another phenomenon: confirmation bias.
This means that the Kid will pay attention to information that confirms
his intuitions and will disregard – consciously or unconsciously – any information that does not fit his opinions. There is therefore a double effect at
work here: filtering of the information used and growing irrationality in the
decision-making process.

---

21. For example, what do you think the order of magnitude is of the US defence budget compared to
the Russian defence budget? Once you have answered, go and check the results on the book's website.

Poor management of losses

Most investors do not exhibit the same behaviour vis-à-vis their potential gains as their actual losses. They tend to hang on to shares that have lost 20%, but will sell shares that have gained 20%. They do something known as **mental accounting**, whereby they believe that losses must be offset by gains. That means that decisions concerning one stock are influenced by the performance of another stock. To be entirely rigorous in finance, one must make each decision independently of all others.

We have mentioned a few biases here, but there are many others. Our purpose has been to show that not only are financial markets not so simple (the complexity of the notion of efficiency), but on top of that the human mind is not as logical as we might like to believe.

So, how do you make money on the stock market?

DIALOGUE
Yin: To sum up, we have learned that nobody can achieve a risk-adjusted performance over the long term that is better than that of the other investors. This is the notion of market efficiency. In addition, there are human biases (conflicts of interests, errors of judgement) that reduce performance. This is all really depressing. You get the feeling that you can never win…
Yang: That's not quite true. Granted, you cannot earn more than everybody else, but when the stock market is rising everybody can make gains (with the risks inherent in the market, because we are dealing with risky assets).
Yin: There are a lot of people offering professional tips and techniques to make money on the stock market.
Yang: True. But be wary of people selling investment schemes. Think about agency theory and ask yourself what their compensation is based on.
Yin: So what is the 'best' way to invest?
Yang: The simplest strategy is one that is known as **index investing** (or **indexing**), whose principles we will now read about.

Index investing

The best investment strategy?

'Gone fishing'

When it comes to the stock market there are two kinds of people: those who do not believe in the efficiency of markets (the majority) and those who do (a minority, including the authors of this book). The former, who we will call 'active managers', try to outperform the market. They read the press, mull over the information for a long time and select a few promising stocks, much the way punters choose their ponies. The second category, who we will call 'passive managers', are convinced that nobody can outperform the market and so they decide to buy... the entire market! In short, the active managers are searching for a needle in a haystack, whereas the passive managers simply buy the entire haystack.

DIALOGUE

Yin: But it's very expensive to buy the entire market! Just for the UK, the FTSE 100 represents 100 stocks to buy, which means 100 commissions to pay! (Not to mention the FTSE 350 ...) And then your portfolio would not even be properly diversified, given that they are all British stocks...

Yang: Luckily, there are products called ETF (exchange traded funds) or trackers, which allow you to buy just one stock (a FTSE 100 tracker, for example) and it's as if you had bought all of the stocks (in this case, FTSE 100 stocks) and you also benefit from dividend payments. There are trackers for different areas of the world and different industries, which allow each individual to buy the haystack they want... without having to buy each wisp of hay individually.

Yin: So why doesn't everybody switch to indexed investing?

Yang: First, because the majority of people do not believe in market efficiency. Second, because in a market that was solely managed passively — an ovine market, one might say — investment opportunities would probably appear. Then it would be in the interests of individualists to spend time searching for needles where everybody else was buying haystacks. So, as we already mentioned when we spoke about market efficiency, it is precisely because the majority of investors are active that markets become efficient and hence passive investing becomes profitable.

8

Cash Management and Risk Management

Annual income twenty pounds, annual expenditure nineteen and six, result happiness.
Annual income twenty pounds, annual expenditure twenty pound ought and six, result misery.

Charles Dickens, *David Copperfield* (1850)

Introduction

The principal cause of business bankruptcy is to be found in the area of cash management. This ostensibly humble and, frankly, arithmetic discipline determines the short-term survival of the company. In the human body, each organ must be regularly supplied with blood, which carries vital oxygen. It is the same for companies: you have to make sure that the cash arrives on time and regularly. It is therefore the job of the company treasurer to avoid any incident that might lead to insolvency – a coronary thrombosis, which often proves fatal for a business.

In fact, the treasurer has several jobs, which we will describe one by one:

- to forecast cash receipts and disbursements in order to anticipate surpluses (which need to be invested) and shortfalls (which have to be financed);
- to identify foreign exchange risks, interest rate risks and other risks;
- to manage these risks.

Making a cash budget

Based in southern Italy, Rolls-Mops is a manufacturer of luxury automobiles that run on fish oil. This is a seasonal business and the company often suffers from cash flow problems. Its management wants to avoid expensive overdrafts and get a better handle on the fluctuations in its bank balance.

FINANCIALESE ——

A **cash flow** is any operation that has an impact on the company's bank balance. A cash flow is recognized on the date of receipt/disbursement. For example, a sale invoiced in June (payment to be made in three months) will be recorded on the books in June, but will generate a cash flow when the payment is actually received in September.

The **cash budget** (also known as a **cash flow budget**) is a table (usually monthly) that recapitulates expected receipts, planned disbursements and the company's **remaining cash balance**.[1] In short, it is 'everything that comes in minus everything that goes out' – in other words, exactly what a shopkeeper does every day with his or her cash register.

Business volume forecasts

> *Of course, you'll understand that this report is merely a synopsis of the expenditures. They are classified, however, and the receipts over there are arranged in such a way that Mr. Jones can very easily verify all the figures set out in the report. For instance, where it says 'cigars,' I have put down the total amount that went up in smoke.*

> George Barr McCutcheon, *Brewster's Millions* (1902)

The treasurer of Rolls-Mops has collected the following projections from the company's various department managers. This is a forecast for the next 12 months.[2]

A few important comments need to be made about Table 8.1. First, let's not forget that Rolls-Mops is going to manage its cash flow on the basis of these figures. It is important therefore to verify the quality of these forecasts – in other words, to check how realistic they are. Some managers may have padded their budgets, others may have been overly

---

1. The cash budget is not to be confused with the cash flow statement (see Chapter 1): the cash budget is a short-term forecast, based on the monthly or weekly figures, and contains more detail on cash receipts and cash expenses than the cash flow statement.
2. Reminder: the presentation of the income statement will differ depending on whether it follows a national GAAP framework or international accounting standards (IFRS). The appendix to Chapter 1 describes the two presentations and their differences.

cautious. The treasurer's first task is therefore one of communication and discussion, to make sure that he/she is working with reasonably reliable figures.[3]

Table 8.1 Projected income statement

	J	F	M	A	M	J	J	A	S	O	N	D	Total
Sales	600	900	1,200	1,500	1,100	800	500	900	1,600	1,700	1,000	800	12,600
– COGS	–480	–720	–960	–1,200	–880	–640	–400	–720	–1,280	–1,360	–800	–640	–10,080
Gross profit	120	180	240	300	220	160	100	180	320	340	200	160	2,520
– Marketing expenses	–60	–90	–120	–150	–110	–80	–50	–90	–160	–170	–100	–80	–1,260
– SG&A	–60	–60	–60	–60	–60	–60	–60	–60	–60	–60	–60	–60	–720
EBITDA	0	30	60	90	50	20	–10	30	100	110	40	20	540
– Depreciation	–30	–30	–30	–30	–30	–30	–30	–30	–30	–30	–30	–30	–360
EBIT	–30	0	30	60	20	–10	–40	0	70	80	10	–10	180
– Tax												–54	–54
Net earnings	–30	0	30	60	20	–10	–40	0	70	80	10	–64	126

Second, we observe that the business is seasonal. Certain lines on the income statement remain stable (SG&A, depreciation) while other items fluctuate a great deal: sales and the cost of goods sold, but also marketing expenses. Apparently, there are two very busy periods during the year: spring and autumn. It is obvious that significant cash flows (and probably requirements) will appear during these periods.

From this observation we conclude that there are in fact two horizons and two types of forecast. The annual figures, which appear in the shaded column on the right, are used to build the forecasts for the next three to five years and serve to formulate capital budgeting strategies (Chapter 3), financial policy (Chapter 5) and business acquisition strategy (Chapter 6). But these forecasts may be misleading because they do not show the monthly fluctuations in business volume, which lead to additional financing requirements. These annual forecasts must therefore be complemented by a 12-month rolling budget.

Finally, looking at Table 8.1, we see that we do not yet have a cash flow framework: this is an initial stage in which we have prepared a **projected income statement** with revenues and expenses. (Depreciation is shown in

---

3. We are firm believers in the GIGO (garbage in, garbage out) model. If a model, however elaborate, is fed with inaccurate figures, it will spit meaningless figures back out – nicely modelled figures, but meaningless just the same.

italics to remind us that these are accounting entries, not cash flows. They are needed to calculate corporate income tax, which we have placed in the last month of the year for the sake of convenience.)

Payment terms

Life on the Mediterranean has its charms... There are also certain downsides, such as the tendency of certain companies not to pay on delivery.[4] A delay of five days in a payment that is due at the end of the month may spark a cash flow crisis. (When such a situation arises, bankers have absolutely no sense of humour.) It is therefore crucial to have good knowledge of your customers' actual (historical) payment dates.

Aware of this, the Rolls-Mops company has tasked an underpaid young intern with calculating a few historical statistics. She comes up with the following information:

Table 8.2 Historical data on cash receipts and disbursements

Receipt of customer payments		Payments to suppliers	
–on delivery	10%	–on delivery	30%
– within 30 days	20%	– within 30 days	70%
– within 60 days	50%		
– within 90 days	20%		

This means that if we look at January's sales (€600), the company will receive €60 (10%) at the time of invoicing in January, then €120 (20%) in February. Sixty days after invoicing, half of the customers paid their bill (50% × 600 = €300 in March). And finally, the last January customers pay after 90 days, in April (20% × 600 = €120). From the viewpoint of Rolls-Mops' accountant, €600 in sales was recorded at the end of January; but from the viewpoint of the company treasurer, the income from those sales has been received over the course of four months. In preparing the cash budget we will adopt the viewpoint of the treasurer, who doesn't count his chickens until they are safely deposited in the company bank account.

---

4. Once they understand how payment terms work, all the CFOs seem to embrace the Mediterranean way. 'When in Rome ...'

Preparing the cash budget

Taking deferred payments into account

> *A customer placed an order with a manufacturer for a large amount of goods worth a great deal of money.*
> *Noticing that the previous invoice hadn't been paid, the collections manager called the customer, saying:*
> *'We can't ship your new order until you pay for the last one.'*
> *The customer's response was succinct: 'In that case, please cancel the order. We can't wait that long.'*
>
> Anonymous

We will use the above-mentioned historical payment data in preparing Table 8.3 of cash receipts and disbursements.

Table 8.3 Cash receipts and disbursements

	J	F	M	A	M	J	J	A	S	O	N	D	Total
Payments received during the month													
– on delivery	60	90	120	150	110	80	50	90	160	170	100	80	1,260
– delivered previous month (M – 1)	140	120	180	240	300	220	160	100	180	320	340	200	2,500
– delivered in month M – 2	450	350	300	450	600	750	550	400	250	450	800	850	6,200
– delivered in month M – 3	200	180	140	120	180	240	300	220	160	100	180	320	2,340
Total receipts	850	740	740	960	1,190	1,290	1,060	810	750	1,040	1,420	1,450	12,300
COGS paid out during the month													
– on delivery	–144	–216	–288	–360	–264	–192	–120	–216	–384	–408	–240	–192	–3,024
– delivered the previous month (M – 1)	–392	–336	–504	–672	–840	–616	–448	–280	–504	–896	–952	–560	–7,000
Total disbursements	–536	–552	–792	–1,032	–1,104	–808	–568	–496	–888	–1,304	–1,192	–752	–10,024

Looking at the payments received, we find €60 invoiced in January paid on delivery in January, €120 invoiced in January paid in February, €300 invoiced in January paid in March and so on. The shaded boxes are sales invoiced in October, November and December of the previous year.[5]

---

5. These sales were not mentioned in the projected income statement (Table 8.1), but they can be found in the files available online.

DIALOGUE	
Nest Egg:	Why is it that the totals for the year in Table 8.3 don't match the totals of Table 8.1?
Unhatched Chicken:	Because of the payment terms (deferred payment period). That's the whole point of making this cash budget. Table 8.1 showed sales and purchase forecasts month by month, reasoning in terms of delivery and invoicing, not payments. But because of payment terms (deferred payment period), we see that the payments for January's sales (€600) are received in January, February, March and April. But what counts for the treasurer are obviously the amounts actually received.
Nest Egg:	So, comparing the two tables, we observe that the company plans to invoice €12,600 in 2016 (projected income statement), but for the same year only €12,300 will actually be received, the remaining €300 to be received the following year.
Unhatched Chicken:	That's right. To be precise, 2016 will also count payments received for some sales made in 2015 (shaded boxes), but the payments for sales made in October, November and December 2016 are missing because they will be paid at the beginning of 2017. The book amount (€12,600) is therefore not equal to the cash amount (€12,300) because we are reasoning in terms of a 12-month rolling forecast.

Other disbursements

We have dealt with the delicate part: the deferred cash receipts caused by payment terms. We will now build the rest of the cash budget. We consider that the marketing and administrative expenses (essentially payroll costs and materials) are paid out in the same month they are recorded on the books – in other words, paid on delivery. This gives us the following cash budget:[6]

Table 8.4   Cash budget

	J	F	M	A	M	J	J	A	S	O	N	D	Total
Payments received	850	740	740	960	1,190	1,290	1,060	810	750	1,040	1,420	1,450	12,300
– COGS paid	–536	–552	–792	–1,032	–1,104	–808	–568	–496	–888	–1,304	–1,192	–752	–10,024
– marketing expenses	–60	–90	–120	–150	–110	–80	–50	–90	–160	–170	–100	–80	–1,260
– SG&A expenses	–60	–60	–60	–60	–60	–60	–60	–60	–60	–60	–60	–60	–720
– Tax												–54	–54
Cash flow	194	38	–232	–282	–84	342	382	164	–358	–494	68	504	242

---

6. This is an assumption. For further details, see our final remarks on preparing a cash budget.

Nest Egg:	We see that the cash flows fluctuate. There is a surplus in December and January and again in June–July–August. On the other hand, there are two periods of deficit: March–April–May and September–October.
Unhatched Chicken:	Yes, those are the two seasonal peaks in sales. And since those sales cause production expenses that are paid quickly, the company finds itself with less cash receipts than disbursements.
Nest Egg:	So they have to fill those gaps in the cash flow, right?
Unhatched Chicken:	Yes, but these are not the final amounts. In fact, the surplus generated in some months can absorb part of the deficit. So we have to take a cumulative approach: add together the results from the different months.

Calculating bank balances

Let's suppose that at the end of last year (2015) the company had a positive bank balance of €15. We begin with this amount and we calculate the company's bank balance at the end of each month.

Table 8.5 Company bank balance

	J	F	M	A	M	J	J	A	S	O	N	D
Opening balance	15	209	247	15	−267	−351	−9	373	537	179	−315	−247
+ Cash flows	194	38	−232	−282	−84	342	382	164	−358	−494	68	504
= Closing balance	209	247	15	−267	−351	−9	373	537	179	−315	−247	257

Thus, in January the company started with €15 in its bank account and the difference between cash receipts and disbursements resulted in a surplus of €194, which was added to the bank balance: 15 +194 = €209. This €209 is the amount carried over to the beginning of February, and so on.

| Nest Egg: | So the closing monthly balance also includes the cumulative amount of all cash receipts and disbursements. For example, January and February added money to Rolls-Mops' bank account. |

Unhatched Chicken:	That's good, because March's cash flow is negative. With the bank balance of €247 the company can absorb the -€232 negative cash flow in March and still manage to end the month with a positive balance of €15.
Nest Egg:	But then April and May are not stellar months...
Unhatched Chicken:	Everything is relative. The company sold a lot of goods, which is why is has temporary cash flow deficits. When the payments are received for those sales, the company will return to a balanced position in early July.

With these bank balance calculations, we have just finished Rolls-Mops' cash budget for the year 2016. Before looking at the various ways of covering cash flow deficits, we have a few suggestions on how to calculate a cash budget.

Final remarks on cash budgets

Never let the future disturb you. You will meet it, if you have to, with the same weapons of reason which today arm you against the present.

Marcus Aurelius (121–80 AD), *Meditations*

The example we have given here is relatively simple. Depending on the complexity of the company's business, the cash budget may be quite a lot more complicated. Here is some general advice:

- Be rigorous so as not to forget anything. This means thoroughly examining the company's bank statements for a year. The treasurer does not want to run an overdraft because one payment was overlooked. All cash expenses and all cash receipts must be included: VAT payments, payroll taxes, social security contributions and other taxes, interest paid and bank charges, and generally any operation that has an impact on the bank account. If investments are planned, these amounts should be counted as disbursements on the actual date of payment. Any new financing (loans, a bond or equity issue) should be counted in the cash receipts. Likewise, loan repayments and dividend payments are cash disbursements that must be counted.
- Pay attention to the precise dates. As we have seen, the date an item is recorded on the books may be very far from the effective date of the cash

flow. The latter is what counts here. Likewise, social security contributions will not have the same impact if paid quarterly or monthly. The same goes for taxes and any kind of direct debit.

- Adapt the budget to the company's business volume. Some companies are happy with a monthly cash budget; others have so much volume that they prefer to operate on a weekly or even a daily basis. Public holidays must also be taken into consideration as well as the other days on which banks or financial markets are closed.
- Adjust the cash budget regularly. Late payments will occur; cash receipts must be adjusted accordingly and the effect on the bank balance estimated. It is always good to have fairly flexible financial resources available and to maintain a minimum, safety balance at the end of each month. As often happens in finance, very precise optimization (aiming for a bank balance of zero, for example) may produce minor savings but may lead to much larger additional costs in the event of a postponed payment.

Balancing the cash budget

The key word here is 'simplicity'. Of course, you have to think about investing cash surpluses and covering deficits, and we will take a look at a few ways of doing that. But you should forget about complex optimizations straight away: they often cause you to waste time and can even lead to a loss of efficiency because they are just too technical. In other words, you don't need a tractor designed by NASA to plough a field. We will therefore begin with a few non-financial ways of optimizing your cash flow.

Non-financial ways of managing cash flows

The simplest way to manage your cash flow is to negotiate the payment terms. This is easier than you may think, provided that you remember a few simple points:

- Customers may agree to speed up their payments, just as suppliers may allow you additional time to pay, but these external parties would like to receive a financial *quid pro quo*: a rebate or a higher price.
- So the question becomes: how much of a rebate can I offer before this deal ceases to be beneficial to my company? The answer is simple enough: collecting the money more quickly helps to avoid bank fees on an overdraft. If the agreed rebate is greater than the estimated fees, then it is not worth it. So you have to estimate the savings and the costs, but these are specific to each partner.

- You are therefore advised to perform a financial analysis of your customers and suppliers, paying particular attention to the following questions: what are their own payment terms for customers and suppliers (and their working capital requirements)? What are their margins? – in other words, how sensitive are they to a variation in price? Do they have cash flow problems or do they regularly have cash surpluses? Is their business seasonal?

- This approach also works for cash flow deficits. Rolls-Mops has surpluses from December to February and from July to September. Rather than invest the cash in the money market, the company could negotiate with its suppliers, offering to pay them on delivery during those months in exchange for rebates. Given the low interest rates offered by money market securities, this strategy may be quite advantageous. Finance plays only a small role in what we are discussing here; rather, it is a matter of reasoned negotiation. You have to find out which factors will influence your business partners' decisions so that you can offer them a solution that will also benefit them.[7]

Short-term borrowing

> *Revolving credit is like a revolving door: if you stay in it too long, you get dizzy and lose your balance.*

There are two periods in the year when Rolls-Mops runs a cash deficit: April to May and October to November. It is therefore not necessary for them to obtain **short-term debt financing** for the entire year, because it would not be used during the other months – but the company would still incur borrowing costs. The simplest financing solution is an **authorized overdraft**. In this case the company asks its bank for temporary overdraft protection and pays interest on the amounts actually used. But when a company is faced with irregular demand (seasonal business), it is better to negotiate a more systematic and less costly solution: a **revolving line of credit**. Once this has been set up, the company can have a negative bank balance without notifying the bank as long as it does not exceed the established limit.

The treasurer is particularly attentive to costs: the interest rate applied by the bank may be fixed or variable (indexed to a market indicator) and several bank charges are added depending on the operation.

---

7. Negotiations with suppliers and customers are not always a zero-sum game, where one party wins and the other loses. A supplier may have a cash flow surplus and low margins. Such a supplier will be amenable to a deal involving longer payment terms in exchange for a higher price, and both companies will benefit from the new arrangement.

Short-term secured borrowing

> *He who drinks on credit gets twice as drunk.*
> Greek proverb

Just as grandpa used to leave his pocket watch with his 'uncle'[8] when times were tough, companies can get short-term financing by putting up certain assets as collateral. This could be either **inventory pledged as security** on a loan or **accounts receivable financing** (also known as **invoice discounting**). Basically, the company says to the bank: 'we have an asset (inventory, receivables) that is worth money and we would like to obtain an equivalent amount in financing – until the asset has been converted into cash.'

SLICE OF LIFE ●
Rolls-Mops has just delivered a 'Silver Herring' Rolls to a customer (invoice = 100) and expects payment in 90 days. But it is April and times are tough. Rolls-Mops' treasurer goes to see their banker with the invoice for 100. The bank discounts the invoice, which means it lends Rolls-Mops the sum of 98 for three months. This is a loan, not a sale. Rolls-Mops still owns the receivable and is responsible in the event that the customer does not pay on time. If the customer pays, the bank takes the 100, which covers the loan (98) and the discounted amount (100 - 98 = 2 for three months). The bank's interest charges have thus been paid up front. If the customer does not pay the invoice, the bank will go after the more solvent of the two: the customer who has not paid what he owes or Rolls-Mops, which still has to pay back the loan!
● ●

These operations are a kind of secondary financing, because the assets were already financed when they first entered the business. They are a type of bridge loan, intended to 'span the gap' while waiting for a payment.

DIALOGUE	
Frank:	So ultimately what is the difference between receivables financing and a short-term loan?
Ava:	Receivables financing is like a secured loan because the asset serves as collateral. There is less risk for the bank and so the interest rate will be lower than for a normal short-term loan (unsecured).
Frank:	Wouldn't it be possible to sell the receivables outright?

---

8. 'Uncle' is old-fashioned slang for a pawnbroker.

Ava:	Yes, that's called factoring, but then it's no longer a loan; it's a sale.
Frank:	So why don't companies get rid of all their receivables by selling them to a factor?
Ava:	First of all, there are financial conditions. For an invoice of 100, a factoring company may be willing to pay only 90. The difference has to cover the cost of financing (2) and the risk of non-payment (8), because there is a transfer of ownership. That said, factoring is very practical and some companies use it all the time. It saves the company from having to deal with accounts receivable management, payment terms, payment reminders and all the associated cash flow problems. But – and this is the second reason – the downside is that the company loses direct contact with its customers, who now deal only with the factoring company.
Frank:	'Losing contact' with certain customers may be a blessing in disguise...
Ava:	That's true, but this blessing also comes with a cost that is not only financial.

In conclusion, in the area of short-term borrowing, the treasurer needs to be attentive to all the costs – financial and non-financial – of the solutions envisaged. Remember this: frantically seeking savings is often a wrong-headed quest. The quality of the relationship with partners (customers, suppliers, bankers) may not be directly quantifiable, but it matters a great deal when the company is going through a tough patch. After all, what is a monthly fee if it helps maintain a relationship that will one day save the company from going bankrupt?

Short-term investments

Once again, simplicity is the operative word. The treasurer is not trying to make fabulous gains from short-term investments; he/she just does not want the money to lie dormant. Apart from the non-financial solutions already mentioned, the simplest investments are interest-bearing accounts or money market securities (mutual funds or OEICs, for instance). The treasurer will be particularly attentive to the **liquidity** of these investments: the ability to get out of them quickly and without cost. Term deposits may offer an attractive interest rate, but you cannot withdraw the money even if cash flow incidents occur (a customer non-payment, an urgent need to buy raw materials, and so on). So this solution can only really be used in businesses where the schedule of cash receipts and disbursements is under control. Likewise, a mutual fund is liquid as long as the shares can be

250

converted into cash quickly, but their price will fluctuate depending on market constraints.

Conclusion on financing and investments

SLICE OF LIFE •
Arlecchino is proud of himself: he has invested his cash surpluses in a term deposit that pays 4% annually. Of course, there are occasional incidents when a customer does not pay on time and the funds cannot be accessed, but Arlecchino has an authorized overdraft (8% interest rate) that enables him to deal with these temporary inconveniences. At the end of the year Arlecchino tallies up his cash budget: income from the term deposit = €100, bank charges and interest on overdraft = -€120. Conclusion: Arlecchino would have been better off leaving the money dormant in the company's current account.
• •

A treasurer's job is not to earn money, but to meet payment obligations. The company's bank account must remain solvent at all times. Unexpected events, which are inevitable, will not cost the company too much as long as a margin of safety has been maintained. The notion of **opportunity cost** is particularly relevant here. And this is the perfect segue to talking about the various cash flow risks and how they are managed by the treasurer.

Risk management

Although the treasurer is not the only one managing the company's risks, there are a number of typical risks associated with this function. The treasurer is also the one who uses traditional risk management tools the most. We will begin by looking at a few types of risk and then the risk management methods.

Different types of risk
Foreign exchange risk

SLICE OF LIFE •
Rolls-Mops is in the process of selling a special edition 'Red Herring' Rolls to a wealthy American mystery writer, Wanda 'Reelemin' Fischer, for €500K. Fischer wants to pay in dollars. The current exchange rate is €1 = $1, which means that the price of the car in dollars is also 500K. Fischer signs the purchase agreement and offers to pay in three months, which Rolls-Mops accepts — in so doing instantly exposing itself to a foreign exchange risk.
• •

This example illustrates two points:

- One is tempted to think that there is a foreign exchange risk when a company is faced with a currency that is not its own. Here, Rolls-Mops, a European company trading in euros, agrees to a contract in dollars.
- But if Rolls-Mops had asked for payment on delivery, there would be no foreign exchange risk because the $500K would be immediately converted into euros at today's exchange rate and would equal €500K. There is a foreign exchange risk when there is uncertainty about the final exchange rate. In this example, nobody knows how much the dollar will be worth in three months.

FINANCIALESE ───────────────────────────────────

The legal tender of a country is known as its **currency**. Currencies are represented by three-letter abbreviations: GBP for the British pound, EUR for the euro, USD for the American dollar, CAD for the Canadian dollar, JPY for the Japanese yen, CNY for the Chinese yuan and so on.

A currency's value relative to another country's currency is given as an **exchange rate**. In **forex** or **FX** (foreign exchange) parlance, we speak of **currency pairs**, such as the British pound/American dollar pair (GBP/USD) or the euro/dollar pair (EUR/USD). The **majors** (the currency pairs that are traded the most) have been given nicknames by forex traders, such as **cable** (GBP/USD) and **fiber** (EUR/USD).

The **spot exchange rate** is the rate at which the currencies are currently trading. The **forward exchange rate** is a future rate that is determined by forex traders, bankers and currency markets and is used in drawing up forward contracts (we will discuss this notion in detail later).

Let's imagine that Rolls-Mops has sold its 'Red Herring' car and the customer pays the $500K after three months. There are three possibilities:

- The euro/dollar pair remains the same and the exchange rate is still $1 = €1, in which case Rolls-Mops gets $500K = €500K and the treasurer can sleep the sleep of the just.
- The euro has depreciated in relation to the dollar and the euro/dollar pair has shifted to a spot exchange rate of, say, $1 = €1.10. In this case, Rolls-Mops will get $500K × 1.10 = €550K, which is made up of the €500K selling price and a €50K foreign exchange gain. The Rolls-Mops treasurer will go out to the local *trattoria* to celebrate and tell everyone that it was all planned and he has everything under control.
- The euro has appreciated, such that the euro/dollar pair has shifted to $1 = €0.80 (for example). Rolls-Mops receives $500K, which is converted

into 500K × 0.80 = €400K, broken down into the €500K selling price and a €100K foreign exchange loss. The treasurer doesn't sleep a wink because this little farce has eaten into (if not obliterated) any profit made on the sale of the car and the CEO is after his blood.

Foreign exchange risk is therefore made up of two components: the time period (already mentioned) and volatility (seen in Chapter 4) or fluctuation. A currency whose value fluctuates a great deal over time carries a greater foreign exchange risk than a 'stable' currency.[9] These risk components (time and volatility) are shared by all the risks presented below and will help us understand risk management methods and tools.

Interest rate risk

'Standard and poor': your life in a nutshell.
'Moody': how your credit score makes you feel.
'Fitchety': your physical state while waiting to find out your credit score.

SLICE OF LIFE •
Rolls-Mops financed its factory with a fixed-rate loan at 4.5% over 12 years. Its main competitor in the market of fish-oil powered cars, Turbot-Traction, has just overhauled and updated its production lines (and its fishing lines) with a long-term loan at a variable interest rate of three-month Euribor + 0.5%.

In the following months, the three-month Euribor drops from 4.5% to 3%. Turbot-Traction now pays 3 + 0.5 = 3.5% on its debt. Rolls-Mops executives are kicking themselves in the gills; they would have loved to benefit from the drop in interest rates!

Then the trend reverses. The three-month Euribor rises to 5%. Turbot-Traction is now paying 5 + 0.5 = 5.5% interest on its debt. Rolls-Mops executives rub their fins together with glee.
• •

This ichthyologic parable teaches us two things:

- Interest rate risk primarily concerns variable rate financing. When a company takes out a variable rate loan (variable rates are often more attractive than fixed rates), it exposes itself to the risk of fluctuations in

---

9. Remember that the value of a currency is always expressed in relation to another currency. The Swiss franc/euro pair (CHF/EUR) may be stable, but the Swiss franc expressed in relation to another currency (the yen, for instance: CHF/JPY) may fluctuate more.

its borrowing costs. The monthly interest payments can change, which leads to a cash flow problem.

- But fixed rates also have their drawbacks. Rolls-Mops has secured an unchangeable rate for itself by contract, but it cannot benefit from fluctuations in the market even when they would be favourable.

These two companies are both faced with interest rate risk, each in its own way. And this issue goes beyond cash management, because it also concerns their cost of capital. This is therefore a problem that affects financial policy and the expected returns calculation (Chapter 5).[10]

FINANCIALESE

Variable rate loans are based on market interest rates. The best known rate in Europe is the **Euribor** (Euro Interbank Offered Rate): this is the rate at which major European banks will lend funds (in euros) to each other. The Euribor fluctuates in relation to supply and demand for bank capital, with several rates depending on the duration of the loan: one-month, three-month, six-month Euribor, and so on. For currencies other than the euro, the **Libor** (London Interbank Offered Rate) is used.

A variable rate is generally made up of a base rate (the reference rate, usually the Euribor or Libor) and a **spread** (or **risk premium**), expressed in hundredths of a percentage point or **basis points** (100 basis points = 1%). In our example, Turbot-Traction borrows at Euribor + 50 basis points (+0.5%). The premium is a function of the company's credit risk, which is expressed in a **credit rating**. Companies with the best credit rating (AAA) can obtain financing at the Euribor rate, that is, without paying a premium. They borrow as if they were high-quality banks. The lower the credit rating (BB, C) the higher the risk premium in basis points and the more costly the loan.

Other types of risk

The other types of risk can be grouped together in two categories: risks that depend on market price fluctuations and the vast shapeless magma of all other risks.

Examples of **risks that depend on market prices** are:

- foreign exchange risk and interest rate risk, as we have already seen;
- procurement risk/risk of raw material price fluctuations;
- energy supply risk (availability, price).

---

10. Another issue, which exceeds the scope of this book, concerns the value of assets. Since an asset is valued as the present value of its future cash flows, any fluctuation in interest rates will have an impact on asset valuation. This concerns financial institutions that are subject to the Basel Accords as well as listed companies that comply with IFRS reporting standards. A glimpse of this is given at the end of Chapter 2 (bond price fluctuation).

Given that these risks concern organized markets, they may be covered by financial products that have been developed for these markets or by non-financial techniques.

Examples of risks that do not depend on market prices are:

- political risk in a country or region: risk of nationalization, limitations on the transfer of funds, corruption and so on;
- social risk: strikes, social movements, worker grievances;
- environmental and societal risk: pollution, media coverage of bad practices, scandals.

As the latter risks do not stem from price fluctuations in the market, they are more likely to be handled through insurance or non-financial techniques.

Various methods for managing risk

Just as we did for cash management, we are going to present the non-financial methods of managing risk first; then we will move on to financial risk management tools. To illustrate these ideas, we will return to the Rolls-Mops case. The company is negotiating a sale with a $500K payment to be made in three months. Given that the company operates in euros, it may find itself facing a foreign exchange risk and is wondering how best to protect itself.

Non-financial risk management techniques

Choose the invoice currency

Rolls-Mops can eliminate any foreign exchange risk by insisting that payments be made in euros. This means that the foreign exchange risk will be shifted to the buyer, Wanda Fischer, because she will have to change her dollars into euros. To compensate Wanda, Rolls-Mops may agree to lower its price slightly at the time of the sale, which would be better than making a bigger loss later due to an unanticipated currency fluctuation.

Index the selling price to the foreign exchange rate

If the buyer insists on paying in dollars, Rolls-Mops may negotiate a clause in the contract, stipulating that in the event of a significant variation in the euro/dollar exchange rate, the price in dollars will be adjusted. For example, if the exchange rate shifts to \$1 = €0.90, the price to pay will be adjusted to €500/0.9 = \$555, so that Rolls-Mops will receive an amount in dollars that is still equal to €500K. One incentive for the buyer to accept this clause might be to have this adjustment work both ways: if the exchange rate goes to \$1 = €1.12, for instance, the price to pay will be €500/1.12 = \$446K. This still equals €500K, but the buyer will pay less in her currency.

Compensation

If Rolls-Mops regularly carries out transactions in regions that accept dollars, there is no need to convert the $500K into euros. They can just keep this money on hand until they need to pay for a future transaction in dollars (and possibly invest it in the meantime). This does not solve the cash flow problem, though, and Rolls-Mops may find itself running an overdraft in euros during this time. The company will have to manage **multi-currency cash flows,** while trying to make sure that receipts in dollars match disbursements in dollars, but now the foreign exchange risk will concern only the difference between receipts and disbursements. Ideally the company would have a supplier that accepts dollars, so that when a customer pays in dollars, they can use those receipts to offset payments to that supplier.

These risk-avoidance techniques – which are not limited to foreign exchange risk – work by either eliminating the risk or shifting it to the customer. They are not always applicable and they involve certain additional costs, but they may be less costly, both in time and money, and just as effective as complex financial techniques.

The classic financial technique: hedging

> For sale: one magnificent bear skin, to be delivered on the first day of the hunting season.
> (A deposit is payable in advance)
>
> L'Os à Moëlle (editor-in-chief: Pierre Dac) (1938)

In the financial world, 'hedging' means making a contract or an investment in order to reduce potential future losses. Hedging is an ancient idea; we find traces of it in Greek antiquity. The notion is inseparable from the concept of futures markets. We will first present these markets and then describe the differences between them and **spot markets** or **cash markets.**

In fact, we have already talked a good deal about spot markets without naming them as such; when we talk about the stock market and the stocks listed on an exchange, we are implicitly referring to a spot market, which is an immediate transaction market. There is a spot market for stocks, bonds, currency, raw materials (**commodities**) and just about everything else whose prices obey the laws of supply and demand.[11]

---

11. Financial markets regularly publish price listings for calves, heifers, feeder calves and other cattle. As you are reading these lines, somewhere in Scotland, there may be a future Rob Roy building an empire out of horns.

Alongside the spot markets, whose function is to facilitate immediate transactions, there are **futures markets**, which handle future transactions. If someone wants to buy cacao in six months, they can place an order today ('open a position', in the lingo) on a raw materials futures market to be fulfilled six months from now. These futures markets replicate most of the products listed on spot markets, especially raw materials, currencies (foreign exchange), gold and other metals. Futures prices are set and fluctuate during the day depending on anticipated future supply and demand. At times there is a lot more activity on the futures market than on the spot market for the same products. So if you want to look clever at a cocktail party when someone asks you the exchange rate for the dollar, just answer: 'Which exchange rate? The spot rate? The three-month forward rate? The six-month forward rate?'[12]

Following this cultural interlude, we return to the notion of hedging.

SLICE OF LIFE ●

Rolls-Mops is supposed to receive a $500K payment in three months. The treasurer has no desire to spend 90 sleepless nights glued to his computer screen watching the fluctuations in the euro/dollar exchange rate, so he calls the bank and immediately opens a forward contract to sell dollars.

The bank guarantees a three-month forward rate of, let's say, $1 = €0.97. Thus the treasurer knows that in three months' time he will sell the $500K to the bank and will receive 500 × 0.97 = €485 in exchange. Three months go by. On payment day, the spot exchange rate is $1 = €0.91, but the treasurer doesn't care; he's covered by the forward contract. He will get €0.97 per dollar as planned (€485).

● ●

DIALOGUE	
Greenback:	First of all, how did their banker arrive at an exchange rate of $1 = €0.97?
Sterling:	He looked up the currency forward rates, specifically the EUR/USD three-month forward rate.
Fiber:	But what certainty does the banker have about what will happen in three months' time?

---

12. Today's homework: get a daily newspaper (preferably a financial one) and find the three-month and six-month forward exchange rates for the euro/dollar pair. Compare these with the spot exchange rate and deduce what investors are anticipating for the coming months.

Cable:	He has no certainty and he is not trying to predict the future. Imagine that he's looking at his screens and he sees that the three-month forward rate for the EUR/USD pair is at $1 = €0.99 today. This is the rate that traders have agreed on today through bidding and asking. The banker decides to make two euro cents of profit and offers Rolls-Mops a forward contract at $1 = €0.99 - €0.02 = €0.97. If Rolls-Mops agrees, the banker immediately opens a selling position on the futures market for $500K at €0.99. He is thus certain to receive $500K from Rolls-Mops and will be able to sell it on the market for €0.99 per dollar (€495K). Out of this sale he will keep 500K × 0.02 = €10K to pay for his cigars and will in due course transfer 500K × 0.97 = €485K to Rolls-Mops.

The treasurer loses a little on this deal in comparison with payment-on-delivery terms. At the time of the car sale, the euro/dollar pair was at $1 = €1 and Rolls-Mops wanted €500K for the car. In the end, though, the treasurer will receive only €485K. But at least he is certain to receive this amount, down to the last penny, thanks to the contract with the bank. Of course, the treasurer could have ignored the risk and not hedged against it. But in the example we have given, the spot exchange rate after three months is $1 = 0.91. If the treasurer hadn't hedged, he would have received $500K in three months' time and then would have had to convert it at the new spot rate: 500 × 0.91 = €455K, so he would have lost even more.

DIALOGUE	
Sterling:	In fact, the solution he chose was the best of a bad bunch...
Fiber:	Umm, you say that with hindsight, but three months earlier he didn't know that the exchange rate was going to plummet to €0.91.
Cable:	Right, so what's the decision-making rule here?
Greenback:	Always hedge. Never rely on luck! By hedging, the treasurer knows right from the outset how much he will get in euros three months down the road. It's a long road and anything could happen. The treasurer can then record this amount in his cash budget and it keeps him from losing sleep and getting grey hair over it.

Fiber:	What if, after the three months have passed, the exchange rate is $1 = €1.05 but he can't take advantage of this attractive spot rate, because he has a contract with the bank at a fixed exchange rate of €0.97? Won't the treasurer be kicking himself?
Sterling:	Not if he's sensible. By hedging, he solved his problem and he moved on.

As we can see, hedging is reassuring because it establishes the terms of the contract right from the outset. But it is also a gilded cage. Whatever happens to the spot rates, the contract must be fulfilled according to the initial terms – which, depending on events, may be advantageous or disadvantageous.

Let's add one more key element: if the customer does not pay the $500K at the end of the three months, the treasurer still has to pay the bank $500K, because that is what is stipulated in the contract. Several possible situations may arise: if the spot rate is $1 = €0.91, the treasurer will rush out to buy $500K at the spot rate (500 × 0.91 = €455K) and deliver it immediately to the bank in exchange for €0.97 per dollar. He will thus make an unexpected gain of €0.06 per dollar = €30K.

But if the spot rate is $1 = €1.05, the treasurer will have to buy dollars at a higher price than he is selling them just to fulfil the contract. He will spend €525K to obtain $500K, which he will immediately transfer to the bank in exchange for €485, making a loss of €40K. Not to mention the fact that the customer still has not paid for the car.

In spite of all its rigid characteristics, hedging (in this case, forward purchase or sales contracts) is a standardized tool and therefore not very costly. The example that we have given on foreign exchange risk can also be applied to interest rates and raw materials prices. Hedging is a way of guaranteeing certain conditions for yourself, no matter how the markets fluctuate elsewhere. It often makes a big difference to have locked in the interest rate on future borrowings or the purchase price of raw materials for the entire duration of a project.

FINANCIALESE ———————————————————————————————————————

Future foreign exchange rates are called **forward rates**, such as the euro–dollar forward rate. The maturity is given as an abbreviation (3M = three months, and so on). For example, the euro–dollar six-month forward rate is written thus: EUR/USD 6M forward rate. Today's exchange rate is called the **spot rate**.

There are forward contracts for many different products. For example, an **FRA** (future rate agreement) is a contract that guarantees a future interest rate, following the same principles described in the foreign currency hedge.

Finally, the success of futures markets has given rise to new financial products called **futures**, which are more practical because they are standardized.

Futures

The present is theirs.
The future, for which I really worked, is mine.
Nikola Tesla (1856–1943)

Let's return to the previous numerical example. We saw that Rolls-Mops' bank opened a forward contract on the market. To do this, they needed to find a **counterparty**, in other words, someone who was willing to buy the $500K in three months. This is not always easy. Even when there are a lot of players on the market with a wide variety of needs, how can a company such as Turbot-Traction be sure to find a counterparty to buy, say, $1,700K in six months? This problem has been solved by the creation of **futures**, which are listed contracts with standardized amounts. For example, there is a $100K three-month future and a $1,000K six-month future. In our example, Rolls-Mops will buy five $100K three-month futures to hedge against $500K. By buying one $1,000K six-month future and seven $100K six-month futures, Turbot-Traction creates a hedge against $1,700K. Since the amounts are standardized (100, 1,000 and so on), anyone can put together a custom hedge – like building something out of Lego bricks, without worrying whether all the building blocks come from the same seller.[13]

An advanced financial technique: options

We have seen one major drawback to forward contracts: once they have entered into the contract, both parties are legally bound to fulfil their obligations, even if the spot market conditions turn out to be better for one of them. Every treasurer in the world had been dreaming of a type of contract

---

13. The other advantage of futures is that either party can exit the transaction when they wish, by selling the contracts on the market. There is no need to wait until the maturity date, as in a forward contract.

where you could have your cake and eat it too ... and that is precisely what has emerged with the development of options.

A few remarks are in order before we move on to the financial jargon section:

- When calculating the net outcome, you must take into account the €20K that was initially paid out to buy the option. The net outcome for scenario 1 is therefore 500 – 20 = €480K, for scenario 2: 550 – 20 = €530K, and for scenario 3: 500 – 20 = €480K.
- The option contract thus begins with a loss (–€20), whereas in a forward contract there is no financial outlay at the beginning. Thus the spot rate at which the company begins to make a gain is not $1 = €1, but $1 = €1.04. This is the rate at which the dollars exchanged will cover the initial €20K premium: $500K × 1.04 = €520K. Subtracting the €20K premium leaves €500K.
- Using an option limits the loss. Even if the exchange rate plummets, the net outcome will never be lower than €480K. But the potential gains are unlimited. For example, if the spot rate goes to $1 = €2, the treasurer will receive $500K × 2 = €1,000K (minus €20K = €980K net).

The terms of the contract specify the **underlying** (the asset that the transaction is based on; in our example it is the exchange rate for the euro/dollar pair[14]), the **expiration date** (three months) and the **strike price** (exchange rate: $1 = €1). An **American option** may be exercised at any time before expiration, while a **European option** may only be exercised (or allowed to lapse) at the expiration date. An option to buy is known as a **call option** or simply a **call**. An option to sell is termed a **put option**.

Finally, an option is said to be **in the money** when it is advantageous to exercise it (the strike price is more advantageous than the spot price, as in our scenario 1); **out of the money** when it is not advantageous to exercise the option (our scenario 2); and **at the money** when the spot price is equal to the strike price (our scenario 3).

We can readily see the utility of options. These instruments are like insurance contracts: you pay a premium in exchange for which you are covered in the event of a setback, but you still have complete freedom if things turn out well. It's having your cake and eating it too.

DIALOGUE
Parsley:	If options are such a cure-all, why don't all treasurers use them? They have the advantages of forward contracts without the drawbacks...
Sage:	Compared with forward contracts, options have one downside: their price (the premium you have to pay).
Parsley:	How is the premium determined?
Sage:	Through the supply and demand for options. Let's say that there are buyers desperately looking for options to buy dollars in six months, but there are no sellers out there, what will happen?
Parsley:	The buyers will offer higher and higher prices until some sellers appear.
Sage:	Exactly. That's the law of supply and demand. The premium you pay for an option is actually its market price: the price at which buyers and sellers are willing to trade that option.
Parsley:	Ok, I can see why you would want to buy an option: you pay a premium to have the right but not the obligation to carry out a transaction. But what benefit is there in being an option seller? The seller is dependent on the buyer's decisions: they have to be ready to fulfil the contract if the buyer exercises the option, but the buyer may also simply decide to allow the option to expire. The seller has everything to lose...
Sage:	They have everything to lose except the premium that has already been paid. Let's look at an example.

---

14. Like futures, options are sold in standardized amounts. For example, an option may give the right to sell $10K, so you would need to buy 50 options to achieve a total of $500K.

Booz is a raw material whose price fluctuates rather a lot. Last year, prices ranged from £80 to £120, and the current price is £105. Call options for Booz (six-month maturity) are detailed in Table 8.6:

Table 8.6   Six-month call options for Booz

Strike price (£)	Premium (£)
107	4.8
106	5.7
105	7.9
103	8.2
102	10.0

This means that if a treasurer pays £4.80 now, he/she will get an option to buy Booz in six months at a strike price of £107. We see that the lower the strike price, the higher the premium. This makes sense; to obtain the right to buy Booz at a low price in the future you are willing to pay more now. Let's see how much investors would have to pay if they wanted to buy Booz in six months. They could opt for the first option and pay £4.80 now + £107 in six months = £111.80. The second option would cost £5.7 + £106 = £111.70. It is not our intention to use this as a system to make predictions, but we can see that the market is setting premiums as if the future price of Booz were to be around £112. The market is probably anticipating a rise in the price of Booz in the coming months.

Now let's don the three-piece suit of a salesperson (we'll call him Sailor) who is selling options at a strike price of £102 (the last line in Table 8.6).

Sailor says to himself: 'If I sell this option, I am committed to delivering Booz in six months' time for £102. But I have no certainty that the buyer will exercise the option.'

In order to be willing to accept such a situation with its uncertainty, the seller determines that he wants a premium of at least £10. This means that Sailor is actually making a bet. Imagine that in six months' time the price of Booz is £106. The buyer (let's call her Byebye) exercises her option because she prefers to buy Booz for £102 (the strike price) rather than £106 (the spot price). Sailor has to buy Booz for £106 and then sell it for £102. Thus he loses £4 per option. But he received 10 when the premium was paid so he makes a net gain of 10 − 4 = £6. As for the buyer, dear me, she made a net loss of the same magnitude. She paid a premium of £10 to ultimately save £4, thus making a net loss of −10 + 4 = −£6. Table 8.7 shows the respective gains and losses depending on the final spot price.

Table 8.7   Net gains at different spot prices

Spot price	100	102	104	106	108	110	112	114	116	118	120
Sailor	+12	+10	+8	+6	+4	+2	0	−2	−4	−6	−8
Byebye	−12	−10	−8	−6	−4	−2	0	+2	+4	+6	+8

DIALOGUE

Sage: So now we see much more clearly how Sailor's bet works. If we go back six months, to when the options were priced, the price of Booz at the time was £105 and Sailor's bet was this: 'I am prepared to take £10 now because I don't think that the price of Booz will rise above £112.'

Parsley: And what is the buyer's bet?

Sage: Byebye says to herself that, given the past volatility in the price of Booz, it could rise to £112 (or more) in six months' time. She prefers to pay a £10 premium now to guarantee a strike price of £102.

Parsley: Basically, Sailor is betting on low volatility and Byebye on high volatility.

Sage: Yes, and that's the basis for option valuation: the more the underlying asset fluctuates, the more the option is worth. And, on the contrary, an option on a very stable underlying asset would be worthless because the future spot price will be very close to the current price.

Valuation of options

We have seen that options are like wagers between sellers and buyers on the future variations in the price of an underlying asset. The **volatility** of the underlying asset is therefore one of the variables in option valuation: the more volatile the asset, the higher the option premium. Another variable is the **expiration date**: the more distant the expiration date, the more time the underlying has to reach a given price. Thus, the further away the expiration date, the higher the premium. Unfortunately, the mathematical formula for option valuation is a little more complicated. It is known as the **Black–Scholes formula,** named after its two inventors, whose efforts were rewarded with a Nobel Prize in Economics. Despite its ultimate complexity, the formula begins with a simple idea: the value of an option depends essentially on one variable: the probability that the price of the underlying asset will move away from the strike price. The greater the probability that the price of the underlying asset will move away from the strike price, the more attractive the option becomes. The formula therefore uses the cumulative distribution function and the probability density function, which are determined in relation to the volatility of the underlying asset and the option's expiration date. Given that only one reader in 17,549 is eager to know the equation for this model, we will not reprint it here. It is enough to know two things:

- The value of an option is a function of five variables: the spot price of the underlying asset, the volatility of the underlying asset, the strike price, the option's expiration date, and the risk-free rate. Once you know these variables, you can plug them into the Black–Scholes formula and obtain the estimated value of the option.
- Starting with the initial formula, one can derive extremely complicated valuation models, because investors will often combine several options (for example, a call option for one date combined with a put option for another date, or two call and put options at the same time to protect the investor against both prices increases and decreases).

Options appear to be a panacea for risk. Do not forget, however, that for every option there is a price to pay: the premium. And any scheme that involves combining several options means that several premiums will have to be paid. The tricky question is to determine whether or not it's worth it. In an efficient market, the amount of the premium should suit both buyers (who don't want to pay too much) and sellers (who want to be properly compensated for risk). If the market is efficient, the amount to pay will match the expectation of future gains, just as it does for a stock. So there is no magic at work here, and once again we come across our old friend, the risk–return trade off.

Conclusion

A wise man also fears a weak enemy.
Publilius Syrus (1st century BC)

The ideal company treasurer is a model of humility. His work is all about planning and managing, prudently and carefully, taking due diligence. Uncertainty must be reduced as much as possible through foresight and rigour. The company should be protected against all uncertainty using risk management tools. Contrary to what some CEOs believe, we feel that a good treasurer is not someone who pulls off amazing 'financial feats', but rather someone who achieves the smallest variance between what is planned and what is realized.

In the area of risk management, company treasurers are not that interested in valuation formulas or models. They just want to have tools than enable them to hedge, fully or partially, against market risks. We have seen two important points:

- It is not necessary to have a great deal of technical skill. Very often, the simplest methods are sufficient to manage the risks.
- Faced with complex situations and requirements, the treasurer will have to agree to pay additional costs. A tailor-made dress fits the individual better, but it costs more than one bought off the peg.

9

Conclusion

We don't know a millionth of one percent about anything.

Thomas Alva Edison (1847–1931)

This chapter contains some advice that could be entitled 'How to Make a Mess of Things by Applying the Models Blindly'. In this section, we will go over a few (perhaps obvious) ideas, working our way through the following statements:

- Finance oversimplifies things.
- Finance overcomplicates things.
- We need to return to basics.
- Not everything in finance is finance.

Finance oversimplifies things

You don't create value with a spreadsheet

No man ever wetted clay and then left it, as if there would be bricks by chance and fortune.

Plutarch (c. 46–120AD)

There is a spreadsheet myth. The young Padawan believes that he controls his future simply because he has managed to insert some (not always correct) numbers and formulas into the cells of a spreadsheet. But we must remember a cruel truth: in real life things never turn out exactly the way the spreadsheet predicted. As we pointed out in Chapter 6, a spreadsheet is a decision-making tool, not a crystal ball.

In other words, making models is a good thing – it helps you understand the problem – but in the end you create value by getting your act together, picking up the phone and going out to meet potential customers. Most great entrepreneurs are salespeople first and foremost, not financiers. And there's no point in trying to optimize your cash management if you don't have any sales people to bring in the orders.

A listed stock is not just a flashing blip on a computer screen

Modelling necessarily entails simplification. And simplification entails a loss of information. Of course, everything could be summed up in financial data, but we must never forget that it is just a summary. A company is made up of investments, employees, managers, competitors and markets – and the whole thing is in constant evolution. So reducing a company to its stock price or an investment project to its NPV is like saying 'Napoleon was a Corsican'. Some people confuse the map with the land...

Finance overcomplicates things

The financialization of the economy: transparency or opacity?

Companies are complex systems – technical and human organizations that sociologists have been studying for centuries. So it is a complicated situation to begin with, which finance has not helped to simplify. Indeed, market finance has introduced more and more abstruse tools for breaking down risks and sharing out responsibility. For example, the **securitization of assets** is a process through which balance sheet assets are converted into listed and tradable securities. This is a good thing, because it promotes the fluidity (liquidity) of trading, but it also leads to the dematerialization of risk, because securitized assets may be combined in portfolios, and then these portfolios may in turn be securitized. In some cases, this is like a game of Old Maid, where the cards are shuffled, dealt, picked up and passed along: the securitized assets have been transformed, bundled and traded so much that in the end nobody knows where the doubtful debt is.

The Curse of King Midas

In the popular imagination, finance is synonymous with complexity, jargon and, let's face it, hidden interests – a view that is perpetuated by the press. This brings us to several issues:

> **A loss of perspective due to simplification.** The stakeholders involved in the management of companies (shareholders, bankers, employees) appear as simplistic caricatures in a drama. Shareholders – usually the villain of the piece – are seen as soulless capitalists whose demands are irresponsible.[1] Bankers, often overlooked in comparison, only appear in

---

1. Remember that anyone who takes out an insurance policy is a de facto shareholder (through the insurance company's investments). Hell may be other people, but everybody is a shareholder.

the final act when a company is on the verge of bankruptcy, whereas in reality they are key partners whose requirements can shape the future of companies. Employees play only a bit part, often reduced to their labour union role – at least, in Mediterranean Europe. Other partners are extras who fade into the background.[2]

A loss of values. Questions about the social purpose of companies are largely pushed aside. Moving away from a historical small business or family business culture (where the firm is a nexus of value creation), we have shifted to a big business, corporate approach (where the main goal of the company is to enrich its shareholders). With this transformation, everything that is a source of profit is captured by the company, while the costs (known as 'externalities') are shifted onto society. For example, a company benefits individually from downsizing its staff, but it is society as a whole that bears the costs of unemployment; a company cuts costs by using technologies that pollute, leaving society to foot the environmental bill...[3] This is coupled with a shortening of the time horizon. Short-term profit-seeking is gaining the upper hand over planning and long-term investment. Basically, short-term local gains are prevailing over long-term global gains.

Mistrust of experts. A public figure who was widely admired yesterday may end up in prison tomorrow. Every opinion seems fit for consumption because the label 'expert' is attached to any person who is viable in the mass media. But the constant bombardment of information and shallow analyses are giving us indigestion, and nobody has the time to step back and consider the big picture. This is not aided by technical jargon, which only adds to the smokescreen. The role of education here is fundamental.

Which brings us to the following idea.

We need to return to basics

Finance is a support function, not a goal in its own right

Although it is regularly cast in a starring role, corporate finance is really nothing more than a support function, just like human resources and

---

2. For example, nobody mentions the responsibility of purchasing departments when talking about the financial difficulties of suppliers (systematic reduction of all prices, imposed payment terms and so on) – all of this being camouflaged under the term 'competition'.

3. In this approach nobody should be exonerated because everybody shares some responsibility. The consumers who demand ever cheaper products, without considering the environmental and social consequences of their choices, are actually aiding and abetting these mechanisms, wittingly or unwittingly.

logistics. It is true that companies put enormous emphasis on financial considerations in their communication. But we must not forget that finance is supposed to be the obedient servant of the company, not the reverse. Without a suitable strategy, a company will lose its bearings and no amount of financial optimization can make up for that (you need only consider the awful misadventures suffered by Captain Jack Sparrow in *Pirates of the Caribbean* for lack of a proper compass).

Common sense is a surprisingly rare commodity

> *I prefer the company of peasants because they have not been educated sufficiently to reason incorrectly.*
>
> Michel de Montaigne (1533–92)

It is better to have a bare-bones model coupled with a lot of common sense than a highly convoluted contraption manipulated by someone with the sense of a goose. Even though models are reassuring and management consultants act as the company's anxiolytics, when push comes to shove it is not the models that make the decisions. It is important, therefore, to act with common sense and to step back and consider the whole situation. A few simple questions can help us reconsider financial decisions from a broader angle:

- **Has the risk been correctly measured?** There is no point in performing complicated present value calculations if you use an 'average' discount rate instead of considering the intrinsic risks of the project.[4]
- **Has the timing been carefully considered?** In addition to performing a sensitivity analysis of financial assumptions (see Chapter 6), be sure to take a close look at timing. For example, what would happen if the project were to fall six months (or a year) behind schedule? It is important to understand the impact on the project's net present value (NPV), but also to measure the consequences that such delays might have on the company's cash flow.
- **Have the consequences of the project been clearly measured?** Are short-term savings being cancelled out by longer-term additional costs? We are thinking, for example, about the strategy of outsourcing certain activities. Moreover, what is the global impact of the project on the company's

---

4. At the very least, it would be wise to determine whether the project is 'more risky than', 'as risky as' or 'less risky than' the assets the company currently has, and then adjust the discount rate accordingly. The right approach is to determine the asset beta of the project, as seen in Chapter 6¾.

other activities? Will the new project cannibalize existing product lines? Is there any cost-sharing? It is always good to step back and consider the global and long-term impact of a project on the company, and not only its individual contribution.

- **Has the market reaction been anticipated?** Finally, common sense tells us that we must take into account the fact that the world is constantly evolving and that the company's competitors will react to any initiative it takes. Launching a new product or service usually occurs in two stages: in the first stage, the company benefits from the element of surprise and gains a head start as well as market share – this is the golden age. In the second stage, the company's competitors react in various ways (price war, innovation, advertising and so on), which will have an impact on the initial forecasts. It may happen that the company does not even get to experience the joys of the golden age, but falls straight into the trenches of an established market. There are still many companies out there making forecasts as though they were sure to be realized. But if there is one certainty in life, it is that there are no certainties.

Not everything in finance is finance

Never forget the taxes

Financial decisions are heavily affected by taxation, both corporate and individual. Characterized as 'market imperfections' by economists, taxes strongly influence the nature of the financial decisions to be made.[5] We have seen this, for example, in cash flow calculations (the fiscal impact of the amortization schedule), in estimating residual values for projects and in determining the company's debt-financing or dividend policy. Taxes can move the goalposts for a lot of financial decisions.

However, it is important not to confuse the effect with the cause. First and foremost, a company seeks value-creating strategies (those with a positive NPV) and while taxes must never be overlooked in estimating the value created, the primary goal of the company is not to reduce its taxes. On the other hand, a tax strategy may have an impact on value creation.

Never forget the human element

The human element should be considered from two angles: as a resource and as a potential fly in the ointment.

---

5. To a lesser extent, legal considerations are also important, for example in terms of control and power, as well as ownership of assets.

Human capital vs financial capital

The five most important things in a startup, in order of importance:
1. *The team*
2. *The team*
3. *The team*
4. *The market*
5. *The product*

Common saying in the venture capital industry

The classic credo in finance goes something like this: 'If you have a promising project (one with a positive NPV), you will always be able to find backers (shareholders, banks) that are willing to finance you.' Although this statement is somewhat debatable – because every company does not have access to a financial market – the underlying message stands: once you have a good business idea, the financing will follow.

And yet, there are numerous companies with exciting development projects that are never launched, even though there are always plenty of investors eager to place their capital. Indeed, the financial view of the world overlooks a key parameter: in order to develop a project you also need people. And even though you can raise funds quickly on the financial markets, it takes time to recruit the right people, train them and oversee their development. As the newspapers remind us regularly, it is easier to raise money than it is to assemble a good team – and keep it. In a world where financial markets seem omnipresent, the notion of **human capital** is becoming more and more prevalent in the literature.[6]

Bounded rationality and personal interests

The oldest and strongest emotion of mankind is fear.

Howard P. Lovecraft, *Supernatural Horror in Literature* (1927)

We have already talked about the human element in Chapter 7 (on the stock market) and it can be summed up in two points:

• Human beings, including decision-makers, are not 100% rational (behavioural finance).

---

6. The notion of human capital was acknowledged in 1992, when the Nobel Prize in Economics was awarded to Gary S. Becker, a professor of economics and sociology. This was one of the first times that the Nobel Foundation extended the sphere of economics to include human behaviour.

- Human beings, including executives, may have personal interests that diverge from the interests of their company (agency theory).

It follows that financial models must be handled with kid gloves: even when the spreadsheet outputs the 'right' decision, the decision-maker should not necessarily follow it. There is an exciting field of research that has been developing for several years now: the goal now is not to mathematically optimize profits, but to understand the control systems (governance) and incentive systems (compensation) that will lead human beings to make the 'right' decisions. It would be an understatement to say that this is an enormous challenge.

Conclusion

The greater good

> *Alice came to a fork in the road. 'Which road do I take?' she asked.*
> *'Where do you want to go?' responded the Cheshire Cat.*
> *'I don't know,' Alice answered.*
> *'Then,' said the Cat, 'it doesn't matter.'*
>
> Lewis Carroll, *Alice's Adventures in Wonderland* (1865)

There is more to life than finance. Indeed, it would be rather disappointing if humanity aspired solely to obtain more profit and better pensions. With a baffling blend of sordid indulgence and divine inspiration, humankind has always oscillated between earthly materialism and lofty ideals. When people are brought together, whether as a company or in a project or a joint venture, the result is certainly more than a community of financial interests. What flows from this coming-together are shared motivation, common aspirations and, finally, value creation, in a process we choose to call 'synergy' – perhaps out of ignorance of what it truly contains. Let's not forget that, beneath its outwardly inhuman appearance, finance actually deals with fundamentally human problems.

Conclusion to the conclusion

> *They deem me mad because I will not sell my days for gold and I deem them mad because they think my days have a price.*
>
> Kahlil Gibran (1883–1931)

If this book were to end with a few general words of advice, they would be the following:

- Do not be slaves to models, even if you have built those models yourself. One ounce of critical thinking is always worth more than three peta-bytes of spreadsheets.
- Always take a bird's-eye view that encompasses everything, instead of being too focused on what's right in front of you. The air is more invigorating higher up.
- Know why you are making a given decision, know how to explain it and how to expound on it.

After all, everyone is a teacher.

> *The teacher, if indeed wise, does not bid you to enter the house of their wisdom, but leads you to the threshold of your own mind.*
>
> Kahlil Gibran (1883–1931)

What? Are you still here? The book is finished. Put it down now and get back to your life.

> *If you say to me, Master, it would seem that you were not very wise in writing to us these flimflam stories and pleasant fooleries; I answer you, that you are not much wiser to spend your time in reading them. Nevertheless, if you read them to make yourselves merry, as in manner of pastime I wrote them, you and I both are far more worthy of pardon than a great rabble of squint-minded fellows.*
>
> François Rabelais, *Gargantua and Pantagruel* (1532–64)

Index

cash flow – *continued*
  end of life, 94
  forecasts, 83, 176
  free, 39, 96
  incremental cash flow, 55, 84
  link with net earnings, 15
  operating, 37–8
  use in valuation, 173, 174–83
  See also price cash flow ratio
cash management, 239
  forecasts, 240–2
cash ratio, *See* ratios
change in working capital, 39, 91, 180–1
  See also working capital
COGS, *See* cost of goods sold
company
  beta of a division, 210
  comparable, 166, 204
  liquidation of, 7, 18
  valuation, 158
comparable company, 166, 204
compounding, 50–3
confirmation bias, 236
constant annuity
  debt repayment by, 58
  formula, 60
constant repayment, *See* debt
cost
  of bankruptcy, 153
  of capital, 139–42, 183
  of equity, 137, 183–4
  of financial distress, 153
  of financing, 132, 142, 183
  of financing (after tax), 152
  of goods sold, 11
cost of equity, 137, 183–4
cost of goods sold, 11
coupon, *See* bond
currency, 252
  risk management, 255
current liabilities, 19
  in days of sales, 26
  in working capital, 21
current ratio, *See* ratios

DCF, *See* discounted cash flow (DCF)
debt
  average cost of, 33
  on the balance sheet, 19
  beta of, 199
  constant annuity, 60
  constant repayment, 58

financing, 145–56
  impact on WACC, 146
  in fine, 58–9
  net, 28–9, 144
  optimum level, 154
  short term, 248–9
debt-to-equity ratio, *See* ratios
default
  on loan, 7
  risk, 48
depreciation
  on balance sheet, 17
  impact on cash flow, 15
  on income statement, 11
differential
  cash flow, 55, 84
  in leverage, 33–4
discount rate, 54, 78, 98, 130,
    142, 183
  See also capital asset pricing model
discounted cash flow (DCF)
  for company valuation, 175
  enterprise value formula, 175, 176
  market value formula, 175, 176
discounting, 51–4
  invoice, 248
distress, *See* cost of financial distress
diversifiable risk, *See* risk, specific
diversification, *See* portfolio, diversification
dividends, 6
  contribution to return, 107, 224
  policy, 145, 225–6
  yield, 107, 223–4
  See also stock dividend
Droids Co., 10

earnings
  per share, 169
  retained, 19
  See also net earnings; price earnings ratio
earnings before interest and tax
    (EBIT), 44
  use in valuation, 164
EBIT, *See* earnings before interest and tax
efficiency, 227–32
  semi-strong form, 228
  strong form, 229
  weak form, 228
efficient frontier of portfolios, 119
efficient market, 227–32
enterprise value, 159
EPS, *See* earnings per share

CPI Antony Rowe
Chippenham, UK
2016-12-27 15:33